"This is a major contribution to the ongoing debate about the relationship between 'personalized medicine' and 'racialized medicine'. Dr. Sun documents how in practice, the two are far more integrated than previous analysts have recognized or acknowledged. Using an international platform, Sun demonstrates how Asian geneticists (Japanese, Chinese, Singaporean, Korean, et al.), in a pushback against US–European domination of human molecular genetics, are often inadvertently re-inscribing ethnic and racial categories generated in the West"

Troy Duster, author of *Backdoor to Eugenics*,
Chancellor's Professor, University of California, Berkeley

"A highly timely counter-weight to the dominance of works on this topic from North America and Europe, Shirley Sun's brilliant and sobering analysis of 'probability medicine' in Singapore will make even the most reflective reader think about the global implications of genomic medicine differently."

Barbara Prainsack, Professor at Social Science,
Health and Medicine, King's College London, UK

"This book addresses a critical but understudied topic: personalized medicine within the context of Asia. Asian countries are key leaders in the move towards personalized medicine but as the author points out, historically, personalized medicine has been viewed through a Western-centric focus. The findings also have implications for the large Asian population residing in the US and other countries. The book is engaging to read and insightful in its interpretations. I recommend it to anyone who wants to understand the global context of the emerging trend towards personalized, precision medicine and how it will change the future of health care."

Kathryn Phillips, Professor of Health Economics and Health Services
Research at the University of California, San Francisco, and Founder/
Director of the UCSF Center for Translational and Policy Research on
Personalized Medicine (TRANSPERS)

"Overall, the book offers intriguing insights about how cutting-edge developments in medicine and scientific research are embedded in complex social and historical contexts. Its sociological and Asian foci are welcome additions to a literature dominated by scientists in Europe and the United States. It should have wide appeal as the number of clinical trials in Asian countries is increasing ... I highly recommend Sun's book to social scientists, doctors, scientists, politicians, and anyone interested in the history and practice of medicine and drug development."

Sociology of Health and Illness, Volume 39, Issue 8, November 2017

"This is a book about an important set of issues that goes beyond the key-words flagged in the title to address the contradictions of biomedical mean-ings of race and population, as well as concerns over the clinical efficacy of genetic testing. It is among the very first books to look at the intersection of these issues using primarily Asian case studies and expert interviews ...There is no question that this book deals with a number of very important issues, for both scholarly and policy communities. It points to a number of new areas where more research is needed and asks questions that will be with us for some time ..."

*East Asian Science, Technology and Society:
An International Journal*, Volume 12, Issue 4, 2018

"The book uses the growth of personalized, or precision, medicine used in the testing and treatment of cancer in Asia to extend one of the more important strands of science and technology studies literature, embodied in scholarship on genetics, race and ethnicity, and health and medicine. In this way it builds on the work of other scholars such as Troy Duster, Dorothy Roberts, Steven Epstein, Sara Shostak, and Ruha Benjamin. STS scholars concerned with these issues are likely to find this book of interest ..."

Contemporary Sociology, Volume 47, Issue 2, March 1, 2018

Socio-economics of Personalized Medicine in Asia

The second decade of the twenty-first century has witnessed a surging interest in personalized medicine with the concomitant promise to enable more precise diagnosis and treatment of disease and illness, based upon an individual's unique genetic makeup.

In this book, my goal is to contribute to a growing body of literature on personalized medicine by tracing and analyzing how this field has blossomed in Asia. In so doing, I aim to illustrate how various social and economic forces shape the co-production of science and social order in global contexts. This book shows that there are inextricable transnational linkages between developing and developed countries and also provides a theoretically guided and empirically grounded understanding of the formation and usage of particular racial and ethnic human taxonomies in local, national and transnational settings.

Shirley Sun is an Associate Professor of Sociology at Nanyang Technological University (NTU), Singapore. Her main research interests are population studies, social inequalities, citizenship and immigration, economic development and social reproduction, and science, technology, and society.

Routledge Studies in the Sociology of Health and Illness

Socio-economics of Personalized Medicine in Asia

Shirley Sun

LONDON AND NEW YORK

First published in paperback 2020

First published 2017
by Routledge
2 Park Square, Milton Park, Abingdon, Oxon OX14 4RN

and by Routledge
52 Vanderbilt Avenue, New York, NY 10017

Routledge is an imprint of the Taylor & Francis Group, an informa business

British Library Cataloguing in Publication Data
A catalogue record for this book is available from the British Library

Library of Congress Cataloging-in-Publication Data
Names: Sun, Shirley Hsiao-Li, author.
Title: Socio-economics of personalized medicine in Asia / by Shirley Sun.
Description: New York : Routledge, 2017. | Series: Routledge studies in the sociology of health and illness | Includes bibliographical references and index.
Identifiers: LCCN 2016005951| ISBN 9781138933835 (hardback) | ISBN 9781315537177 (ebook)
Subjects: LCSH: Personalized medicine–Social aspects–Asia. | Personalized medicine–Economic aspects–Asia. | Social medicine–Asia. | Medical economics–Asia.
Classification: LCC RA525 .S86 2017 | DDC 362.1095–dc23
LC record available at https://lccn.loc.gov/2016005951

ISBN: 978-1-138-93383-5 (hbk)
ISBN: 978-0-367-35442-8 (pbk)
ISBN: 978-1-315-53717-7 (ebk)

Typeset in Galliard
by Apex CoVantage, LLC

For Alexander and Troy

Contents

Acknowledgments

I owe many people my deepest appreciation. The following paragraphs gratefully acknowledge just some of those colleagues and friends.

I thank the anonymous reviewers of the manuscript and my colleagues in Singapore, Hong Liu, Francis Khek Gee Lim, Alex Law, Hallam Stevens, Lisa Onaga, Sulfikar Amir, Hyung-Wook Park, Lyle Fearnly, Wei Peng Seeto, and Tiow Yong Lee in particular, for their insightful, thoughtful and always helpful feedback and encouragement. Additionally, I would like to thank Ruha Benjamin, Catherine Bliss, Lundy Braun, Duana Fullwiley, Joan Fujimura, Joseph Graves, Amy Hinterberger, Ying-Yi Hong, Jay Kaufman, Michael Montoya, Ann Morning, Dorothy Roberts, Keith Wailoo, and Ken Weiss for their knowledgeable and challenging comments on issues related to social diversity, genetics, and society.

Portions of this book were presented at numerous conferences and seminars, and I am grateful for the questions and comments I received at each. Partial drafts of Chapter 2 were presented at the workshop "The Interface of Humanities and Genomics," organized by Yasuko Takezawa and held at Kyoto University in Japan (January 2011), as well as at the "Reconsidering Race: Cross-Disciplinary and Interdisciplinary Approaches," co-organized by Kazuko Suzuki and Diego von Vacano and held at Texas A&M University in the USA (May 2013). Partial drafts of Chapter 3 were presented at the workshop "Biology, Medicine and Race beyond the Genome," co-organized with Hallam Stevens and held at the School of Humanities and Social Science (HSS) at the Nanyang Technological University in Singapore (January 2013), as well as in the seminar on "Personalized Medicine and Asian DNA: Pharmacogenomics and Market Forces," organized by Susan McDaniel and held at the Prentice Institute for Global Population and the Economy, University of Lethbridge, Canada (April 2015). A draft of Chapter 4 was presented at the workshop "Genomic Sovereignty in a Global Context: Comparative Exchanges in Justice, Ethics and Genomic Medicine," co-organized by Amy Hinterberger and Ernesto Schwartz Marin and held at the Brocher Foundation, Switzerland (December 2014). Sections of this book were also presented at the annual meetings of the American Sociological Association and the International Sociological Association.

I am indebted to the utmost professional, clear, and careful guidance of the editors at Routledge, Yong Ling Lam and Samantha Phua in particular.

My appreciation also goes to the Singapore Ministry of Education and the School of Humanities and Social Sciences at the Nanyang Technological University (NTU) for the research grant. I am very grateful for the superb research assistance provided by Yanru Lek, Zoe Ong, Lynette Chan, Filzah Amalia Rahmat, Peili Pey, Mohammad Syafiq Bin Mohammad Suhaini, Prashant Deepak Waikar, Kian Yong Goh, and Chua Wei Min.

Of course, this project would not have been possible without the generosity and kindness of all 31 human genetic scientists and clinicians who shared their rich experiences, views, and opinions, amid their extremely busy schedules. It is my hope that their voices will be heard. My heartfelt thanks also go to my family and close friends, Alexander Sun, Chen-Feng Shen, Bin Sun, Annie Park, Tony Park, Vickie Kuo, Eleanor Yeh, Tom Lai, and Junmin Wang, who have provided love, all around good cheer, and the unwavering support that was vital to the completion of this project. Finally, this book is written in the spirit of Ms. Ida B. Wells (1862–1931), and I dedicate it to Professor Duster's prescient warning on the reification of race in science and the hope of a brighter future for all.

1 Introduction

When the mapping of the human genome was completed in 2003, the notable conclusion was that humans across the globe are 99.9 percent the same at the DNA level. However, in the last decade, two remarkable developments have ensued. First, human molecular genetics has generated a focus on personalized medicine (PM; also known as precision medicine or stratified medicine), with the promise and claim to use the analysis of an individual's unique genetic makeup to enable more precise diagnosis and treatment of diseases and illnesses around the globe. Second, there is increasing "molecularization of race," such that human taxonomies that the Human Genome Project had declared null and void are re-inscribed via the DNA (Duster, 2006a; Fullwiley, 2007). In this book, I further explore and document the tensions and contradictions in these two developments and delineate how they have become dangerously intertwined.

To begin with, the European Science Foundation (ESF) published a comprehensive report, "Personalised Medicine for the European Citizen: Towards More Precise Medicine for the Diagnosis, Treatment and Prevention of Disease (iPM)," in December 2012.[1] In the United States, PriceWaterhouseCoopers estimated that the personalized medicine market was worth about $232 billion in 2009 and would exceed $450 billion by 2015.[2] In January 2015, the President of the United States announced that he is setting aside more than $200 million for scientists to pursue "precision medicine." Similarly, applications of genomics that enable personalized health interventions have expanded in the Asia-Pacific region.[3] Indeed, Ozdemir et al. (2011:1) note that Asia-Pacific is a "new frontier for post-genomics medicine." For instance, it was reported in *Nature News* that China is expected to announce its precision medicine initiative in March 2016, and analysts predict that the cost would be more expensive than the $210 million initiative in the United States (Cyranoski, 2016).

Personalized medicine and population-based research and development

According to the Personalized Medicine Coalition (2014):

> In a time of unprecedented scientific breakthroughs and technological advancements, personalized health care has the capacity to detect the onset of

disease at its earliest stages, pre-empt the progression of disease, and, at the same time, increase the efficiency of the health care system by improving quality, accessibility, and affordability.

In the 10 years since the completion of the Human Genome Project (HGP), advances in genome technology have led to an exponential decrease in sequencing costs (more than 16,000-fold). Patients have benefited from major biological insights and medical advances, including the development of more than 100 drugs whose labels now include pharmacogenomic information.

There is, however, a palpable tension between the rhetoric of "individualized" medical intervention, based on DNA analysis of an individual's unique genetic makeup, and large-scale genome variation studies that attempt to assess drug responses and disease susceptibility of specific "populations." As Hinterberger (2012a:74) puts it, "while contemporary genomic research promises personalized medicine (or measures of risk) targeted at the level of the individual, it is primarily the comparison of groups and populations that drives human genome research." Moreover, amid the excitement concerning personal genomics and "personalized medicine," Lee (2003:385) suggests that "in the absence of cost-effective, ubiquitous genome scanning tests, it may be more accurate to describe the next wave of genomic medicine as population-based rather than one focused on individual differences." In other words, once we reject the scenario of blockbuster drugs (i.e. the same drug for everybody with the same illness), the issue becomes population-targeted drugs. The key question is, what is a population? The primary concerns are how to target a population correctly, how to ensure that a drug goes to the population that is most likely to respond positively, and how to avoid giving drugs to the population that is likely to respond negatively.

In these pages, I offer an explanation for how dominant social actors and institutions involved in the creation, development, and implementation of promised personalized medicine think about "population" in Asia and beyond, particularly in relation to cancer prevention and treatment. Drugs like Herceptin and Gleevec for treatment of breast cancer and chronic myeloid leukemia, respectively, are evidence of targeted therapies that pave the way toward personalized treatment. Moreover, the cost of sequencing an individual's genome has decreased to approximately US$1000, which is a small fraction of the initial cost of about $3 billion in 2003 (Hayden, 2014). While this book primarily discusses PM for cancer, the issues identified might be relevant for the development of personalized medicine for other diseases as well.

What is a population? Race and genetics in North America

A key question of contemporary human molecular genetics involves determining what constitutes an appropriate reference population for the purposes of drug development and disease prevention. The boundary-making of such populations raises both theoretical and empirical questions to be examined in specific social contexts. In line with this concern, a significant body of research, carried out primarily in North American contexts, has shed light on social forces that shape the construction of various population categories within the realm of human genetic/genome knowledge production (Duster, 2003, 2006a, 2006b; Fullwiley 2007; Hinterberger, 2010, 2012b; Fujimura and Rajagopalan, 2011). These studies are of seminal importance because they demonstrate, empirically, that the deployment of seemingly neutral human genome sequencing technology is necessarily a social and cultural phenomenon. Amid the projected high market value and enthusiasm for personalized medicine, Kato, Kano, and Shirai (2010) point out, correctly, that "while determining genomic sequence data is becoming faster and more accurate, *interpretation* of the clinical significance of genomic information is dependent on a science that is still immature and potentially changeable over time" [emphasis in original]. This is because the interpretation of the genetic code itself (as well as the act of genotyping using particular categories and criteria) is a human endeavor and, thus, an inevitable function of the lived experiences, beliefs, and values of the interpreters, as well as the institutional and structural constraints they face.

For example, the National Institutes of Health (NIH), one of the largest funders of medical research in the United States, requires all of the projects that it funds to gather information on the race and ethnicity of their subjects using categories set forth by the White House Office of Management and Budget (OMB) – the same categories used by all federal agencies, including the US census. However, in the book *Inclusion: The Politics of Difference in Medical Research*, US sociologist Steven Epstein (2007) demonstrates that attention paid to gender, race and ethnicity, and age differences in biomedical research is less a function of the "natural" differences of these groups than of successful political mobilization efforts by advocacy groups, experts, and members of US Congress. Such efforts have culminated in the rise of a new "inclusion-and-difference" policy regime in the United States. In other words, the axis of difference for biomedical research is significantly determined by politics. Moreover, Fullwiley (2007) shows that one of the unintended consequences of such a policy regime is the "molecularization of race" in pharmacological laboratory settings – that is, "through practices of recruiting, organizing, storing, and comparing human DNA by US race categories mandated by the Office of Management and Budget and the National Institutes of Health, US racial distinction is conserved in the laboratory (Fullwiley, 2007:22)."

This book attempts to contribute to this growing body of literature by tracing and analyzing prominent genetic and genomic projects related to personalized medicine as they have unfolded in Asia. While various social actors, including patients, can participate in "the molecular biopolitics of life itself" (Rose, 2006), the playing field is not level. Here, I will take a closer look at the fuller realm of claims-making about genome-based personalized medicine by dominant social actors including scientists, physicians, pharmaceutical companies, and state authorities. In so doing, I hope to illustrate specific political, economic, cultural, and social forces shaping the co-production of science and social order in transnational settings. As Clancey, Graham, Bishop, and Fischer (2013:3) point out, "'race and ethnicity' issues [have been] discussed largely in terms of Europe, the Americas, and Africa; the potentially very significant and interesting relationships between biotechnology and society in this half of the world [i.e. Asia] have been comparatively under-researched." I offer an explanation of how populations become ethnically and racially labeled in the contexts of a globalized genome science and pharmaceutical industry, as well as in national public health policies. Moreover, I draw on literature in the social sciences to illustrate the actual histories of the formation of ethnic categories in these contexts. Finally, drawing on extensive interview data with physicians, I highlight the problems of translating such knowledge regarding the distribution of a particular genetic marker or allelic frequencies among ethnic and racial groups at the level of everyday clinical practices and the implications for potential discrimination at the societal level.

Personalized medicine, pharmacogenomics, and pharmacoethnicity

The idea underlying the field of inquiry known as pharmacogenomics is that drug response is personal and genetics plays a part in that response. As Xie and Frueh (2005:325) succinctly put it: "the goal of personalized medicine is to maximize the likelihood of therapeutic efficacy and to minimize the risk of drug toxicity for an individual patient. One of the major contributors to this concept is pharmacogenomics." According to the US National Library of Medicine:[4]

> Pharmacogenomics is the study of how genes affect a person's response to drugs. This relatively new field combines pharmacology (the science of drugs) and genomics (the study of genes and their functions) to develop effective, safe medications and doses that will be tailored to a person's genetic makeup.

As such, pharmacogenomics promises to help identify relevant genetic information that will make prescribing drugs safer and more effective and potentially save the health care industry millions of dollars. Indeed, Allen Roses of Glaxo-SmithKline asserts that "more than 90 percent of drugs only work in 30–50 percent of people" (BBC News, 2003). It is reported that less than 60 percent of patients respond to drugs prescribed via the "trial and error" method in the United States (Aspinall and Hamermesh, 2007). This raises the question: who might be in the 30–50 percent?

The authors of a 1999 *Science* article with the practical title "Pharmacogenomics: Translating Functional Genomics into Rational Therapies" predicted the explosion of industry interest in using genomic strategies to discover new drug targets (Evans and Relling, 1999:487–491). They acknowledged that developing medications for every member of a population was a "pharmacological long shot" and recommended, instead, developing drugs "targeted for specific, but genetically identifiable, subgroups of the population." They note that "all pharmacogenetic polymorphisms studied to date differ in frequency among ethnic and racial groups" and concluded that this "marked racial and ethnic diversity" in drug-metabolizing enzymes "dictates that race be considered in studies aimed at discovering whether specific genotypes or phenotypes are associated with disease risk or drug toxicity" (Evans and Relling, 1999:487–491). Similarly, "[p]harmacoethnicity, or ethnic diversity in drug response or toxicity," O'Donnell and Dolan (2009:4808) write, "results from the combined interaction of many factors, principally differences in environment, local practice habits and regulatory control differences, drug-drug interaction differences, and genetic differences."

Such a complex array of contributing factors, however, easily gets lost when there is an almost exclusive focus on searching for genetic factors – which is the mandate of pharmacogenomic pharmacoethnicity studies – that may or may not explain observed differences across racially and/or ethnically designated population groups. Moreover, as Wailoo (2011) has argued, "the story of cancer and the color line therefore becomes the story of cancer's transformation and of *racialization*," which he defines as "the processes by which scientists used the disease to create narratives of difference" (p. 181). Finally, as will be shown in the following pages, some medical geneticists and oncologists mentioned the problems in attributing the causes of cancer to either genetics or race/ethnicity – and they further pointed out that, in some studies, race and ethnicity are actually used as a statistical proxy for environmental exposures and dietary contributory factors to cancer.

Nevertheless, the way forward for the study of pharmacoethnicity in cancer therapeutics proposed by O'Donnell and Dolan (2009:4810) provides clues to its appeal to non-Western countries as they try to attract foreign investments and develop knowledge-based economies. O'Donnell and Dolan (2009:4808) provide several suggestions for putting the notion of pharmacoethnicity into action, including, but not limited to, the following two components: 1) international collaboration and repeat trials in multiple different countries so that diverse populations can be utilized for clinical trials concerning pharmacoethnicity, and 2) studying ethnic populations enriched for the phenotype of interest. Thus, the concept of pharmacoethnicity encourages the active search for potentially "druggable" or drug-actionable genetic markers and the determination of their frequencies among populations categorized by ethnicity, with an end point of an identifiable pharmaceutical market.

The approval of BiDil by the US FDA as the first "ethnic" drug to treat heart failure in self-identified African Americans is a case in point. BiDil was seen to be a significant step toward personalized medicine (Stein, 2005). Yet, upon closer inspection, BiDil is not a pharmacogenomic drug. It is a combination of two generic drugs, hydralazine and isosorbide dinitrate, intended to treat all people suffering from heart failure. Both drugs have been used to treat heart failure in people of all races (U.S. Food and Drug Administration, 2005). Race was the key factor that ensured the success of BiDil even though there were no concrete trials or research conducted to prove its superior efficacy for African Americans compared to other races (Roberts, 2011; Kahn, 2013).

Why Asia?

There are several reasons to pay special attention to the development of postgenomic medicine in Asia. First, cancer is an increasing burden, particularly in developing countries. As the International Agency for Research on Cancer (IARC) has stated:

> In 2012, the worldwide burden of cancer rose to an estimated 14 million new cases per year, a figure expected to rise to 22 million annually within the next two decades. Over the same period, cancer deaths are predicted to rise from an estimated 8.2 million annually to 13 million per year. Developing countries are disproportionately affected by the increasing numbers of cancers. More than 60 percent of the world's total cases occur in Africa, Asia, and Central and South America, and these regions account for about 70 percent of the world's cancer deaths.
>
> (International Agency for Research on Cancer, 2014)

Second, in June 2000, President Bill Clinton (United States), Prime Minister Tony Blair (United Kingdom), and two molecular geneticists who had led public and private sector human genome projects announced the first mapping and sequencing draft of the human genome. However, "Asians must be aware that there should be three players," Ryoji Noyori, the 2001 Nobel Prize winner in Chemistry, notes, "America, Europe and Asia" (Nature, 2007). As we shall see, molecular geneticists and medical researchers in Asia are contending that Asia is a key player.

Third, I suggest that we will advance our understanding of the fluidity and complexity of the categories of ethnicity and race when we examine how "othering" is done when the "self" is "Asian." That is, historically, the "Asian" has been defined through a "Western"-centric lens and has been seen and treated as the non-Western "other." This book seeks to understand what happens if and when the producers of knowledge for genome-based medicine are primarily located in Asia. At the same time, the arguments advanced in this book might have implications for the "Asians" in the United States as well. The US Census Bureau projected that "between 2013 and 2050, the Asian population (one race) is expected to increase 115 percent to 34.3 million," making it the fastest growing minority group in the US (Pew Research Center, 2008).

Time, space, and the emergent other

Many social scientists have explored the concept of "othering" or "the other," which is said to have been coined by philosopher Georg Wilhelm Friedrich Hegel. Berenson (1982) believes that the determining factor of one's self-consciousness lies in whether one has recognition for the "being of the Other." Edward Said further popularized the concept in *Orientalism*, which spurred the development of postcolonial theory. Said explains the "other" in the following manner:

> The construction of identity – for identity, whether of Orient or Occident, France or Britain, while obviously a repository of distinct collective experiences,

is finally a construction – involves establishing opposites and "others" whose actuality is always subject to the continuous interpretation and re-interpretation of their differences from "us". Each age and society re-creates its "Others". Far from a static thing then, identity of self or of "other" is a much worked-over historical, social, intellectual, and political process that takes place as a contest involving individuals and institutions in all societies.

(Said, 2003:333)

Moreover, Said writes, "the Orient was almost a European invention, and had been since antiquity a place of romance, exotic beings, haunting memories and landscapes, remarkable experiences" (1978:1). The essentialist boundary between the Orient and the Occident has been, that is, the result of human fabrication rather than nature. What might be the purpose for these categories?

Said argues that *Orientalism*, orchestrated by the Western powers, serves as a "regime of knowledge" or "ideological suppositions, images and fantasies about a currently important and politically urgent region of the world called the 'Orient'" (Said, 1978). In Western discourse, thus, the East is constructed as the inferior other. For instance, Lee (1999:ix) writes about perceptions of Asians in United States:

"Orientals are rugs, not people," says my student, summing up Asian American history. As she knows, it is the common experience of all Asian Americans – recent immigrant or fourth-generation American born, university professor or garment worker – to be asked by other Americans, "*Where do you come from?*" My student knows that the question, while often benign, is never completely innocent. "Oakland" or "Oshkosh" is never the acceptable answer, and its rejection reveals at once that the question is not about hometowns. The repeated question always implies, 'You couldn't be from here.' It equates the Asian with alien.

This viewpoint concerning the discursive practices of domination by the West on the East is not without its critics. These man-made categories suggest an ontological instability (Bhabha, 1994). Indeed, it should be emphasized that Bhabha (1994) sees beyond the sole domination of Western ideology and points to the involvement of the alienated Oriental Self in the construction, reinforcement, and circulation of Orientalist discourse. In other words, it should be emphasized that the othered takes part in the othering process.

More recently, Mountz defines the term "other" as both a noun and a verb. As a noun, the "other" always constitutes the outside and is therefore "a person or group of people who are different from oneself." As a verb, "other means to distinguish, label, categorize, name, identify, place and exclude those who do not fit a societal norm" (Mountz, 2009:328).

One may then raise the questions of who gets to define whom, what fits into the "us" and "other," and what purpose does this distinction serve in this millennium, which is significantly characterized by the rise of data-driven genomic science and medicine? Castell proposes that our identity construction within this network society is intertwined with questions like "how, from what, by whom and for what?" (Castell, 2004:7). In this regard, there is an emphasis not only on power being enmeshed within our self-conception and conception of the "other," but also on the location of the power. Once outside of the socio-geographic realms where the definition of "other" originates, the term loses its meaning (Chatterjee, 2012). In short, othering may be a tool within an age-old toolbox of discrimination and exclusion, but its effective use is contingent on spatial and temporal contexts.

Genomics in Asia and the unfolding dynamics of othering

One prominent example of othering, which has been occurring for centuries, is the dichotomy of "West versus non-West/Asian." European explorers imagined themselves as superior to all of the peoples they encountered, such that these people have been "othered" by European imperialism and colonialism (Hudson, 1996). In Asia, as elsewhere, othering was a key component of colonial administration; artificial boundaries based on "real or imagined attributes such as language, customs, religion and indigenousness" were created to meet the exigencies of daily rule (Spaan, von Naerssen and Kohl, 2002:163). For instance, "the colonial economy marked the origin of the Malaysian multi-ethnic society" (Spaan, von Naerssen and Kohl, 2002:163); that is, members of each "race" had certain characteristics or mannerisms that made them "suitable" to work in certain occupations. Later on, the advent of the nation-state necessitated the formation of the "native" and the "other" (Rabinowitz, 2010).

While othering processes have been studied in health care settings pertaining to interactions between health care providers and minority patients, these studies have been conducted mostly in advanced developed countries, and such processes have not been examined in terms of genomic science and its relation to personalized medicine. As alluded to above, however, the genomic revolution is taking hold in Asia; thus, we can raise the question: how are the 'self' and 'other' defined and constructed when the actors 'defining the situation' are located in Asia?

Drawing on primary interview data with more than thirty top geneticists and medical oncologists in Japan, Korea, Hong Kong, Taiwan, and Singapore,[5] as well as published documents used as secondary sources, I illustrate how the empirical phenomenon of the making and unmaking of "Asian" DNA can be best understood as responses to being othered, and, as such, these responses unfold in different contexts. We will examine both a project primarily concerned with migration patterns (the HUGO Pan-Asian Single Nucleotide Polymorphism Consortium)[6] and one focused on disease treatment (the IRESSA Pan-Asia Study).[7] The former is suitable for investigation not only because it is the first inter-Asian genomics collaboration, but also because it is seen as laying the foundation for postgenomic medicine in Asia (Ozdemir et al., 2011), while the latter facilitated the marketing of the EGFR (Epidermal growth factor receptor) biomarker-based personalized anti-lung cancer drug IRESSA, to be sold not only in Asia, but also in Europe and Canada.

As will be discussed, the development of the HUGO Pan-Asian SNP Consortium was partly driven by scientists attempting to take control of the definition of "Asian" genome variation and, thereby, counter the perceived hegemonic authority of the West in genomic science. Such counter-hegemonic movements do not have a monolithic base, however, and can take form as regional or national initiatives. In other words, one can begin to speak of the rise of multiple centers in genomic science and medicine. In line with this observation, I will explore the relationship between ethnic and racial categories and genomic public health policies in the nation-state of Singapore, a former British colony and the current location of the Human Genome Organization's (HUGO) international headquarters.

Though the main empirical site of the investigation is Asia, this book engages the literature on genomic applications in developing countries. Séguin et al. (2008) point out that developing countries – Mexico, Thailand, South Africa, and India – are initiating their own genotyping projects, and characterize such investment in, and adoption of, innovative genomic science and technology as "breaking the cycle of dependence on industrialized countries." Instead of assuming that this relationship is one of dependence, I will explore the complex connections between developed and developing countries. Daar and Singer (2005:241) argue that "pharmacogenetics has significant relevance to the health of people in developing countries. . . . [F]or this benefit to be realized, we need to take into account not just differences between the genotypes of individuals. . .but the differences in genotypes between different *population groups.*" Séguin et al. (2008:487) further suggest that, "at the very least, such approaches will help [us to] understand disease susceptibility and drug responses in the local population." Integral to all of these projected developments is, again, the fluid nature of the relevant "population" in which a (prospective) patient is located.

There are patterned genetic and genomic differences among human population groups –for example, one can talk about clinal variations. However, this book alerts the readers to other worrisome developments. For instance, one possibility for constituting a "population" is a racialized formulation (e.g. Caucasian versus non-Caucasian), as hinted by Daar and Singer as such (2005:243):

> For pharmaceutical companies worldwide, developing countries are not only potentially huge markets for drug therapeutics but are also depositories of important human genetic diversity. Understanding this diversity is valuable because it better defines those population subgroups that will benefit more from a particular drug than others, and allows the detection of side-effects that might not be seen in populations that are mainly Caucasian. . . . It will therefore be increasingly important to include non-Caucasian populations in clinical trials.

Benjamin (2009:341) conceptualizes "postcolonial genomics as a nationalist project with contradictory tendencies – unifying and differentiating a diverse body politic, cultivating national scientific and commercial autonomy *and* dependence upon global knowledge networks and foreign capital." In other words, to fully appreciate the construction of the population category, one needs to understand the forces that "unify and differentiate." In this book, I explore the ways in which racial and ethnic variability operate.

Current research infrastructure and development concerning personalized medicine in Asia

It is clear that Asian countries are interested in and have invested in research and development of genome-based personalized medicine. For instance, the International Cancer Genome Consortium (ICGC) is a global collaboration aimed at research on various cancers and the development of potential personalized treatment (Jain, 2015a:368–369). Currently, four Asian nations serve as both members and research hubs: China (Chinese Cancer Genome Consortium), India (Department of Biotechnology, Ministry of Science and Technology), Japan (RIKEN and National Cancer Centre), and Singapore (Genome Institute of Singapore). Each research project is estimated to cost US$20 million. Nations funding the projects include China, India, Japan, Saudi Arabia, and South Korea.

The Pan-Asian SNP Consortium (PASNP), a transnational research team within the Human Genome Organization (HUGO), mapped genetic variation and migration patterns in 75 populations, with data from ten countries: Japan, Korea, China, Taiwan, Singapore, Thailand, Indonesia, Philippines, Malaysia, and India. I will briefly review the development of personalized medicine in the ten countries that participated in the HUGO PASNP below.

In Japan, the most notable project is the "BioBank Japan Project on the Implementation of Personalized Medicine," led by researchers at the RIKEN Center for Integrative Medical Sciences. The project began in 2003 and is now in its third phase (starting in 2013).[8] In addition, in a partnership with Seattle Genetics Inc., the Tokyo-based Takeda Pharmaceutical Company Limited is in the midst of developing both specific personalized medication and the means to clinically execute it (Jain, 2015b).

China is involved with major global collaborative efforts, including the Pharmacogenetics for Every Nation Initiative (PGENI) (Pasha and Scaria, 2013; Jain, 2015c), the 1000 Genomes Project (Pasha and Scaria, 2013; Jain, 2015d), HapMap (Mitra, Gope and Gope 2013; Pasha and Scaria, 2013), and, as noted above, the ICGC (Jain, 2015e). PGENI is a collaboration involving 104 nations. China plays a crucial role as one of the five key coordinating bases with the goal of integrating pharmacogenetics with public health care and enabling the spread the spread of genome research to the Global South. The 1000 Genomes Project, with an estimated US$30 to US$50 million in funding, is a collaboration between the Beijing Genomics Institute, the US National Genome Research Institute, and the UK Wellcome Trust's Sanger Institute. Its goal is to sequence the genome of 1000 people across the world and produce a petabyte worth of data. The HapMap project, started in 2002, seeks to uncover genetic variation between individuals by pinpointing the haplotype. One of its goals is to understand the relationship between genetic variations and drug responses. It is an extensive collaboration between China, Japan, the United States, Canada, the United Kingdom, and Nigeria. A 2012 news article from the Asia-Pacific Biotech News entitled "Personalized Medicine Receives a Boost" noted that, "Affymetrix Inc. (NASDAQ: AFFX) recently announced that its GeneChip System 3000Dx v.2 (GCS 3000Dx v.2) has been approved by China's State Food and Drug Administration (SFDA) for *in vitro* diagnostic use." Affymetrix Inc. is the genome technology partner of HUGO PASNP Consortium. Andy Last, executive vice president of the Genetic Analysis and Clinical Applications Business Unit at Affymetrix, is reported to have said that "this registration clearance is a significant accomplishment for Affymetrix and supports our global clinical strategy. It connects us more closely to physicians in China wanting to utilize clinically relevant genomic biomarkers that improve their patients' health and wellness" (Asia-Pacific Biotech News, 2012).

Similarly, according to the Korean government's official website, "demand for personalized medicines [sic] . . . has been on the rise" in South Korea[9]. Korea has a strong local research foundation. The Korean Genome Project "is an open access endeavor to collect, analyze and distribute Korean genomes" (Pasha and Scaria, 2013). Its objective is to enable both researchers and the general public to access personal genomic information. Furthermore, the Korean Pharmacogenomics Research Network is acclaimed for having "laid a strong research infrastructure" at Seoul National University (Reddy et al., 2011:161). The network also works with the Korean Ministry of Health and Welfare and established a genomic bio-bank in 2011. Currently, it is involved with researching means to translate genomic research into clinical and medical applications.

In Taiwan, Chen and Chen (2010) have explored practical approaches necessary to enable Taiwanese hospitals to establish the clinical practice of pharmacogenetic tests. The current status of health care expenditure is centralized with the Bureau of National Health Insurance (NHI). Given Taiwan's policy of universal health care, the assumption is that the NHI functions as the reimbursement agency for all patients. However, in 1998, the NHI plunged into a financial crisis, annotating a growing concern within the state that "the premium received from the payer is insufficient to cover the expenses of NHI" (Chen and Chen, 2010:503). Thus, it has been proposed that reimbursements be reserved for patients "who have wild-type K-ras gene and epidermal growth factor receptor (EGFR) expression" (Chen and Chen, 2010:503). These two biomarkers – the wild-type K-ras gene and the EGFR mutation – and their relationship with the efficacy of cancer treatments have been established and replicated.

In India, *BioSpectrum* reports that "the future of pharmacogenomics in India is bright and will be the key in bringing the reality of personalized medicine to the masses in India" (Murarka, 2012). The essential purpose of the Indian Genome Variation database (IGVdb) is to "further research on disease predisposition" (Séguin et al., 2008:489), with the hope that available data lead "to improved diagnostics for treatment of patients" (Séguin et al., 2008:490). The government's Department of Biotechnology (DBT) is also funding the $20 million Indian Genome Initiative (IGI) (Acharya et al., 2004). This has enabled the establishment of the Center for Human Genetics (Bangalore) in order to introduce a credible bioinformatics infrastructure. The Center for Human Genetics "was set up to enhance Indian contributions to computational genomics, proteomics and drug design" (Asia Pacific Biotech News, 2004:949). Other well-funded organizations in India's genome research infrastructure include the Research Centers of the Indian Council for Medical Research (ICMR), the Center for Cellular and Molecular Biology (CCMB), and the Institute of Genomics and Integrative Biology (IGIB) (Asia Pacific Biotech News, 2004:950–955).

In Singapore, according to an article in *The Business Times*:

> [E]ven as pharmaceutical giant Novartis remains focused on producing blockbuster drugs in the next five years, Singapore's biomedical research – linked to economic outcomes and investment dollars in recent years – heads down a narrower path of personalized medicine. A new program called *Polaris*, which receives $20 million from the [national] Agency of Science, Technology and Research (A*Star) over three years, is the starting point for stratified medicine where drugs are matched to a patient's biomarker.
>
> (Kan, 2012)

Thailand's involvement in genomic research is also momentous. The hope, it appears, is for Thailand to benefit from the superior research infrastructure of its partner countries in the HUGO Pacific Pan-Asian SNP Initiative (Séguin et al., 2008). Apart from this partnership, the Thailand Center for Excellence in Life Sciences (TCELS) Pharmacogenomics Project has undertaken an SNP genotyping project vis-à-vis drug response. Examples of diseases tested include HIV and leukemia. TCELS is also "collaborating with the RIKEN institute in Japan" to study the relationship between genetics and post-traumatic stress disorder (Seguin et al., 2008:490). Finally, the Thai SNP Discovery Project is one that partners state organizations, academic and medical institutions, and the private sector with research centers in France.

Malaysia, Indonesia, and the Philippines are also in the developing stages. For instance, the "Malaysia Human Genome Variation Consortium" (the Malaysian node of the Human Variome Project) is concerned with mapping genome diversity in the country (Pasha and Scaria, 2013). Also, it specifically "aims to determine the migratory history of the country's populations, the genetic similarities between them and the implications of these variations on the various facets of research including pharmacogenomic" (Pasha and Scaria, 2013:197).

As investments in research in Asia have risen in recent years, scientists with Asian backgrounds who have been trained in Europe and the United States are returning to Asia. In an article entitled "Flocking to Asia for a Shot at Greatness" (Normile, 2012) published in *Science* on 7 September 2012, Dr. Tan Chorh Chuan, President of the National University of Singapore (NUS), was quoted as saying, "conditions are right for Asian universities to attract top faculty from the rest of the world." Indeed, it was reported in the same article that:

> Hong Kong and Singapore schools aren't alone in recruiting globally. The National Research Foundation of Korea has committed $728 million for a 5-year World Class University Project that has attracted 321 foreign academics, most on full-time appointments. Three years ago, Japan's Ministry of Education began a program to internationalize both the faculty and the students at its universities, although budget constraints have crimped the effort. And Taiwan's Ministry of Education has an Aim for the Top University Project that supports overseas recruitment. China has employed a variety of schemes in the past decade to lure back scientists who went overseas for advanced degrees or jobs. These include the Ministry of Education's Changjiang Scholars Program and the Chinese Academy of Sciences' 100 Talents Program.

Finally, given the region's remarkable economic growth and aging populations, the Asia-Pacific region has become a major block in the global oncology market. According to IMS Health, a provider of pharmaceutical and health care market analysis, in 2009, the Asia-Pacific region's oncology market was worth US$10.97 billion, and "by 2011, the global oncology market was growing by 6.8 percent, driven by 15.2 percent growth in emerging markets. . . . Japan, China, and Australia together represented more than 85 percent of the oncology market share within the Asia-Pacific region." The IMS report lists the top ten countries in terms of market shares in 2009 as follows: Japan (63.7 percent), China (15.6 percent), Australia (6.5 percent), Korea (4.6 percent), Taiwan (3.6 percent), Thailand (1.5 percent), Hong Kong (1.0 percent), Singapore (0.6 percent), India (0.6 percent), and Indonesia (0.6 percent). Indeed, negotiations for drug commercialization rights have resulted in an agreement wherein "firms are funding development costs on a 50:50 basis worldwide," with the exception of Japan along with the United States and Canada (Jain, 2015a:336).

But as we highlighted earlier, Kato et al. (2010) write that "while determining genomic sequence data is becoming faster and more accurate, *interpretation* of the clinical significance of genomic information is dependent on a science that is still immature and potentially changeable over time" [emphasis in original].

Existing social-science studies of science and medicine performed in Asia

There is a comparatively small but growing number of studies of human genome science by researchers from backgrounds in the humanities and social sciences in Asia. However, these studies have yet to subject notions of "Asian" and "ethnicity" to close and systematic examination. This is an important task, however, given the possibility raised by Ong (2013) that "with Genome-wide Association Studies (GWAS) as a guiding tool, drugs can be determined as safe or dangerous for some patients but not others, *depending on their ethnic group*" (Ong, 2013:79, emphasis mine). Indeed, as Daar and Singer (2005:241) point out, "we need to explore the nexus between pharmacogenetics, genotyping projects in developing countries, and the evolution of the pharmaceutical industry in both the developed and developing worlds."

Within Asia, there are country-level analyses that are instructive concerning the problematic nature of population categories in genomic science and medicine. In the case of Japan, Kuo (2008:500) writes that "anthropologists Hiroshi Wagatsuma and Toshinao Yoneyama argue that *minzoku* includes all qualifications of being Japanese that, like staves, together make up a barrel called *nihonjin* (the Japanese). . . . [T]he staves include holding Japanese citizenship, following Japanese etiquette, speaking Japanese, having Japanese bodily characteristics, having been born in Japan, understanding traditional Japanese stories, *naniwabushi*, living in Japan, eating sashimi, and other Japanese traits." In studying Taiwan's biobank, Tsai (2010:433) points out that Taiwan's "four great ethnic groups (*sida zuqun*) – the Hoklo, Hakka, Mainlanders, and aboriginal peoples – exist only as a social construction that arose in the 1990s in a specific political-cultural context." In South Korea, Hyun (2015:1) showed that "[antidoping scientists] used racial categories in their studies of the UGT2B17 gene without concern, and their research reinforced the shaping of racialist discourses on the idea of Asians as a doping-friendly race in the media and cyberspace."

My hope is to provide an empirically grounded understanding of the formation and usage of specific human taxonomies in the development and implementation of personalized medicine as it unfolds in Asia. Here, we raise questions such as: if there is no consistent and standardized genetic basis for classifying populations based upon race/ethnicity, then why do large-scale mapping projects continue to use such categories in identifying research populations? Personalized medicine for whom? Is it possible to reconcile claims that "there are no genes for race" (Dupré, 2008) with the notion that "ethnic groups are genetically different" (Evans and Relling, 1999)? Finally, who gets to determine and define the category Asian? Who is Caucasian, and why does it matter?

The illuminating question could be, when are you from?

Instead of an almost exclusive focus on the question of where a person is from, Duster (2015:84) has pointed out that "when we shift and raise the question 'when are you from?' we become far better equipped, conceptually, to see and examine the inexorable convergence of science and society." Kahn (2015) suggests that the time period in which scientists and researchers constructed ideas of "pure" race and/or ethnicity matters:

> The idea that there are somehow 'pure' types of African, European, or Asian DNA is a fiction, constructed not only by artificially bounding geographic areas but also by arbitrarily designating distinct points in time as marking the temporal moment of purity.

In other words, it is of fundamental importance for the analyst to take a step back and to examine the social histories embedded in the population categories that scientists and medical researchers in contemporary times take for granted in their laboratories. This task is essential because it allows us to then critically reflect upon what the scientists and researchers are telling us about those categories, what they are doing with those categories, and what ethical and social implications may flow from those assumptions and practices.

Following this line of inquiry, it is important to note, first of all, that the modern nation-states in Asia that this book discusses are primarily creations of the twentieth century. Moreover, as shown in Appendix A, most nation-states have colonial histories. Secondly, a rich body of literature has demonstrated that the contemporary ethnic categorizations in postcolonial nation-states have been significantly shaped by the Western colonial administrations. India, Malaysia, and Singapore were under British colonial rule. The Spanish and American colonial administrators in the Philippines and their Dutch counterparts in Indonesia all actively engaged in the naming and labeling of peoples under their colonial rule. Nation-states that have not been colonized by "the West" have their own political histories. For example, between 57 BCE–668 BCE, the three kingdoms of Goguryeo, Baekje, and Silla dominated the Korean Peninsula and parts of Manchuria, the area now known as "Korea." Before turning to illuminate and explain the emergence of these issues as they relate to Asia, in Chapter 2, I first draw analogies and parallels to how Europe went through remarkably similar processes of ethnic and racial "emergence." Then, in Chapters 2 and 3, I further suggest that the dynamic construction of ethnic and racial categories in the contexts of a global genomic science and the pharmaceutical industry is not only about the relationship between the contemporary Asia and "the West," but also regional dynamics within Asia. In Chapter 4, I elaborate on the point that ethnicity is a function of the construction of "nationhood" as well.

What is at stake when populations are ethnically or racially labeled?

While large-scale genetic variation projects calculate allelic frequencies of genetic variants among racial and ethnic groups, Marcus Feldman, a biologist, and Richard Lewontin, a population geneticist, have stated that "the actual distribution of human genetic variation, including the distribution of genotypes that are directly relevant to the diagnosis and treatment of disease, is such that race is not a useful biological concept when applied to humans" (Feldman and Lewontin, 2008:98). Indeed, humans are essentially identical in about 99.5 percent of their DNA (Weiss 2007). More fundamentally, "it is possible to make arbitrary groupings of populations defined by geography, language, self-identified faiths, other identified physiognomy and so on and still find statistically significant allelic variations between these groupings" (Duster, 2006a:434). In Asia, for instance, Takezawa et al. (2014:3) note that "even among mainland Japanese, statistically meaningful genetic differentiation was found among individuals in different regions, such as Tohoku, Kanto, Kinki, and Kyushu."

Perhaps, most importantly, as anthropologist of science Jonathan Marks (2006:6) explains:

> [P]roviding health care can obviously benefit by knowing something of the self-identification of the subject, given that different groups have different risks, due to their histories or life circumstances. But that does not presuppose that there are fundamental biologically-based divisions between the groups. . . . The therapeutic intervention would have to be based on genotype, not on any racialized identity. Otherwise it would be far more likely to kill people than to cure them.

The main point that these first four chapters makes is that identity categories of "Asian" or "Caucasian," "Japanese" or "Malay," are demonstrably integral to the social process of "(self-)othering" in particular contexts, such as colonialism or establishing the boundaries of the nation-state, and yet some researchers are uncritically using these categories as if they were intrinsically biomedical. Chapter 5 problematizes such widespread usage of ethnic and racial categories as proxies for human genetic variation and provides the turning point in this book. In particular, I draw on interviews with oncologists to explain and highlight the serious limitations of using patterns of genomic differences that seem to differ between ethnic and racial groups in their clinical practices. In other words, even though population-based genomic research is couched in the rhetoric of advancing cancer treatment and prevention, this chapter delineates physicians' concerns about using findings from such a research agenda. Chapter 6 further emphasizes the ethical dilemmas that physicians face in the delivery of genome-based medicine for cancer patients, as well as their concerns for potential discriminatory practices at the societal level.

Chapter outline

Chapter 2 – Regionalism and the study of human genetic variation in a transnational context: Asianism, nationalism, and the racialization of ethnicity

The first phase of the HUGO Pan-Asian SNP Consortium (PASNP) project was completed in 2009. The primary conclusion that "there is substantial genetic proximity of SEA [Southeast Asian] and EA [East Asian] populations" was presented in "Mapping Human Genetic Diversity in Asia," published in *Science* (The HUGO Pan-Asian SNP Consortium, 2009). The Pan-Asian Population Genomics Initiative (PAPGI) is the next phase of PASNP.

This chapter analyzes this influential publication in *Science* along with the contexts of the production of such scientific knowledge. Specifically, drawing on interviews with leading geneticists in the HUGO PASNP Consortium and on documentary analysis, it describes how and why the PASNP study changed from a disease-oriented study to a study of migration history, and how participating scientists used "ethnicity" as a population sampling frame while defining it subjectively.

Reacting against Western domination in human genome science, human geneticists in Asia organized themselves to gain control over the definition of "Asian" genome variation. Moreover, this chapter provides descriptions of historical, political, and legal processes that have shaped the "ethnic" groups used in the genome variation analysis. It concludes that the PASNP's work engages a dynamic tension that simultaneously undermines (for some) and reifies (for others) the biological bases of socially constructed notions of race and ethnicity, and highlights the implications for pharmacogenomics studies and personalized medicine.

Chapter 3 – Capitalizing on being "othered": precision medicine and race the context of a globalized pharmaceutical industry

Before genome-based personalized medicine can be administered in clinical settings, the question is what shapes drug marketing and development. This chapter closely examines the story of gefitinib (IRESSA, marketed by the pharmaceutical company AstraZeneca), a targeted drug for treating non-small-cell lung cancer patients with EGFR mutations. It suggests that the case of IRESSA deserves a closer look, not least because it has been hailed as an exemplary case of personalized medicine. It illustrates that, in some instances, lurking just beneath the surface of molecular-based personalized medicine is the reality of racially and ethnically designated population-based drug development in the context of a globalized pharmaceutical industry. In addition, this chapter analyzes the ways in which some geneticists and medical oncologists in Singapore have re-centered Asia in their empirical pharmacogenomic studies of cancer drug toxicity with an emphasis on ethnic diversity, typically adopting comparisons between "Asians" and "Caucasians" in the context of Phase IV clinical trials. As such, it provides examples of the transnational implications of racially and ethnically framed pharmacogenomic studies for countries beyond Asia.

Chapter 4 – Managing otherness: genomics and public health policy in Singapore

This chapter describes the ways in which Singapore's government is incorporating genomic science for public health policy decision-making. In the national context, the internal social diversity of the "nationally Asian" population is highlighted in studies of genomic medicine in terms of cost-effectiveness. Specifically, the chapter explores the ways in which medical doctors and health economists try to use census population categories such Malay, Chinese, and Indian, and how these health professionals think in terms of sampling (as if these were distinctive populations), providing the basis for ethnically- or racially-based public health policy guidelines. Moreover, the chapter offers a social-historical-political account of the unfolding character of the category of the "Malay" population to suggest that while medical researchers are actors of contemporary times and do not think in terms of historical contingencies, we can see the complexities inherent in these population categories once we examine the actual history.

Chapter 5 – Cancer genomics in clinics

Chapter 5 returns to the key promise of genomic science in advancing human health. I suggest that "making genomic medicine" is not only about acquiring and understanding knowledge about human genome variation, but also about judgment as to whether and how to translate knowledge into practice. This chapter describes the ideal of personalized medicine that most medical oncologists in Singapore hold – which is to use the molecular characteristics of individuals to improve the prevention, detection, and treatment of cancer. As such, the chapter highlights the tensions between the racial and ethnic categories constructed in the contexts of global genomic science, the pharmaceutical industry, and national genomic public health policies at the macro level, and clinical practice at the micro level. Doctors are on the front lines of delivering health care, and they articulated their concerns about using ethnic or racial identities as proxies in deciding drug efficacy, drug toxicity, and preventive medicine for individual cancer patients. This chapter identifies some of the social and economic conditions under which racial and ethnic patient identities shape treatment decisions, which are seen as suboptimal by most, if not all, clinicians.

Chapter 6 – Socio-economic factors and ethical dilemmas in personalized medicine provision

Socio-economic factors are ultimately related to ethical issues. This chapter highlights the lessons learned from medical oncology in terms of the promise and limitations of collective interventions at the molecular level, as opposed to the environmental level, to address the complex disease of cancer. It suggests that genome-based personalized medicine is expansive, but not curative. Given this characteristic, we focus on the ethical dilemmas and knowledge gaps of personalized medicine provision from the perspectives of physicians. In relation to bioethics, for example, should doctors recommend genetic testing, and, afterwards, should they recommend certain kinds of genome-based personalized medicine? As a doctor, should one provide all available information or only information as needed by the patient? Doctors have different ways of resolving such ethical dilemmas, and their resolutions can, potentially, be challenged. With regard to biopolitics, we discuss some concerns potential discriminatory practices against ethnically or racially identified groups. This issue is important because of how population-based genomic studies identify and construct reference populations along racial and ethnic lines that are significantly a function of history and politics.

Chapter 7 – Conclusion: personalized medicine and population-based genetic/genomic studies

No two patients are alike, even if they come from the same racial or ethnic population. In the (post-)genomic era, will medicine be "personalized" according to an individual's unique genetic makeup, or will it be developed and administered in relation to that individual's racial and ethnic identities? This book analyzes social forces shaping possible outcomes. Moreover, it provides empirical evidence to suggest that the emergence of "Asia(n)" DNA or ethnically demarcated genomics is partly a function of various strategies of centering Asia in the genomic science and medical fields, and partly a function of the ways in which population geneticists and medical researchers in Asia cope with otherness. As such, these racial and ethnic categories have no *a priori* naturalness, even though, at first glance, they may appear to. Thus, the majority of the medical oncologists interviewed do not support using race or ethnicity as a proxy in their clinical decision-making, not least because, as they put it, genetic mutations do not recognize racial or ethnic boundaries. Through closely examining what is happening in Asia, this book hopes to contribute to our understanding of the co-creation of racial categories and production of knowledge in this global era.

Notes

1 European Science Foundation. 2012. "Personalised Medicine for the European Citizen – Towards More Precise Medicine for the Diagnosis, Treatment and Prevention of Disease (iPM)." *ESF Forward Look* (November 2012):1–62. France: European Science Foundation. Retrieved January 18, 2015 (http://www.esf. org/fileadmin/Public_documents/Publications/Personalised_Medicine.pdf).
2 PriceWaterhouseCoopers. 2009. "The New Science of Personalized Medicine: Translating the Promise into Practice." Retrieved November 20, 2015 (http:// capitalgroupholdings.com/files/The-New-Science-of-Personalized-Medicine.pdf).
3 Ozdemir, Vural, David H. Muljono, Tikki Pang, Lynnette R. Ferguson, Aresha Manamperi, Sofia Samper, Toshiyuki Someya, Anne M. Tassé, Shih-Jen Tsai, Hong-Hao Zhou and Edmund J. D. Lee. 2011. "Asia-Pacific Health 2020 and Genomics Without Borders: Co-Production of Knowledge by Science and Society Partnership for Global Personalized Medicine." *Current Pharmacogenomics and Personalized Medicine* 9(1):1–5.
4 U.S. National Library of Medicine. Genetics Home Reference: Your Guide to Understanding Genetic Conditions. 2015. "What is pharmacogenomics?" Retrieved November 20, 2015 (http://ghr.nlm.nih.gov/handbook/genomicre search/pharmacogenomics).
5 See Appendix A for details.
6 PASNP. 2010. "Pan-Asian Single Nucleotide Polymorphism Consortium." Retrieved November 20, 2015 (http://www4a.biotec.or.th/PASNP).
7 IRESSA. 2014. "The IPASS Study." Retrieved January 28, 2015 (http://www. iressa.com/ipass-study.html).
8 RIKEN Center for Integrative Medical Sciences. "The BioBank Japan Project on the Implementation of Personalized Medicine (Establishing techniques for personalized medicine)." Retrieved November 20, 2015 (http://www.ims.riken.jp/ english/projects/pj02.php).
9 Invest Korea. 2012. "Promising Investment Opportunities." *Overview of Korea's Industries 2012: Medical/Bio*. Retrieved November 20, 2015 (http://www. investkorea.org/ikwork/iko/eng/com/fileDown.jsp?filename=data/content_ file/20130121/07_Bio.pdf.).

References

Acharya, Tara, Nandini K Kumar, Vasantha Muthuswamy, Abdallah S Daar and Peter A Singer. 2004. "Harnessing Genomics to Improve Health in India – An

Executive Course to Support Genomics Policy." *Health Res Policy Sys* 2(1). doi: (10.1186/1478-4505-2-1).

Asia Pacific Biotech News. 2004. "Public Research & Infrastructure Development." *Asia Pacific Biotech News* 8:948–959.

Asia Pacific Biotech News. 2012. "Personalized Medicine Receives Boost in China." *Asia-Pacific Biotech News* 16(3). Retrieved November 24, 2015 (http://www.asiabiotech.com/publication/apbn/16/english/preserved-docs/1603/1603.pdf).

Aspinall, Mara G. and Richard G. Hameresh. 2007. "Realizing the Promise of Personalized Medicine." *Harvard Business Review* 85(10):109–117.

BBC News. 2003. "Drugs 'Don't Work on Many People'." *BBC News,* December 8. Retrieved November 23, 2015 (http://news.bbc.co.uk/2/hi/health/3299945.stm).

Benjamin, Ruha. 2009. "A Lab of Their Own: Genomic Sovereignty as Postcolonial Science Policy." *Policy and Society* 28(4):341–355.

Berenson, Frances. 1982. "Hegel on Others and the Self." *Philosophy* 57(219):77–90.

Bhabha, Homi K. 1994. *The Location of Culture.* New York: Psychology Press.

Castell, M. 2004. *The Power of Identity.* Oxford: Blackwell Publishing.

Chatterjee, Ipsita. 2012. "How Are They Othered? Globalisation, Identity and Violence in an Indian City." *The Geographical Journal* 178(2):134–146. doi: 10.1111/j.1475-4959.2011.00427.x.

Chen, Hsiang-Yin and Li-Chia Chen. 2010. "Implementation of Innovative Pharmacogenetic Tests into Practice in Taiwan: An Institutional Perspective." *Drug Development Research* 71:502–506.

Clancey, Gregory, Connor Graham, Ryan Bishop and Michael M.J. Fischer. 2013. "Asian Biopoleis: Practice, Place, and Life." *East Asian Science, Technology and Society: An International Journal* 7(1):1–6.

Cyranoski, David. 2016. "China Embraces Precision Medicine on a Massive Scale." *Nature News & Comment,* 529(7584), 9–10/. doi:10.1038/529009a.

Daar, Abdallah S. and Peter A. Singer. 2005. "Pharmacogenetics and Geographical Ancestry: Implications for Drug Development and Global Health." *Nature Reviews Genetics* 6:241–246.

Dupré, John. 2008. "What Genes Are and Why There Are No Genes for Race." Pp. 39–55 in *Revisiting Race in a Genomic Age,* edited by B.A. Koenig, S.S. Lee and S.S. Richardson. New Brunswick, NJ: Rutgers University Press.

Duster, Troy. 2003. *Backdoor to Eugenics.* 2nd ed. New York and London: Routledge.

Duster, Troy. 2006a. "The Molecular Reinscription of Race: Unanticipated Issues in Biotechnology and Forensic Science." *Patterns of Prejudice* 40(4):427–441.

Duster, Troy. 2006b. "Lessons from History: Why Race and Ethnicity Have Played a Major Role in Biomedical Research." *The Journal of Law, Medicine & Ethics* 34(3):487–496.

Duster, Troy. 2015. "Response to Comments on 'A Post-Genomic Surprise'." *British Journal of Sociology* 66(1):83–92.

Epstein, Steven. 2007. *Inclusion: The Politics of Difference in Medical Research.* Chicago and London: The University of Chicago Press.

European Science Foundation. 2012. "Personalised Medicine for the European Citizen – Towards More Precise Medicine for the Diagnosis, Treatment and Prevention of Disease (iPM)." *ESF Forward Look* (November 2012):1–62. France: European Science Foundation. Retrieved January 18, 2015 (http://www.esf.org/fileadmin/Public_documents/Publications/Personalised_Medicine.pdf).

Evans, William E. and Mary V. Relling. 1999. "Pharmacogenomics: Translating Functional Genomics into Rational Therapeutics." *Science* 286(5439):487–491.

Feldman, Marcus W. and Richard C. Lewontin. 2008. "Race, Ancestry, and Medicine." Pp. 89–101 in *Revisiting Race in a Genomic Age*, edited by B.A. Koenig, S.S. Lee, S.S. Richardson. New Brunswick, NJ, and London: Rutgers University Press.

Fujimura, Joan H. and Ramya Rajagopalan. 2011. "Different Differences: The Use of 'Genetic Ancestry' Versus Race in Biomedical Human Genetic Research." *Social Studies of Science* 41(1):5–30.

Fullwiley, Duana. 2007. "The Molecularization of Race: Institutionalizing Human Difference in Pharmacogenetics Practice." *Science as Culture* 16(1):1–30.

Hayden, Erika Check. 2014. "The $1,000 genome." *Nature* 507:295.

Hinterberger, Amy. 2010. "The Genomics of Difference and the Politics of Race in Canada." Pp. 147–186 in *What's the Use of Race? Modern Governance and the Biology of Difference*, edited by I. Whitmarsh and D.S. Jones. Cambridge: MIT University Press.

Hinterberger, Amy. 2012a. "Investing in Life, Investing in Difference: Nations, Populations and Genomes." *Theory, Culture and Society* 29(3):72–93.

Hinterberger, Amy. 2012b. "Publics and Populations: The Politics of Ancestry and Exchange in Genome Science." *Science as Culture* 21(4):528–549.

Hudson, Nicholas. 1996. "From 'Nation' to 'Race': The Origin of Racial Classification in Eighteenth-Century Thought." *Eighteenth-Century Studies* 29(3): 247–264.

The HUGO Pan-Asian SNP Consortium. 2009. "Mapping Human Genetic Diversity in Asia." *Science* 326(5959):1541–1545. doi: 10.1126/science.1177074.

Hyun, Jaehwan. 2015. "Asians – A Doping-Friendly Race?: Antidoping Research and Popular Discourse on Race in the Postgenomic Era." *East Asian Science, Technology and Society: An International Journal* 10:1–23.

International Agency for Research on Cancer. World Health Organisation. 2014. "Global Battle Against Cancer Won't Be Won With Treatment Alone: Effective Prevention Measures Urgently Needed To Prevent Cancer Crisis." *Press Release*, February 3. Retrieved November 23, 2015 (https://www.iarc.fr/en/media-centre/pr/2014/pdfs/pr224_E.pdf).

Invest Korea. 2012. "Promising Investment Opportunities." *Overview of Korea's Industries 2012: Medical/Bio*. Retrieved November 20, 2015 (http://www.investkorea.org/ikwork/iko/eng/com/fileDown.jsp?filename=data/content_file/20130121/07_Bio.pdf.).

IRESSA. 2014. "The IPASS Study." Retrieved January 28, 2015 (http://www.iressa.com/ipass-study.html).

Jain, Kewal K. 2015a. *Textbook of Personalized Medicine*. Basel, CH: Humana Press.

Jain, Kewal K. 2015b. "Basic Aspects." Pp. 1–34 in *Textbook of Personalized Medicine*. Basel, CH: Humana Press.

Jain, Kewal K. 2015c. "Development of Personalized Medicine." Pp. 589–654 in *Textbook of Personalized Medicine*. Basel, CH: Humana Press.

Jain, Kewal K. 2015d. "Future of Personalized Medicine." Pp. 693–708 in *Textbook of Personalized Medicine*. Basel, CH: Humana Press.

Jain, Kewal K. 2015e. "Personalized Cancer Therapy." Pp. 199–382 in *Textbook of Personalized Medicine*. Basel, CH: Humana Press.

Kahn, Jonathan. 2013. *Race in a Bottle: The Story of BiDil and Racialized Medicine in a Post-Genomic Age*. New York: Columbia University Press.

Kahn, Jonathan. 2015. "'When Are You From?' Time, Space, and Capital in the Molecular Reinscription of Race." *The British Journal of Sociology* 66(1):68–75.

Kan, Lynn. 2012. "Singapore Place Bet on Personalised Drugs" *The Business Times*, November 10. Retrieved November 24, 2015 (https://www.healthxchange.com. sg/News/Pages/singapore-places-bet-personalised-drugs.aspx).

Kato, Kazuto, Kei Kano and Tetsuya Shirai. 2010. "Science Communication: Significance for Genome-Based Personalized Medicine – A View from the Asia-Pacific." *Current Pharmacogenomics and Personalized Medicine* 8(2):92–96.

Kuo, Wen-Hua. 2008. "Understanding Race at the Frontier of Pharmaceutical Regulation: An Analysis of the Racial Difference Debate at the ICH." *The Journal of Law, Medicine & Ethics* 36(3):498–505. Retrieved November 24, 2015. (http:// soc.thu.edu.tw/professors/Professoracadmic/feiwen/sts/%E7%9B%B8%E9%9 7%9C%E8%AB%96%E6%96%87/Kuo-J%20of%20Law,%20Med&%20Ethics%20 paepr.pdf).

Lee, Robert G. 1999. *Orientals: Asian Americans in Popular Culture*. Philadelphia, PA: Temple University Press.

Lee, Sandra Soo-Jin. 2003. "Race, Distributive Justice and the Promise of Pharmacogenomics: Ethical Considerations." *American Journal of Pharmacogenomics* 3(6):385–392.

LePoer, Barbara Leitch, ed. 1991. *Singapore: A Country Study*. Washington, DC: Federal Research Division, Library of Congress, Government Printing Office Catalog.

Marks, Jonathan. 2006. "The Realities of Races." Social Science Research Council. *Is Race "Real"?* Web Forum. Retrieved November 24, 2015 (http://raceandge nomics.ssrc.org/Marks/).

Mitra, Rohan., Mohan Lal Gope and Rajalakshmi Gope. 2013. "Personalized Genome, Current Status and the Future of Pharmacogenomics." Pp. 19–38 in *Omics for Personalized Medicine*, edited by D. Barh, D. Dhawan and N.K. Ganguly. New Delhi: Springer (India) Private Limited.

Mountz, Allison. 2009. "The Other." Pp.328–338 in *Key concepts in political geography*, edited by C. Gallaher, C.T. Dahlman, M. Gilmartin, A. Mountz and P. Shirlow. London: SAGE Publications Ltd.

Murarka, Vipul. 2012. "Personalized Medicine Picks Up Pace in India." *BioSpectrum*, August 23. Retrieved November 24, 2015 (http://www.biospectrumasia.com/ biospectrum/analysis/3147/one-size-fit-anymore/page/3).

Nature. 2007. "Asia on the Rise: The Balance of Scientific Power Is Moving East as Scientists in the Asia-Pacific Region Learn to Collaborate More Effectively." *Nature* 447(7147):885. doi: 10.1038/447885a.

Normile, Dennis. 2012. "Flocking to Asia for a Shot at Greatness." *Science* 337(6099): 1162–1166.

O'Donnell, Peter H. and M. Eileen Dolan. 2009. "Cancer Pharmacoethnicity: Ethnic Differences in Susceptibility to the Effects of Chemotherapy." *Clinical Cancer Research* 2009(15):4806–4814. doi: 10.1158/1078-0432.CCR-09-0344.

Ong, Aihwa. 2013. "A Milieu of Mutations: The Pluripotency and Fungibility of Life in Asia." *East Asian Science, Technology and Society: An International Journal* 7:69–85.

Ozdemir, Vural, David H. Muljono, Tikki Pang, Lynnette R. Ferguson, Aresha Manamperi, Sofia Samper, Toshiyuki Someya, Anne M. Tassé, Shih-Jen Tsai, Hong-Hao Zhou and Edmund J.D. Lee. 2011. "Asia-Pacific Health 2020 and Genomics without Borders: Co-production of Knowledge by Science and Society Partnership for Global Personalized Medicine." *Current Pharmacogenomics and Personalized Medicine* 9(1):1–5.

Pasha, Ayesha and Vinod Scaria. 2013. "Pharmacogenomics in the Era of Personal Genomics: A Quick Guide to Online Resources and Tools." Pp. 187–214 in *Omics for Personalized Medicine*, edited by D. Barh, D. Dhawan and N.K. Ganguly. New Delhi: Springer (India) Private Limited.

PASNP. 2010. "Pan-Asian Single Nucleotide Polymorphism Consortium." Retrieved November 20, 2015 (http://www4a.biotec.or.th/PASNP).

Personalized Medicine Coalition. 2014. *The Case for Personalized Medicine*. 4th ed. Washington, DC: Personalized Medicine Coalition.

Pew Research Center, 2008. *U.S. Population Projections: 2005–2050.* Retrieved 30 January, 2015 (http://www.pewsocialtrends.org/2008/02/11/us-population-projections-2005–2050/.)

PriceWaterhouseCoopers. 2009. The new science of personalized medicine: Translating the promise into practice. Retrieved November 20, 2015 (http://capital groupholdings.com/files/The-New-Science-of-Personalized-Medicine.pdf).

Rabinowitz, D. 2010. "Oriental Othering and National Identity: A Review of Early Israeli Anthropological Studies of Palestinians." *Identities: Global Studies in Culture and Power* 9(3):305–325.

Reddy, Panga Jaipal, Rekha Jain, Young-Ki Paik, Robin Downey, Adam S. Ptolemy, Vural Ozdemir and Sanjeeva Sricastava. 2011. "Personalized Medicine in the Age of Pharmacoproteomics: A Close up on India and Need for Social Science Engagement for Responsible Innovation in Post-Proteomic Biology." *Current Pharmacogenomics and Personalized Medicine* 9(3):159–167.

RIKEN Center for Integrative Medical Sciences. n.d. The BioBank Japan Project on the Implementation of Personalized Medicine (Establishing Techniques for Personalized Medicine) Retrieved November 20, 2015 (http://www.ims.riken.jp/english/projects/pj02.php).

Roberts, Dorothy. 2011. *Fatal Invention: How science, Politics and Big Business Re-Create Race in the Twenty-First Century.* New York and London: The New Press.

Rose, Nikolas. 2006. *The Politics of Life Itself: Biomedicine, Power, and Subjectivity in the Twenty-First Century.* Princeton and Oxford: Princeton University Press.

Said, Edward. 1978. *Orientalism.* New York: Pantheon Books.

Said, Edward. 2003. *Orientalism.* London: Penguin Books.

Séguin, Béatrice, Billie-Jo Hardy, Peter A. Singer and Abdallah S. Daar. 2008. "Genomic Medicine and Developing Countries: Creating a Room of their Own." *Nature Reviews Genetics* 9(6):487–493.

Spaan, Ernst, Ton Van Naerssen and Gerard Kohl. 2002. "Re-Imagining Borders: Malay Identity and Indonesian Migrants in Malaysia." *Tijdschrift voor economische en sociale geografie* 93(2):160–172.

Stein, Rob. 2005. "FDA Approves Controversial Heart Medication for Blacks." *The Washington Post*, June 24. Retrieved Dec 05, 2015 (http://www.washingtonpost.com/wp-dyn/content/article/2005/06/23/AR2005062301762.html).

Takezawa, Yasuko, Kazuto Kato, Hiroki Oota, Timothy Caulfield, Akihiro Fujimoto, Shunwa Honda, Naoyuki Kamatani, Shoji Kawamura, Kohei Kawashima, Ryosuke Kimura, Hiromi Matsumae, Ayako Saito, Patrick E Savage, Noriko Seguchi, Keiko Shimizu, Satoshi Terao, Yumi Yamaguchi-Kabata, Akira Yasukouchi, Minoru Yoneda and Katsushi Tokunaga. 2014. "Human Genetic Research, Race, Ethnicity and the Labeling of Populations: Recommendations Based on an Interdisciplinary Workshop in Japan." *BMC Med Ethics* 15:33. doi: 10.1186/1472–6939–15–33.

Tsai, Yu-Yueh. 2010. "Geneticizing Ethnicity: A Study on the 'Taiwan Bio-Bank'." *East Asian Science, Technology and Society: An International Journal* 4:433–455. doi: 10.1007/s12280–010–914.

U.S. Food and Drug Administration. 2005. "FDA Approves BiDil Heart Failure Drug for Black Patients." *News Release*, June 23. Retrieved November 23, 2015 (http://www.fda.gov/NewsEvents/Newsroom/PressAnnouncements/2005/ucm108445.htm).

U.S. National Library of Medicine. 2015. "Genetics Home Reference: Your Guide to Understanding Genetic Conditions." *What Is Pharmacogenomics?* Retrieved November 20, 2015 (http://ghr.nlm.nih.gov/handbook/genomicresearch/pharmacogenomics).

Wailoo, Keith. 2011. *How Cancer Crossed the Color Line.* Oxford: Oxford University Press.

Weiss, Rick. 2007. Mom's genes or Dad's? Map can tell. *Washington Post*, September 4, A1. http://www.washingtonpost.com/wp-dyn/content/article/2007/09/03/AR2007090301106.html.

Xie, Hong-Guang and Felix W Frueh. 2005. "Pharmacogenomics Steps toward Personalized medicine." *Personalized Medicine* 2(4):325–337. doi: 10.2217/17410541.2.4.325.

2 Regionalism and the study of human genetic variation in a transnational context

Asianism, nationalism, and the racialization of ethnicity

Introduction

> *How do you define an ethnic group? . . . We decided we won't define. We will have the scientists define an ethnic group. Because they know best how to define an ethnic group.*
>
> HUGO PASNP interviewee Dr. Zhang

Over the past decade, advances in human genomics work in Asia have been rapid and expansive. In 2009, the Pan-Asian SNP Consortium (PASNP), a transnational research team within the Human Genome Organization (HUGO), mapped genetic variation and migration patterns in 75 populations, with data from 10 countries: Japan, Korea, China, Taiwan, Singapore, Thailand, Indonesia, Philippines, Malaysia, and India. The primary conclusion that "there is substantial genetic proximity of SEA [Southeast Asian] and EA [East Asian] populations" was presented in "Mapping Human Genetic Diversity in Asia," published in *Science* (The HUGO Pan-Asian SNP Consortium, 2009). In alluding to this genetic proximity while excluding Australia, this high-impact publication seemed to lend support to the argument that "Asian" is a coherent racial/ethnic category.

This chapter revisits this premise that "Asian" is a coherent racial/ethnic category and analyzes the social and political contexts of the production of scientific knowledge in human genetics. Most notably, it addresses how a scientific collaboration has reshaped epistemological claims in medical science about the significance of ethnic and racial differences between and among Asians. More specifically, I begin here to explain and reconcile the seemingly contradictory claims made by some scientists that, genetically, "all Asians probably came through South-east Asia and migrated northward . . . as one people" (Singh, 2009), on the one hand, and that "notable genetic differentiation from Korean and Chinese populations has been found" (Fujimoto et al., 2010:931), on the other.

If geneticists are simply concerned with diversity, why does "Asian" enter as a category at all? This chapter highlights the role of regionalism with respect to Asia and how it has generated a new version of the "Molecular Reinscription of Race" (Duster, 2006), which might be called "regional racialization" in genomics. Moreover, I suggest that we cannot fully understand scientists' current attempts at regional integration without an understanding of the larger historical contexts and developmental phases of regionalism. As Sun (2007:9) suggests, "the discussion of Asia [has] involved not only the question of Eurocentrism, but also the question of hegemony within the East." This was perhaps most notable in Japan's attempt at regional integration before World War II. Saaler (2007:1) writes: "Pan-Asianism [is] an ideology that served not only as a basis for early efforts at regional integration in East Asia, but also as a cloak for expansionism and as a tool for legitimizing Japanese hegemony and colonial rule."

In addition, this chapter documents how, within the HUGO PASNP, ethnic variation was molecularized. Drawing on existing literature, I illustrate how the "ethnicities" that HUGO PASNP Consortium members used were politically, socially, and historically constructed. In addition, drawing on interview data, I note that the molecularization of ethnicity in Asia by the Consortium is significantly a function of the members' decision to switch from an initial plan for a project to understand the genetic causes of diseases to one focused on migration history in Asia, and the concomitant ways in which the population sampling for the migration project was done.

This chapter begins by drawing on the dominant scientific literature of the mid- to late-twentieth century, which suggests that nation states and ethnicities are primarily social-political constructs. It then shifts to explain how the historical phase of Japanese colonialism crystallized what had been the fluid boundaries of ethnic identities, including some of those that ultimately were used by the HUGO PASNP Consortium members.

However, before turning to illuminate and explain the emergence of these matters as they relate to Asia, it will be of heuristic value to draw analogies and parallels to Europe's remarkably similar processes of ethnic and racial "emergence."

The fundamental question of, when are you from?

Despite the widely publicized conclusion – based on the human genome map – that race does not exist at the molecular level, Duster (2015) articulates how some developments in molecular genetics research continue to re-inscribe race as a biological category. Moreover, there are fundamental problems with the ways in which racially and ethnically labeled populations are used for research focusing on differences, such as "admixture research" (Duster, 2015; Kahn, 2015). As Duster puts it:

> Since there was no such thing as "Germany" before 1871, should Prussian and Bavarians be categorized as "admixture" in 1873, but then would each be conceptualized as a "purer" version of "ethnicity" in 1850? Since there was no such thing as "Italy" in 1858, what, genetically, were Milanese and Romans and Neapolitans with respect to their regional "ethnic admixtures" once the nation state was unified? And who gets converted into single genetic ethnic category in 1865?

Indeed, the terms "Germany" and "Germans" would have had different meanings before 1871. At that time, "Germany" was fragmented, with independent kingdoms, city-states, and empires (O'Brien, 1992), its boundaries changing under different rules and war conditions. Deciding whether Prussians should be considered an "admixture" or "German" is not a straightforward task. Prussia had long been affiliated with Poland, but was later integrated into "Germany" in 1871 (Friedrich, 2004). Would a "Prussian" ancestry render an individual an "admixture" or "German" in today's context? Furthermore, in 1947, Prussia was legitimately abolished by an Allied decree (Friedrich, 2004). What would it mean to be a "Prussian" should the name "Prussia" lose its official legitimation?

In other words, intricate power relations, with wars and conflicts, are bound to influence the naming, identifications, and categorizations of people. This is no less true in the context of the region known as "Asia." For example, Okinawa was known as the Ryukyu Kingdom before becoming the Okinawa prefecture of Japan in 1879; the first Sino-Japanese war happened between 1894 and 1895. Similar examples can be found in the partition of India into Pakistan and India in 1947, the split between Bangladesh (East Pakistan) and Pakistan (West Pakistan) through the Bangladesh Liberation War, and so on and so forth. . . .

In the following section, I illustrate the emergent and fluid nature of the "Japanese" category.

Once upon a time: the unfolding character of the "Japanese" category

Japan was first politically unified in the seventh and eighth centuries, with the introduction and implementation of institutions of central government modeled after China (Jansen, 2002). However, similar to European history, with its medieval period following the fall of the Roman Empire, Japan went through its own medieval period between, approximately, the twelfth and seventeenth centuries. In 1600, the military government of the Tokugawa shoguns, with the support of regional lords, successfully reunited Japan (Howell, 1994). February 11 was officially declared a "Japanese" national holiday in 1872. To construct the categorization of "Japanese" and the boundaries of "Japan," the government strategically employed different terms. The term "Japanese" (*nihonjin*) can mean "a citizen of Japan" (*kokumin*, which can include people of different ethnic backgrounds, though this is uncommon) or a person of the Japanese ethnic group (*minzoku*, which can include people who are not citizens of Japan). The Ainu inhabiting Hokkaido, inhabitants of the Ryukyu Islands (Okinawans), and outcasts (*Burakumin*) scattered throughout the main islands were denied membership in the Japanese population in the nation's initial stage (Howell, 1994). In other words, the Ainu, the Ryukyuans, and the Burakumin are what Winichakul (2000:41) has termed "the Others Within."

More recently, the situation has changed, as these groups now fall within the broad category of "Japanese" (*Nihonjin-minzoku*). However, such minority groups remain internal others (non-*Wajin*). *Wajin* is the dominant majority group among all who are regarded as Japanese citizens. Japanese law has supported and privileged the promotion of *Wajin* ideology (大和民族意識), contributing to the idea of a "mono-ethnic order" (Levin, 2008:10). Importantly, the national narrative of homogeneity and monoethnicity emerged after Japan's defeat in World War II (Arudou, 2013). Drawing on critical race theory scholarship on whiteness, Levin (2008:11) argues that "Wajin are . . . Japan's white people." The *Wajin* majority is, according to Arudou (2013:162), "largely ignorant about the realities of life for Japan's 'invisibilized' minorities, and generally views Non-*Wajin* residents as elements exogenous to Japanese society."

In other words, the non-*Wajin* have been rendered invisible and/or treated differently from the *Wajin* through official policies. In fact, it was only in 2008 that the Ainu were recognized as an indigenous people by the Japanese government. Looking back at Japan's history, the changing classification of minority groups has also been influenced by external factors. For example, the Ainu population has come a long way toward being recognized as an indigenous population. In 1855, in response to Russia threatening Japan's sovereignty over Hokkaido, the shogunate government assumed direct administration and began assimilation programs in Hokkaido so as to secure territorial rights to the island (Howell, 1994). Later, when the Meiji state came to power, the cultural norms of the Ainu were suppressed (Howell, 1994), as they were forced to give up their hunter-gatherer lifestyle to learn farming (McGrogan, 2010). The Ainu were officially renamed "former aborigines" in 1878 and gradually became subject to the same laws governing the "Japanese" (Howell, 1994). It was not until 2008 that the Ainu were officially recognized and granted the status of an indigenous people.

According to McGrogan (2010), indigenous rights have become an increasingly prevalent international norm, and Japan wanted to adhere to such norms and be seen as an advanced country. Japan was also facing explicit pressure from United Nations member countries that were raising Ainu issues. These factors, together with activism on the part of the Ainu, contributed to the shift in Japan's official position. The Ryukyuans, however, at the time of this publication, are not recognized as an indigenous people by the Japanese government. While it is beyond the scope of this chapter to address the question of why some groups actively fight to be assimilated while others want to be treated as separate, the relevant observation here is that these groups were assigned minority group status for profoundly historical, economic, political, and social reasons. Moreover, the majority Japanese identity was formed through the othering of minority groups.

Effects of Japanese colonialism and regional integration on the notion of "Japanese"

In addition, complex relationships exist between Japan, South Korea, and Taiwan, and answers to the questions of who is Japanese, who is Korean, and who is

Taiwanese/Chinese depend on historical and political contexts. Japan was an imperial and colonial power during the first half of the twentieth century. According to Robertson (2002:192):

> [T]he new scientific order in Japan was introduced under the aegis of nationalism and empire-building. Beginning with the colonization of Okinawa in 1874 followed by that of Taiwan in 1895, Korea in 1910, Micronesia in 1919, Manchuria in 1931, North China by 1937, and much of Southeast Asia by 1942, the state consolidated through military force a vast Asian-Pacific domain, the so-called Greater East Asia Co-Prosperity Sphere (Dai-tō-a Kyōeiken), a rubric coined in August 1940.

The dominant view among Koreans is that they all belong to a "unitary nation," descending from a common ancestor, and, thus, are ethnically homogenous. According to Shin (2006), however, this sense of ethnic homogeneity was created only in the colonial era as a response to Japan's assimilationist policies. Specifically, Korea was colonized by the Japanese in 1910. Japanese colonial rulers claimed that Koreans and Japanese were of common origin, but the latter were superior. Hence, Japanese rulers took the position that Korean cultural traditions should be replaced with Japanese ones in order to achieve parity between the two groups. Korean nationalists countered that view with an alternative myth, claiming connection to the primordial mythical figure Dangun, from whom all Koreans are supposedly descended (Myers, 2010; Hong, Song and Park, 2012), suggesting a distinct and homogenous nation. Tikhonov's (2012) analysis of race and racial discourses in the two decades prior to the annexation of Korea by Japan also supports the argument that the narrative of Korean ethnic homogeneity took root only in the early twentieth century. Following World War II, antagonism toward the "Japanese other" has continued to be instrumental to the strengthening and maintenance of Korea's national identity (Lee, 2013). For example, there are three national holidays that commemorate anti-Japanese resistance.[1] On every *Gwangbokjeol* (Liberation Day), the president addresses the people with a speech that includes prominent references to Japanese colonialism.

During the Japanese colonial era, Japanese identity (*nihonjin*) was conferred on Japan's subjects in Korea and Taiwan, and a sizeable number of these "imperial subjects" went to reside and work in Japan. When Japan lost its colonies following World War II, Japanese citizenship was stripped from these people, and they became "non-Japanese." In an incisive analysis of how the Japanese colonial regime urged Taiwanese aboriginal groups to die as Japanese (*nihonjin*) for the Japanese empire, Ching (2001) has described the colonial cultural constructions of "Japanese" (*nihonjin* as *nihon minzoku* and/or as *kokumin*), which had life-and-death implications for the colonized:

> The dominant Japanese colonial discourse of *doka* (assimilation) and *kominka* (imperialization) does not simply signify a shift or a conversion from

one category of identity to another, such as from "aborigines" and "Taiwanese" to "Japanese" or from "colonized peoples" to "imperial subjects." Rather, these are ideological formations that purposely obfuscate and deflect the issue of the legal and economic rights of the colonized to that of some generalized cultural process of becoming "Japanese" and "imperial subjects." Doka and kominka, by urging and then insisting that the colonized become "Japanese" (*nihon minzoku*), conceal the inequality between the "natural" Japanese, whose political and economic privileges as citizens (*kokumin*) are guaranteed, and those "naturalized" Japanese, whose cultural identities as Japanese (*nihonjin*) are required, but whose political and economic rights as citizens are continuously denied. . . . The instrumentality of this Japanese colonial discourse is remarkably demonstrated in the encounter between the Taiwanese aborigines and the guardian of Japanese nationalism.[2]

The crucial distinction made by Japanese colonialism between "natural" Japanese and "naturalized" Japanese is also instructive in understanding the *Zainichi* in Japan. Most of the *Zainichi* (Korean-Japanese) were involuntary migrants to Japan between 1910 and 1945, and were required to use Japanese names.[3] After World War II, they lost Japanese citizenship and were given alien status. To be sure, a legal identification of a person as "Japanese" (*ninhonjin-kokumin*) is not equivalent to being treated as "Japanese" (*Ninhonjin-minzoku*), and the answer to the question of who is "Japanese" continues to be shaped by historical, political, economic, social, and cultural forces.

Understanding ethnicity and race as an "emergent" phenomenon is crucial as we now turn to an analysis of the HUGO PASNP Consortium's work. As I shall show, one of the main findings in the interview data with Consortium members is that the scientists have uncritically adopted the given racial (i.e. "Asian") and ethnic categories in Asia (e.g. the "Japanese") in their construction of population in genome science, the foundation of genome medicine. However, as I have attempted to illustrate in discussing "who is Japanese," such ethnic categories are historically and politically constructed, sometimes through colonial encounters. By looking into the history of Asia and using the case of Japan, I attempt to make three points: first, there is a continuity in the contexts of Western domination and the usage of "Pan-Asianism" as an ideology, which helps to explain the appeal and adoption of the "Asian" category in earlier Japanese regional integration and, again, in current genomic science. Second, racial and ethnic categories are historically and politically constructed; for example, "Koreans" and "Taiwanese" were considered "Japanese" during the Japanese colonial era. Finally, it is not merely that the category of the "Japanese" has been taken for granted and treated as if it were a biological category by scientists; the internal "others" – the Ryukyuan and Ainu ethnic minorities in Japan, for example – have also been "geneticized" because geneticists have used such social diversity categories as proxies for genetic diversity in Japan.

Resisting being "othered": scientists in Asia define "Asian" genome diversity

As Cho, Bullock, and Ali (2013) point out, the HUGO PASNP Consortium is the first intra-Asian genomics collaboration. It had its genesis in the dissatisfaction of Asian researchers with international genomics projects. For example, the International HapMap Project's use of only Chinese and Japanese DNA samples as representatives of Asia was "seen by some researchers as a semi-imperialistic essentializing of Asia" (Cho, Bullock, and Ali, 2013:295). Thus, "Asian" solidarity served as a rallying point against the Eurocentrism of prevailing scientific discourse and being "othered" in genomic science, and Consortium members gathered to define "Asian" genomic variation. One of the founding members, Dr. Zhang, a self-identified Asian geneticist, emphasized this sense of collectivism among researchers: "Importantly, I developed a network of friends across Asia. *This was a work that was conceived by Asians, executed by Asians, funded by Asians as a collective*" [emphasis mine].

This emphasis on how "Asians" managed to conceive, fund, and complete the project from beginning to end reveals the researchers' pride in this being an "Asian" project, which highlights the continuing relevance and importance of Pan-Asian ideology. It is important to note, however, that Japan's colonialism, with its goal of constructing a "New East Asian Order" and "Greater East Asia Co-Prosperity Sphere," was also tightly linked to Pan-Asian ideology as a reaction against "Western" domination (Hotta, 2007). In other words, the actions taken and leadership roles involved have changed, but the essential idea of coming together as "Asians" to showcase that "Asians" are not inferior to "Westerners" remains a recurrent theme. Hence, it is no surprise that the HUGO PASNP's project of studying migration history in Asia was proudly acclaimed by many as an "independent" Asian breakthrough in human genome science. However, I will highlight three dimensions through which the Consortium had deep transnational connections, particularly with the United States.

First, the Consortium's primary technology partner was Affymetrix (Agency for Science, Technology and Research Singapore, 2009; HUGO Pan-Asian SNP Consortium, 2009), a company based in the United States that develops and provides technologies that aid in analyzing biological data at various levels, including at the genetic level. Consortium researchers used GeneChip Human Mapping 50K Xba array sets provided by Affymetrix (HUGO Pan-Asian SNP Consortium, 2009). In addition, Affymetrix provided these arrays at a discounted price or for free, funded a research lab, sponsored one of the Consortium's meetings in San Francisco, and provided staff training in eight genotyping centers (Cho, Bullock and Ali, 2013). Thus, Affymetrix played a key role in many ways. Indeed, since the establishment of the Consortium, Affymetrix has moved more of its operations to Singapore. The HUGO PASNP Consortium used a technology platform, developed by Affymetrix, which is used and understood by most professionals conducting genome-wide association studies (GWAS).

Second, the Consortium used the Bayesian analytical software program *Structure* (HUGO Pan-Asian SNP Consortium, 2009), which was developed in the United States as well. The software helps users to investigate and infer population structure and assigns individuals to populations (Bolnick, 2008; Cho, Bullock and Ali, 2013). One of *Structure*'s developers has warned that inferring the value of K (i.e. the number of population cluster in the sample) can be difficult and contentious (Pritchard, Stephens and Donnelly, 2000). Specifically, when researchers choose different values of K, *Structure* can produce substantially different results, and the same person may be assigned to different population groups. Also, even with one value of K, a rerun can generate different results, as there may be two or more possibilities of maximizing the Hardy–Weinburg equilibrium in each population (Bolnick, 2008). However, such human agency gets lost, and the published result becomes "the one and only" scientific statement, even if there is a lapse in reporting all existing biological information and data (Bolnick, 2008). For instance, in the Consortium, values of K = 2 to K = 14 were used to run analyses, in accordance with the geographic divisions deemed meaningful by the researchers (Cho, Bullock, and Ali, 2013). With the different runs, there were different results, and researchers might or might not agree on which value of K was most suitable. Jong Bhak, the Director of the Korean Bioinformation Center, has said that his group deemed K = 12 to be the best descriptive value, but the Chinese group chose another value (Cho, Bullock, and Ali, 2013).

Third, a number of professionals involved in the Consortium received their professional training in or were affiliated with universities in the United States. Most notably, Dr. Edison Liu, who successfully led the first phase of the Consortium's investigation, with its resulting publication in *Science*, is a graduate of Stanford University, and he eventually returned to the United States to head the Jackson Laboratory, in Sacramento, California (Teater, 2012). Other Consortium members, such as Li Jin and Mark Seielstad, were trained under Luigi Luca Cavalli-Sforza, a founder of the Human Genome Diversity Project (HGDP) and renowned population geneticist and linguistic anthropologist, who is also at Stanford (Cho, Bullock, and Ali, 2013).

Hence, the perception of the HUGO PASNP Consortium as an independent "Asian" project conducted by "Asians" is only partially accurate, given that the primary technology partner, technological software, and expert training came mostly from the United States.

The transnational links presented above facilitated the Consortium's work, but the internal dynamics between researchers from various countries in Asia should not be neglected. Researchers in the HUGO PASNP Consortium who were interviewed mostly emphasized the cooperative nature of their relationships. Dr. Kang said: "So HUGO Pan-Asian was to me . . . absolutely 100 percent cooperation. I was not interested in competing with anybody." He added that the PASNP Consortium helped to uplift the capabilities of some Asian countries in genomic research:

> . . . *India, and Pakistan, all these countries, instead of being left out, which has always happened in the past by the Western countries and researchers. Now they*

feel that they are also in the mainstream. So we have our own genomic community in Asia, at least PASNP. So we have this fabric, a network. Although the actual outcome[s] aren't so significant yet, definitely we laid the foundation, in Malaysia and definitely in Korea as well. Although the success was fairly moderate, there was indeed, huge progress making these emerging Asian countries embrac[e] these technologies [emphasis mine].

The scientists also highlighted the so-called "host-guest" arrangement as instrumental in fostering a "Pan-Asian" partnership. The essence of this arrangement was for more advanced research institutions ("hosts") to provide assistance in genome sequencing to less advanced institutions ("guests"). The crux of this arrangement was that the ownership of DNA samples and data would reside with the "guest."

As noted by Dr. Zhang, the "host-guest" arrangement created the impression of a partnership of equals within the Consortium, despite significant differences in technological and financial capabilities between its member institutions:

> The idea [of the host-guest relationship] solved the problem of chain of custody of the DNA. So a country like Indonesia which didn't have these technical capabilities, the scientists would carry the DNA with them to a host nation. And so the host nation says two things. Number one, I will do it, the genotyping, and I will pay for it and I will teach you how to do it. . . . [I]t was structured so that even the people who were least enabled to do the science were equal partners . . . this was a win-win situation, they brought samples, they didn't relinquish any control, but they learned how to do the work.

In other words, the host-guest framework invented by the HUGO PASNP Consortium helped reduce the problem of hegemony in Asia and served to mitigate the national genomic sovereignty issue (Benjamin, 2009). Dr. Kang said that this arrangement will similarly be employed in the second phase of work of the PASNP, known as the Pan-Asian Population Genomics Initiative (PAPGI):

> [For] PAPGI we're trying to have this special scheme called [the] guest-host scheme. So the guest is this poor lab [that] doesn't have much sequencing resources and money, but they have good samples, and good biologists, and excellent biological research, but they don't have much funding from the government. Because they are in say, Thailand, or Indonesia. And the rich labs [are in] say Japan, Korea, or Saudi Arabia, Singapore. We have funding, but to do really good . . . Consortium work, we need really good samples and biological background information. So these host labs invite these guest labs, work together. So one gives samples, the other one gives money, and sequencing, and then they analyze together, and then automatically this goes to [the] PAPGI Consortium. No one actually dominates anything.

While the PASNP members emphasized "Pan-Asianism" in their intellectual collaboration, and their findings even seem to suggest that there appears to be a genetic basis for being Asian, as the following interview data shows, regional politics and histories shaped the process of data sharing. Moreover, the perceived neutrality of Singapore allowed it to play an important role in the Consortium. According to Dr. Zhang:

> . . . in order to really take the lead, Singapore volunteered and [it] turns out that Thailand, Malaysia and Indonesia all used us as their host. . . . Actually, Philippines even came to Singapore, so basically, we were the major hosts. . . . Koreans had some Mongolians, the Chinese had some central Asians, the Indians had the great diversity of themselves but in actual fact Singapore played the major role. . . . Singapore played the role that Brussels plays in the EU. It's a neutral, small, non-threatening, you know – so *if Japan wanted to lead it, the Japanese-Koreans would have a problem and if China wanted to lead it, some others would have a problem.* So Singapore was a neutral body and they accepted that [emphasis mine].

Concrete examples of the positive aspects of the Consortium's work can be seen in its effects on genome science in Malaysia and the Philippines. This is particularly true in the case of the Philippines. Because of the guest-host relationship, its success, and what was learned, the government contributed money to setting up infrastructures for Philippine researchers to examine the genetic structure of indigenous populations. Because Consortium researchers in Malaysia published a high-impact paper, the government decided to dedicate a significant amount of money to genomics; therefore, the country is now more or less independent in terms of doing genome sequencing. In this sense, PASNP did act as a catalyst.

Moreover, national pride and national identities seemed to be equally important within the HUGO PASNP Consortium. After the initial publication in *Science*, researchers published offshoot papers analyzing the data pertaining to their respective countries.

In the case of Japan, some spin-off studies focused on the "others within" – namely, the Ainu and Ryukyuan populations. For instance, in "The History of Human Populations in the Japanese Archipelago Inferred from Genome-wide SNP Data with a Special Reference to the Ainu and the Ryukyuan Populations" (Jinam et al., 2012), researchers made use of several datasets, including those from International HapMap and the HUGO Pan-Asian Consortium, to conduct both individual and population analyses to garner insights into the genetic histories of these populations in Japan. The conclusion of the study was that, genetically, the Ainu are closer to the Ryukyuan than they are to the Mainland Japanese population. This result was interpreted as indicating that the Ainu and Ryukyuan possibly share a common ancestry, which is different from that from the Mainland Japanese. From a scientific viewpoint, these results could be considered substantial, as indicated by publication in the peer-reviewed *Journal of Human Genetics*. However, upon closer inspection, one should note that the study hinged upon the use of social constructs (the categorizations of the Ainu,

Ryukyuan, and Mainland Japanese populations). It is not unreasonable to suggest that not only the ethnic groups, but also their ancestral linkages and histories, are being geneticized.

Ethnicity as a proxy for genetic diversity and the molecularization of ethnicities in Asia

Several HUGO PASNP Consortium geneticists interviewed expressed the view that ethnicity has a genetic basis. Dr. Sato, a self-identified Japanese geneticist, and Dr. Lee, a self-identified Chinese geneticist, were particularly convinced. Dr. Sato said, ". . . one of the biggest findings from the Pan-Asian Consortium is just [that] ethnic classification correspond[s] to the genetic classification very well." Dr. Lee expressed a similar conviction: "What is the implication of demarcation? Well, *ethnic populations are genetically different. It's true*. Right, if you talk about even Koreans and Chinese, you can still see difference, the point is how different [when] you talk about on the world scale" [emphasis mine].

While acknowledging genetic similarities among different ethnic groups, Dr. Kang was confident about finding genetic markers that differentiate between two ethnic groups: "One ancestor, but sufficiently different to define ethnicity. So Koreans are very similar to Chinese. However, I can define it. Physically. Actually a lot of people are trying to find the markers [that differentiate the] Koreans from Japanese."

Thus, for some scientists, the "findings" of the PASNP Consortium study appear to suggest that there is a genetic basis to ethnicity. Indeed, Yang et al. (2014) published a paper entitled "Identification of Ethnically Specific Genetic Variations in Pan-Asian Ethnos" in *Genomics and Informatics*. It seems important to ask: how and why did this genetic attribution happen? In the following paragraphs, I suggest that "how" this genetic attribution happened has to do with the Consortium's use of ethnic diversity as a proxy for human genetic diversity, and that "why" can be attributed to the study's shift from a disease-oriented project to one investigating population diversity and migration history in Asia. Most importantly, the interview data reveal that Consortium researchers treated contemporary ethnic categories as static when they claimed to have found "ethnically specific genetic variants" (Yang et al., 2014), even though, as noted in the introduction to this chapter, such categories are "emergent" and "unfolding."

The PASNP Consortium originally intended to undertake a disease study, but key members determined early on that choosing which disease to study would prove problematic. There were also concerns about sovereignty and, thus, control of genetic data, which reinforced a lingering concern that researchers from technologically developed countries could gain at the expense of their technologically backward counterparts. Dr. Sato articulated the complex difficulties of a disease-oriented study design:

> Actually before starting this [HUGO PASNP Consortium] cooperation, we discussed very much about the project, whether we can start with some disease studies, or if we should start with population studies. And finally we

start with population studies. How to explain? Less biased. Some people like to study hypertension, others want diabetes . . . maybe [in] some countries diabetes [has] become more serious, but other countries [are] more interested in infectious diseases. So population studies are rather unbiased [,] you know?

In short, to embark on a disease-specific study was seen as almost impossible, and the alternative of a population study was comparatively appealing. Dr. Zhang explained this:

It [the HUGO PASNP Consortium] started out as a disease-specific discussion and it started in 2002 in Shanghai. . . . They wanted to find a disease. But it became very clear from the onset, several things were problematic. Number one, there were a lot of haves and have-nots. The have and have-not divide was huge in Asia. [The "have and have-not" refers to] technologies. In those days, things were not quite standardized, so there were only a few institutions, like . . . mainly Japan. . . . [But] countries didn't want to send DNA to Japan or anywhere else. There was this issue of genetic sovereignty that was rising. . . . So no country wanted to give their genetic treasure to Japan so that they would have a patent on the diagnostic. It's an issue of where your funding comes from.

[For t]hose countries with aspirations in genetics, most of the research was funded in Asia by trade and industry, not by health [institutions]. Or if it is by education [institutions], it usually has an industrial KPI.

To summarize this section, political, logistical, and financial factors dictated the failure of a disease-oriented study. For example, while Japan had technological competence, no countries were eager to share their genetic materials with Japan. Recruiting clinicians and hospitals presented another formidable obstacle. Finally, research for treatment of diseases, a public health matter, is largely funded by industry rather than public health institutions in Asia.

It was for these reasons that the PASNP study eventually morphed into a population study, a shift of focus also partly motivated by the practicability of the population diversity design. Dr. Zhang said:

The first thing when I realized what was happening, I started to talk to key players, to suggest that we move away from disease and do population genetics, which has a much easier design. You don't have to have cases and controls; you just basically have people's DNA. As long as you know what dialect they speak, and who their grandparents are, which virtually everybody can tell you. Furthermore you don't need big numbers, you just need to have diversity, because it's a sampling issue . . . in actual fact it doesn't matter how many people you have in your country. It matters more how diverse they are. So countries like Thailand and Indonesia and India became much more important than Korea and Japan. So the ease of design was a key driver. . . . We put a framework and the framework was that we don't do disease, we do diversity.

In short, the fact that the goal of understanding the relationship between disease and genes was dropped and replaced with the goal of understanding migration history in Asia had to do with the belief that the latter (migration history) was easily achievable and would require little effort. Specifically, obtaining samples for a population study would be easier, particularly when one assumed that social diversity represented genetic diversity. Dr. Zhang went on to explain ethnicity as a proxy for genetic diversity: "*I need a surrogate for genetic diversity in order to get my first sampling. So the surrogate is ethnicity. . . . You stratify according to ethnicity within the states*" [emphasis mine].

As it turned out, using ethnicity as a proxy was crucial and motivated "hosts" to help "guests" because such cooperation could increase the diversity of samples for the study. Dr. Zhang noted, "those who were least enabled tended to be people with the greatest diversity of samples, so they were valuable."

However, the interviews provide extensive documentation of the extent to which there is no coherent definition of ethnicity, but only varied local interpretations. As shown in Dr. Zhang's interview, the term "ethnicity" could draw no consensus: "So we [the HUGO PASNP Consortium members] had a discussion. How do you define an ethnic group? . . . We decided we won't define. We will have the scientists define an ethnic group. Because they know best how to define an ethnic group."

DR. ZHANG WENT ON TO HIGHLIGHT COUNTRY-LEVEL VARIATIONS IN DEFINING ETHNICITY: Ethnicity is defined locally by language and geographical localization, and then lastly, race. [Referring to the use of Chinese, Indian, and Malay to define diversity in Singapore's population] That's race, right? That's usually a race construct. . . . You don't define diversity in Singapore by whether you're North Indian or South Indian. . . . Now if you're in China, you define by what language you speak and where your parents lived, or where your grandparents came from.

Along the same lines, Drs. Kang, Sato, and Chua explained local bases for defining ethnicity, which rely essentially on self-identification:

DR. KANG: The way we define[d] [who] the Koreans were at that time [was] people who had three generations of knowledge that they have been in Korea, no external influence, and people who are from two cities, one called Ansung, the other one Ansan. . . . We took the original samples from a previous study in Korea, Korean Study, so they collected this. So essentially they just defined geographically, these two cities.

DR. SATO: Usually we consider about three generations back . . . or just ask the person if your father, mother, grandparents reside in the same area. Not very complicated. Because Japan has not much immigrants in recent years.

DR. CHUA: We use the three generations. So this is for HUGO Pan-Asian. And also our definition of Han Chinese. In all my studies when we talk about Han Chinese, this is the definition. For us, [it is] difficult to get the four generations because nobody knows the four generations. Difficult to find. I mean . . . you know your parents are Chinese, your parents will know whether their parents are Chinese, but your grandparents may not be there to know the fourth [generation]. . . .

Self-identification plays a large part in defining ethnicity – if subjects considered themselves, their parents, and their grandparents to belong to a particular ethnic group, then for the purposes of the PASNP, they belong to that ethnic group. In sum, ethnicity became a locally defined term in the PASNP study. It is important to note that the researchers took ethnic categories such as "Japanese", "Korean", and "Han" for granted, bracketing the historical and political histories embedded in them. As demonstrated earlier in this chapter, "Japanese" is a historically, politically, and culturally constructed category. Similarly, Chow (1997) has demonstrated the ways in which ancestral worship was deployed as a crucial concept in discourses to create the "Han" race as different and superior to the Manchus in China in the twentieth century.

Dr. Zhang was correct that, in Singapore, ethnicity is commonly used to refer to three main population groupings: Chinese, Indian, and Malay. As PuruShotam (1998:51) has brilliantly demonstrated, however, while "the most commonsensically available ethnic names in Singapore that are applied to self and others are 'Chinese,' 'Malay,' 'Indian,' and 'other'[CMIO]," such categories emerged out of a long political and historical process of expansion and consolidation. According to PuruShotam (1998), the first census in Singapore, produced in 1871, consisted of 33 ethnic categories: "Europeans and Americans, Armenians, Jews, Eurasians, Abyssinians, Achinese, Africans, Andamese, Arabs, Bengalis and other natives of India not particularized, Boyanese, Bugis, Burmese, Chinese, Cochin Chinese, Dyaks, Hindoos, Japanese, Javanese, Jaweepekans, Klings, Malays, Manilamen, Mantras, Parsees, Persians, Siamese, Singhalese, Military – British, Military – Indian, Prisoners – Local, Prisoners – Transmarine" (PuruShotam, 1998:61). In the census of 1881, a decade later, there were 47 ethnic categories. These categories were "reclassified . . . under six main categories . . . these six categories were "European and Americans," "Eurasians," "Chinese," "Malays and Other Natives of the Archipelago," "Tamils and other natives of India," and "Other Nationalities." Once instituted in this way, these six divisions were retained in this form for the following two censuses" (PuruShotam, 1998:61–62). Further differentiations of race categories were made in all categories except for "Eurasians." Then, the census of 1921 identified 56 races, and the number increased yet again in the 1931 census – it was reported that over 70 races had been identified by Vlieland (the census superintendent at the time). The contemporary Chinese-Malay-Indian-Others (CMIO) model to which Dr. Zhang referred was a result of administrative consolidation of these earlier categories.

Yet another example of socially constructed ethnic labels is the manner in which ethnicity in Thailand was defined by Consortium members – the ethnic groups identified are "Hmong, Yao, Tai Lue, Tai Yong, Tai Kern, Tai Yuan, Mlabri, H'Tin, Plang, Lawa, Keran, and Palong." Upon closer examination, most of these groups are "hill tribes" or forest people in Thailand. As Winichakul (2000:41) articulates, however, the labeling and official treatment of these tribes is a project concerning "Others Within." Specifically, Winichakul (2000) writes:

> Ethnographic construction, generally speaking, was part of the colonial project to formulate and control the Others of the West. Alongside the colonial enterprise, the Siamese rulers had a parallel project of their own . . . a project which reaffirmed their superiority, hence justifying their rule, over the rest of the country within the emerging territorial state. . . .
>
> The two principal categories of people, of 'Others Within,' are the *chao pa*, the forest, wild people, and the *chao bannok*, the multi-ethnic villagers under the supremacy of Bangkok [emphasis in original].

What may be some implications of the PASNP Consortium's work? It has been established that the genetic makeup of a patient, *as an individual*, can affect drug efficacy and drug toxicity in the case of certain drugs. Based on the purported or assumed genetic basis of ethnicity among Asians, could the development of medicine for different ethnic groups become possible? The geneticists interviewed agreed on the importance of taking genetic diversity into account in drug development. Most argued that it is inappropriate to lump Chinese, Koreans, Japanese, Indians, and so on under one "Asian" framework, as is often the practice in clinical trials conducted in the United States. Dr. Zhang remarked:

> When I was growing up as a young researcher . . . when we did stratifications in American clinical trials, it was Asian, Africans, African Americans, Hispanics, and Caucasians. They *cannot* do that! My point here is that . . . they threw Japanese and Chinese and Indians altogether under one Asian framework. . . . In the past, if you were doing a study in the US, you called Indians, Japanese, Chinese, Malays . . . all Asians and you lumped them under one ethnic demarcation in your clinical trial studies . . . you can't do that [emphasis mine].

However, the researchers had different views as to whether drugs should be developed along ethnic lines. On the one hand, geneticists like Dr. Kang hold the view that there is sufficient diversity to merit the development of ethnicity-specific drugs, even while acknowledging that, genetically, human beings have far more similarities than differences:

> . . . we're very similar to each other. That's for sure. Because we are human beings, we're not some ants. . . . So that means a lot of drugs we share, have

good impacts. . . . However, we are sufficiently different to have Chinese specific and Korean specific drugs.

Dr. Chua, for his part, did not see any problem with a population-based (ethnicity-based) approach to drug development:

> I really don't see any tension. Basically new drugs in the clinical trial, now you have to do in different populations . . . different population[s] have different safety profile[s] and different toxicity. . . . [T]he US FDA require[s] the different population statement. And when they [the drugs] come to Singapore, Singapore may ask [for] a bridging study if they don't think there's . . . enough data for [the] "Chinese" population. . . .

Dr. Chua cited examples of drug efficacy (BiDil and IRESSA) and drug toxicity (carbamazepine) to emphasize the importance of a population-based approach that would involve conducting clinical trials along ethnic lines:

> If the [carbamazepine] clinical trial were done in [a] Chinese population, that drug [would] never have gone to the market. That particular drug is a major cause of the Stevens-Johnson syndrome in Southeast Asia. But it is very very safe in [a] Caucasian population. And this was 30–40 years ago when the clinical trial was done, and that primarily was done in the Caucasian populations, so [it was] approved and [brought] to the Asian market and everybody use[d it]. . . .
>
> By using this population-based knowledge, one may able to, to revive those already dead drugs. Because one drug may not be good for Caucasian populations. Usually they're testing on Caucasian populations. Efficacy is not good, discard. But recently, a drug for treating heart failure in African Americans [BiDil] . . . that is the example that you can actually stop the clinical trial but you can come back to [it], to test on other population[s].
>
> IRESSA . . . drug was off the [US] market. Because the EGFR mutation of lung cancer is very rare, it's less than 10 percent. But in [the] Chinese population, 30–40 percent of our lung cancers [patients] carry this mutation. But this IRESSA is no longer in the market of the US, but it's here, it's available for Asians. Asians have a much higher, higher mutation.

Dr. Zhang noted that genetic diversity contributes to scientific discovery, but also cautioned against overemphasizing genetic differences between different ethnic groups:

> Diversity provides discovery . . . IRESSA is a great example. IRESSA is a dead drug in the US, but it became alive because of the responses they saw in Asians. It is fallacious to think that just because of that one example, we are completely different from our Caucasian counterparts. We're all human. But there is diversity and that diversity has some order to it.

At the same time, Dr. Zhang expressed ambivalence about developing ethnicity-specific drugs. His reservation stems from the difficulty of defining ethnicity, which is perhaps an implicit acknowledgment that ethnicity is, in fact, a social-political construct rather than genetically based:

> [W]hat you're asking is . . . "is there ever going to be ethnic specific therapy?" Let me ask you what's ethnicity then. You define for me ethnicity. . . . There is no question that there will be genetically-based therapeutics. But if you ask me if there's going to be ethnically-based therapeutics, then I have a real problem answering, because I don't know what your term of ethnicity is. . . . If ethnicity is a surrogate for genetics, then I would say there is a possibility. But I think it's a very weak surrogate for genetics.

On the subject of genetic diversity in China, Dr. Zhang drew connections to a case study modeled after the HUGO PASNP Consortium's study of diversity in Asia:

> . . . there's another study that is an offshoot of this [HUGO PASNP Consortium model], [which looked] at the diversity in China and found that there's a clear north-south variation and diversity [is] greater in the south than in the north. China is a microcosm of the whole Asian migration issue and therefore genetic stratification is a problem within a nation-state. That is, you can't lump all Chinese together now.

In other words, genetic differences could almost inevitably be "found" due to the sampling methodology that researchers adopted, whether between racial or ethnic categories or geographical locations. As such, it remains to be seen whether and how racially and ethnically labeled populations may contribute to the development of personalized medicine in the postgenomic era, a topic we will explore further in the next chapter.

Conclusion

In this chapter, I emphasize the importance of empirically-grounded understanding of "biocuration" (Howe et al., 2008), that is, researchers decoding the human genome make choices regarding what to interpret (and what *not* to interpret), as well as how to interpret, analyze, and present data (Fullwiley, 2007, 2008; Fujimura and Rajagopalan, 2011; Shim et al., 2014). More fundamentally, as Duster (2006:434) points out:

> [I]t is possible to make arbitrary groupings of populations defined by geography, language, self-identified faiths, other-identified physiognomy, and so on, and still find statistically significant allelic variations between those groupings. . . . When researchers claim to be able to assign people to groups based on allele frequency at a certain number of loci, they have chosen loci that show differences between the groups they are trying to distinguish.

In other words, such groupings – even when they are social rather than biological – can be *molecularized* in the laboratory, and it is critical to understand how and why scientists decide to define a population group in a specific way. Along similar lines, while one often hears that science and society are co-produced, as Reardon (2011:327) suggests, "it is at the point of emergence, when actors are deciding how to recognize, name, investigate, and interpret new objects, that one can most easily view the ways in which scientific ideas and practices and societal arrangements come into being together." For instance, in her analysis of the construction of populations using the latest "admixture" technology, Fullwiley (2008:706) concludes:

> It should be clear by now that the very continents and people chosen for this product [for ancestry determination] were selected due to their perceived proximity to what we in North America imagined race to be. . . . In other words, the assumed bounded groups on which the AIMs draw (African, European, Native American and Asian) correspond to American cultural ideas of race, which, in the case of many scientists, also ends up shaping where across the globe they collect the DNA of 'populations.'

In her examination of the case of the "Quebec founder population" at a private genome research laboratory in Canada, Hinterberger (2012:82) demonstrates that "the emphasis on the homogeneity and purity of the Quebec founder population . . . is laden with historical negotiations of racialized population mixing in the settlement of the new world." Montoya (2007) examines how scientists used "Mexican" in genetic epidemiology of type 2 diabetes, demonstrating that the varied social and historical forces shaping the life histories of groups remain key elements in scientists' decisions to use a particular category. He coins the term "bioethnic conscription" to highlight the point that genetic differences between ethnoracial groups bear not only descriptive but also attributive significance.

These groundbreaking studies – primarily carried out in North American contexts – show us the ways in which racial differences are constructed within human genome science. While they are attentive to the national and global contexts of the practice of science, few researchers have incorporated regional-level factors into their analysis, which is the emphasis of this chapter. Moreover, a conventional idea distinguishes the notion of "race" from the notion of "ethnicity." According to McIntyre (2011):

> Race is a socially constructed attribute that is tied to beliefs about differences in the physical makeup of different individuals. Ethnicity is different. When most people speak of "ethnic differences," they are referring specifically to cultural differences. Thus, ethnicity has to do with shared cultural heritage.

In this chapter, I have tried to show how "ethnicity" and race become equivalent in the PASNP's work, and that ethnicity was given genetic attributes due simply to the fact that geneticists used it as their population sampling frame and a proxy for genetic diversity. It is in this context that we can say that a process of the molecular racialization of ethnicity has occurred.

Additionally, the eugenics movement of the late nineteenth and early twentieth centuries was seen by some scientific and political leaders as holding the key to future human progress. It was believed that the eugenic ideal could be pursued in two ways: by restricting the reproduction of persons believed to be of inferior genetic potential (negative eugenics) and, conversely, by encouraging individuals thought to possess desirable genetic characteristics to increase their fertility (positive eugenics) (Bittles and Chew, 1998). Hereditarian theory was the foundation of the eugenics movement in the United States that inspired ideals of "racial hygiene" in Nazi Germany (Proctor, 1988). To put it differently, one of the possible implications of treating racial or ethnic categories as if they were biologically or genetically determined categories is the elimination of socially or politically undesirable groups. In the (post-)genomic era, according to Duster (2003), "the front door to eugenics is closed," but it may open again "under the guise of disease prevention policies." In light of this concern, and to lower the chances of molecular science being used for inhumane political purposes, perhaps it is useful to remind ourselves that countries in Asia have, historically, had their own share of eugenic policies and practices. A succinct review in the cases of Japan, Korea, China, and India is provided in Appendix C.

Notes

1 The three public holidays are: (1) *Gwangbokjeol* (Liberation Day of Korea); (2) *Samiljeol*, which celebrates Korea's declaration of independence from Japan on March 1, 1919; (3) *Hyeonchung-Il*, a memorial day honoring those who died not only in military service but also in independence efforts.
2 Aboriginal soldiers who were "Japanese" (*nihonjin*) during the war are collectively enshrined in the Yasuguni, just like other Japanese soldiers. However, survivors and their families continue to be denied the reparations and redress given to citizens of Japan, as they are no longer "Japanese." In both the colonial and post-colonial eras, culture (being "Japanese" or non-"Japanese") continues to arbitrate and deny access to legal procedures and economic benefits.
3 Korea's own colonial government in Korea also imposed *sōshi-kaimei* in 1939–1940, a policy of pressuring Koreans to adopt Japanese names.

References

Agency for Science, Technology and Research Singapore. 2009. *Scientific Consortium Maps the Range of Genetic Diversity in Asia, and Traces the Genetic Origins of Asian Populations.* Singapore: Agency for Science, Technology and Research. Retrieved January 19, 2016 (http://www.a-star.edu.sg/Media/News/Press-Releases/ID/1158/Scientific-consortium-maps-the-range-of-genetic-diversity-in-Asia-and-traces-the-genetic-origins-of-Asian-populations.aspx).

Arudou, Debito. 2013. "'Embedded Racism' in Japanese Law: Towards a Japanese Critical Race Theory." *Pacific Asia Inquiry* 4(1):155–168.

Benjamin, Ruha. 2009. "A Lab of Their Own: Genomic Sovereignty as Postcolonial Science Policy." *Policy and Society* 28(4):341–355.

Bittles, A.H. and Y.-Y. Chew. 1998 "Eugenics and Population Policies." Pp.272–287 in *Human Biology and Social Inequality*, edited by S.S. Strickland and P.S. Shetty. New York: Cambridge University Press

Bolnick, Deborah A. 2008. "Individual Ancestry Inference and the Reification of Race as a Biological Phenomenon." Pp.70–85 in *Revisiting Race in a Genomic Age*, edited by B.A. Koenig, S.S. Lee and S.S. Richardson. Piscataway, NJ: Rutgers University Press.

Ching, Leo T.S. 2001. *Becoming 'Japanese': Colonial Taiwan and the Politics of Identity Formation.* Berkeley, Los Angeles and London: University of California Press.

Cho, Philip S., Nathan Bullock and Dionna Ali. 2013. "The Bioinformatic Basis of Pan-Asianism." *East Asian Science, Technology and Society: An International Journal* 7:283–309. doi: 10.1215/18752160–2142980.

Chow, Kai-Wing. 1997. "Imagining Boundaries of Blood: Zhang Binglin and the Invention of Han 'Race' in Modern China." Pp. 34–52 in *The Construction of Racial Identities in China and Japan*, edited by F. Dikötter. Honolulu, HI: University of Hawaii Press.

Duster, Troy. 2003. *Backdoor to Eugenics.* 2nd ed. New York and London: Routledge.

Duster, Troy. 2006. "The Molecular Reinscription of Race: Unanticipated Issues in Biotechnology and Forensic Science." *Patterns of Prejudice* 40(4):427–441. doi: 10.1080/00313220601020148.

Duster, Troy. 2015. "A Post-Genomic Surprise: The Molecular Reinscription of Race in Science, Law and Medicine." *British Journal of Sociology* 66(1):1–27.

Friedrich, Karin. 2004. " 'Pomorze' or 'Preussen'? Polish Perspectives on Early Modern Prussian History." *German History* 22(3):344–371. doi: 10.1093/0266355403 gh314oa.

Fujimoto, Akihiro, Hidewaki Nakagawa, Naoya Hosono, Kaoru Nakano, Tetsuo Abe, Keith A Boroevich, Masao Nagasaki, Rui Yamaguchi, Tetsuo Shibuya, Michiaki Kubo, Satoru Miyano, Yusuke Nakamura and Tatsuhiko Tsunoda. 2010. "Whole-Genome Sequencing and Comprehensive Variant Analysis of a Japanese Individual Using Massively Parallel Sequencing." *Nature Genetics* 42:931–936. doi: 10.1038/ng.691.

Fujimura, Joan H. and Ramya Rajagopalan. 2011. "Different Differences: The Use of 'Genetic Ancestry' Versus Race in Biomedical Human Genetic Research." *Social Studies of Science* 41(1):5–30.

Fullwiley, Duana. 2007. "The Molecularization of Race: Institutionalizing Human Difference in Pharmacogenetics Practice." *Science as Culture* 16(1):1–30.

Fullwiley, Duana. 2008. "The Biologistical Construction of Race: Admixture Technology and the New Genetic Medicine." *Social Studies of Science* 38(5):695–735.

Hinterberger, Amy. 2012. "Investing in Life, Investing in Difference: Nations, Populations and Genomes." *Theory, Culture and Society* 29(3):72–93.

Hong, Yihua, Changzoo Song and Julie Park. 2012. "Korean, Chinese or What? Identity Transformations of Chosŏnjok (Korean Chinese) Migrant Brides in South Korea." *Asian Ethnicity* 14(1):29–51.

Hotta, Eri. 2007. *Pan-Asianism and Japan's War 1931–1945.* New York: Palgrave Macmillan US.

Howe, Doug, Maria Costanzo, Petra Fey, Takashi Gojobori, Linda Hannick, Winston Hide, David P. Hill, Renate Kania, Mary Schaeffer, Susan St Pierre, Simon

Twigger, Owen Whilte and Seung Yon Rhee. 2008. "Big data: The Future of Bio-curation." *Nature*, 445 (4 September), pp. 47–50.

Howell, David L. 1994. "Ainu Ethnicity and the Boundaries of the Early Modern Japanese State." *Past & Present* 142:69–93.

The HUGO Pan-Asian SNP Consortium. 2009. "Mapping Human Genetic Diversity in Asia." *Science* 326(5959):1541–1545. doi: 10.1126/science.1177074.

Jansen, Marius B. 2002. *The Making of Modern Japan*. Cambridge, MA and London, UK: The Belknap Press of Harvard University Press.

Jinam, Timothy, Nao Nishida, Momoki Hirai, Shoji Kawamura, Hiroki Oota, Kazuo Umetsu, Ryosuke Kimura, Jun Ohashi, Atsushi Tajima, Toshimichi Yamamoto, Hideyuki Tanabe, Shuhei Mano, Yumiko Suto, Tadashi Kaname, Kenji Naritomi, Kumiko Yanagi, Norio Niikawa, Keiichi Omoto, Katsushi Tokunaga and Naruya Saitou. 2012. "The History of Human Populations in the Japanese Archipelago Inferred from Genome-Wide SNP Data with a Special Reference to the Ainu and the Ryukyuan Populations." *Journal of Human Genetics* 57:787–795. doi: 10.1038/jhg.2012.114.

Kahn, Jonathan. 2015. "'When Are You From?' Time, Space, and Capital in the Molecular Reinscription of Race." *The British Journal of Sociology* 66(1):68–75.

Lee, Jerry Won. 2013. "Legacies of Japanese Colonialism in the Rhetorical Constitu-tion of South Korean Identity." *National Identities* 16(1):1–13.

Levin, Mark A. 2008. "The Wajin's Whiteness: Law and Race Privilege in Japan." *Horitsu Jihō* 80(2):80–91. Retrieved January 17, 2016 (http://papers.ssrn.com/sol3/papers.cfm?abstract_id=1551462).

McGrogan, David. 2010. "A Shift in Japan's Stance on Indigenous Rights, and Its Implications." *International Journal on Minority and Group Rights* 17(2):355–373.

McIntyre, Lisa. 2011. *The Practical Skeptic: Core Concepts in Sociology*. 5th ed. Colum-bus, OH: McGraw-Hill.

Montoya, Michael J. 2007. "Bioethnic Conscription: Genes, Race, and Mexicana/o Ethnicity in Diabetes Research." *Cultural Anthropology* 22(1):94–128. doi: 10.1525/can.2007.22.1.94.

Myers, Bryan Reynolds. 2010. *The Cleanest Race: How North Koreans See Themselves – and Why It Matters*. Brooklyn, NY: Melville House Publishing.

O'Brien, Peter. 1992. "German-Polish Migration: The Elusive Search for a German Nation-State." *The International Migration Review* 26(2):373–387.

Pritchard, Jonathan K., Matthew Stephens and Peter Donnelly. 2000. "Inference of Population Structure Using Multilocus Genotype Data." *Genetics* 155(2): 945–959.

Proctor, Robert. 1988. *Racial Hygiene: Medicine under the Nazis*. Cambridge, MA: Harvard University Press.

PuruShotam, Nirmala Srirekam. 1998. *Negotiating Language, Constructing Race: Disciplining Difference in Singapore*. Berlin: Walter de Gruyter.

Reardon, Jenny. 2011. "The Human Genome Diversity Project: What Went Wrong?" Pp. 321–342 in *The Postcolonial Science and Technology Studies Reader*, edited by S. Harding. Durham, NC: Duke University Press.

Robertson, Jennifer. 2002. "Blood Talks: Eugenic Modernity and the Creation of New Japanese." *History and Anthropology* 13(3):191–216. doi: 10.1080/0275720022000025547.

Saaler, Sven. 2007. "Pan-Asianism in Modern Japanese History: Overcoming the Nation, Creating a Region, Forging an Empire." Pp. 1–14 in *Pan-Asianism in*

Modern Japanese History: Colonialism, Regionalism and Borders, edited by S. Saaler and J.V. Koschmann. New York and London: Routledge.

Shim, Janet K., Sara L. Ackerman, Katherine Weatherford Darling, Robert A. Hiatt and Sandra Soo-Jin Lee. 2014. "Race and Ancestry in the Age of Inclusion Technique and Meaning in Post-Genomic Science." *Journal of Health and Social Behavior* 55(4):504–518.

Shin, Gi Wook. 2006. *Ethnic Nationalism in Korea: Genealogy, Politics and Legacy*, Stanford, CA: Stanford University Press.

Singh, Seema. 2009. "Early Human Settlers Used Southern Coastal India to Enter Asia." *Livemint*, December 10. Retrieved January 17, 2016 (http://www.livemint.com/Politics/1vDe4TLrcXV5k8XBU98p6M/Early-human-settlers-used-southern-coastal-India-to-enter-As.html).

Sun, Ge, trans. 2007. "How Does Asia Mean?" Pp. 9–58 in *The Inter-Asia Cultural Studies Reader*, edited by K.H. Chen and B.H. Chua. New York and London: Routledge.

Teater, Barry. 2012. "Leading Up." *The Search Magazine*, March 01. Retrieved January 19, 2016 (https://www.jax.org/news-and-insights/2012/march/leading-up-a-profile-of-ceo-ed-liu).

Tikhonov, Vladimir. 2012. "The Race and Racism Discourses in Modern Korea, 1890s-1910s." *Korean Studies* 36:31–57. doi: 10.1353/ks.2012.0008.

Winichakul, Thongchai. 2000. "The Others Within: Travel and Ethno-Spatial Differentiation of Siamese Subjects, 1885–1910." Pp.28–62 in *Civility and Savagery: Social Identity in Tai States*, edited by A. Turton. London: Curzon Press.

Yang, Jin Ok, Sohyun Hwang, Woo-Yeon Kim, Seong-Jin Park, Sang Cheol Kim, Kiejung Park, Byungwook Lee and The HUGO Pan-Asian SNP Consortium. 2014. "Identification of Ethnically Specific Genetic Variations in Pan-Asian Ethnos." *Genomics & Informatics* 12(1):42–47. doi: http://dx.doi.org/10.5808/GI.2014.12.1.42.

3 Capitalizing on being "othered"

Precision medicine and race in the context of a globalized pharmaceutical industry

Introduction

Lurking just beneath the surface claim of molecular-based personalized medicine is the reality of racially and ethnically designated population-based drug development in the context of a globalized pharmaceutical industry. In contrast to the previous chapter, in which the term "Asian" was deconstructed in the context of globalized genome science, the following pages reveal a scenario in which "Asian" and "Caucasian" are reinterpreted and injected with a heavy dose of genetic reification.

Before genome-based "personalized medicine" can be administered in clinical settings, the question of what shapes drug marketing and development needs to be addressed. Existing studies have shown that population groups can be strategically appropriated by interested parties to the detriment of the health care of individuals designated as members of said groups. For example, Kahn argues that "the primary forces driving the re-invention of BiDil [a drug for treating heart failure] as an ethnic drug . . . were legal and commercial, rather than biomedical" (Kahn, 2004, 2013). Indeed, rather than receiving more affordable treatments, the targeted population found that costs increased (Sankar and Kahn, 2005).

While the case of BiDil is now relatively well known (Roberts 2011a, 2011b; Kahn 2013), how IRESSA (for treatment of non-small-cell lung cancer) became an Asian-focused drug has attracted less critical examination. We suggest that the case of IRESSA deserves a closer look, not least because it has been hailed as an exemplary case of personalized medicine. As noted in the European Science Foundation publication *Forward Look*, health care professionals must "raise awareness of examples in which stratified approaches have already begun to be used effectively in the clinic as precursors of a wider vision of personalized medicine" (European Science Foundation, 2012:15). "Drugs such as gefitinib and erlotinib, for instance, are being used to treat patients with non-small-cell lung cancer who have mutations in the epidermal growth factor receptor (EGFR)" (European Science Foundation, 2012:13).

Moreover, from 2005 to 2012, a global migration of clinical trials occurred (Drain, Robine, Holmes and Bassett, 2014). While the United States conducted the largest number of clinical trials (58,980, or 30 percent of all trials) during this period, there was an absolute increase in the number of clinical trials conducted outside of the United States, Canada, and Europe. Most significantly, "the absolute increase was greatest for the Asian region (489 percent)" (Drain et al., 2014:166).

Lung cancer has been the most common cancer worldwide for several decades[1]. In 2012, out of an estimated 14 million new cases of cancer worldwide[2,3], 13 percent were new lung cancer cases (approximately 1.8 million). In the United States alone, it was expected that there would be 224,210 new cases and 159,260 deaths from lung cancer in 2014[4]. Lung cancer, classified as either non-small-cell lung cancer (NSCLC) or small-cell lung cancer (SCLC), is estimated to be responsible for about one-fifth of deaths from cancer worldwide (approximately 1.59 million deaths)[5]. More than 80 percent of patients suffer from NSCLC[6,7].

IRESSA is the trade name for gefitinib, marketed by AstraZeneca. The following is from AstraZeneca's website (2014):

> IRESSA (gefitinib) is a once-daily 250 mg oral medication that targets and blocks the activity of the EGFR-TK, an enzyme that regulates intracellular signalling pathways implicated in cancer cell proliferation and survival. . . . Studies have shown that tumours with an EGFR mutation are particularly sensitive to IRESSA. A mutation in the EGFR is a characteristic occurring in about 10–15 percent of non-small cell lung cancers (NSCLC) in Europe and around 30–40 percent in Asia. . . .

AstraZeneca secured regulatory approval for IRESSA in Japan in 2002. In the United States, IRESSA was first approved by the Food and Drug Administration (FDA) in May 2003, under accelerated approval regulations. Accelerated approval is granted on the condition that the manufacturer will continue testing the drug in clinical trials to demonstrate that it indeed provides a clinical benefit to patients.

Then, on June 17, 2005, the FDA disallowed the administration of IRESSA to new patients. This was because clinical trials did not show that IRESSA benefited patients, as noted on the US National Cancer Institute (NCI) website (2011):

> The FDA has carefully reviewed data from two failed clinical studies of gefitinib, one of which was required by the agency as part of the drug's accelerated approval. This trial enrolled patients with regionally advanced or metastatic NSCLC who had failed one or two prior treatment regimens. In this large study, 1,692 patients were given either gefitinib or [a] placebo. There was no significant survival benefit either in the overall study population or in patients who had high levels of a surface marker called "EGFR."
>
> In the second trial in patients with stage III NSCLC, after completion of induction and consolidation chemotherapy and radiation therapy, patients were given either gefitinib or placebo maintenance therapy. No gefitinib survival benefit could be demonstrated.

When these results were announced, the FDA began a review to assess whether the drug should be pulled from the market. However, when the data were reassessed by race and ethnicity, scientists found that "Asians" had a 9.5 month prolongation of life on the medication, which was nearly double the 5.5 month average for the general population. AstraZeneca touted these findings as significant and began marketing strategies and sales in Asian countries (Zamiska and Whalen, 2005).

Then, in 2009, researchers in Hong Kong, China, Thailand, Taiwan, and Japan conducted the IRESSA Pan-Asia study (IPASS), with participation from 87 medical research centers in 9 Asian countries. The main findings of this study were: "Gefitinib [i.e. IRESSA] is superior to carboplatin-paclitaxel [i.e. chemotherapy] as an initial treatment for pulmonary adenocarcinoma [a type of lung cancer] among nonsmokers or former light smokers in East Asia. The presence in the tumour of a mutation of the EGFR gene is a strong predictor of a better outcome with gefitinib." The IPASS results were subsequently published in the prestigious medical journal *The New England Journal of Medicine* (Mok et al., 2009).

Partly as a result of this new study, the European Commission approved the marketing of IRESSA for EGFR-mutation-selected patients with non-small-cell lung cancer in July 2009. In 2010, Health Canada also approved IRESSA as a first-line treatment for locally advanced or metastatic non-small-cell lung cancer in patients positive for the EGFR mutation.

These regulatory approvals were landmark achievements for IRESSA, now seen as a first step toward personalized medicine in oncology. For instance, Hughes (2009:758) suggests that the success of IRESSA and the IPASS means that there is "a need for [pharmaceutical] companies to identify the right patients for targeted therapies." Mok et al. (2009) call the IPASS "a small step towards personalized medicine for non-small cell lung cancer," further describing its importance as such:

> Personalized medicine for NSCLC is now a reality. . . . [The] IPASS and three other randomized studies have confirmed higher tumour response rates, longer PFS, and less toxicity with EGFR TKI over empiric cytotoxic chemotherapy as first-line therapy for EGFR mutation-selected patients. This small step may eventually lead to a big leap towards personalized medicine for NSCLC.

Part of what is striking about the changing fortunes of IRESSA is the drug's troubled history in Japan; as of March 2010, there were 810 reported deaths due, allegedly, to adverse reactions to IRESSA. Patients and their bereaved families lodged lawsuits against AstraZeneca and the Japanese government for failing to include proper warnings about IRESSA's serious side effects. The Osaka District Court ruled in favor of patients and their families in February 2011, but in May 2012 the Osaka Court of Appeals overturned this judgment and ruled in favor of AstraZeneca (*The Pharma Letter*, 2012).

In addition to a closer examination of the IRESSA case, on a broader scale, we hope to contribute to a discussion of the question, whose interests are being served by pharmacogenomic and pharmacogenetic studies that focus on inter-racial or inter-ethnic differences of drug responses? As mentioned in the introductory chapter, according to Daar and Singer (2005:241), we need to take into account not only differences between the genotypes of individuals, important as they are, but also differences in genotypes between different population groups. Moreover, Suarez-Kurtz (2008:337) writes that "pharmacogenomics' conceptual development and praxis remain contingent upon a better understanding of human genomic diversity and its impact on drug pharmacokinetics and pharmacodynamics. Ethnic specificity has become an integral part of pharmacogenetic/pharmacogenomic research."

Indeed, as Tate and Goldstein (2008) note, "there is no shortage of gene variants known to influence drug response that have substantial differences in frequency among racial or ethnic groups." That such differences are found should not surprise us, as noted in the introductory chapter. As Duster (2006:434) points out: "it is possible to make arbitrary groupings of populations defined by geography, language, self-identified faiths, other identified physiognomy and so on and still find statistically significant allelic variations between these groupings." The key question is, why is there a strong interest in searching for such differences at the level of populations categorized by race and ethnicity?

Drawing on interviews with medical oncologists, we argue that such knowledge regarding the distributions of genetic variants among ethnic or racially labeled groups is being pursued as a key coping strategy adopted by pharmaceutical companies to deal with the high unpredictability of the success or failure of their often billion-dollar investments in drug development.

What is at stake? As Kahn (2013:234) points out:

> The issue . . . is not whether commerce should affect biomedical research or practice, but what the proper balance between commerce and science is. . . . Certainly the choice of which drugs or diagnostics to develop has always been influenced by commercial considerations, but *when commercial considerations affect not only the choice but the actual framing, interpretation, and presentation of scientific data, then something is wrong.* Such has been the case, witting or not, with the distinctive rise of 'ethnic' biomedicine in a postgenomic era [emphasis mine].

In addition, Chin (2011) notes the internationalization of clinical trials and suggests that issues of cost, availability of patients, and quality of research results are the main factors driving this current trend. Our data and argument here complement Chin's work by adding that, in so far as the increasing volume of clinical trials in Asia is concerned, the picture involves a particular (re)formulation of the American racial taxonomic system as adopted by the FDA in the United States, ambitions and policies of local governments, and an emerging sense of self-determination and assertion among scientists.

Before turning to whether or not pharmaceutical companies stand to benefit from profiling (potential) patients racially and ethnically, it is important to first draw attention to the ways in which the genomics revolution is being felt by the pharmaceutical industry.

The first important theme emerging from the interview data, ironically, is that it is not in the apparent interests of pharmaceutical companies to develop drugs that are effective for patients with specific biomarkers, particularly when these markers may be only present in a small subset of the whole patient population – such subsets can be demarcated along biomarker lines and/or race and ethnicity lines.

There have been noted efforts by pharmaceutical companies to produce biomarker-based personalized medicine, in addition to "blockbuster" drugs (i.e. generic medicines for everyone). However, in general, the relationship between pharmaceutical companies and the making of drugs based on either biomarkers or racialized categories is neither simple nor straightforward.

As Dr. Hsu put it:

In fact, drug companies are the ones that are trying to resist all these [genetic] tests. Actually, even the drug company . . . [has] this dichotomy. The marketing people . . . don't want these tests, because the more you define the group to be narrower and narrower, fewer people buy the drug. So you're actually reducing the market size. [For] example, the Erbitux. Erbitux used to be used for 100 percent of colon cancer. Since the KRAS testing came out, only 60 percent of [patients] will use [it]. Now [with] NRAS [testing] and all that, now only 42 percent will use [it]. So if there are more tests coming out, eventually maybe only 20 percent will use [it]. So the more tests you do, the fewer people will buy your drug, but that is from the marketing point of view.

The corporate headquarter[s], as well as the medical people, like to do the test, because it is the politically correct thing to do. And you cannot run away from the test, because the scientists will be asking to test them. The scientist will challenge you: I found this test in the lab, and I tested it in mice . . . can you show me data in human[s]? So *drug companies are held [for] ransom*, because they cannot avoid doing tests. . . .

Dr. Hsu continued:

Would the drug company purposely as a business strategy try to limit their use to a certain ethnic group? [W]hy would they? They wouldn't. Unless, by not limiting it, other people get side effect[s]. . . . [T]hat's a different story, because they are liable to be sued. But if the drug [is being used, but] is not very effective, they will say, bad luck. So I think drug companies, if possible, they like the drug to be used by everybody in the world. The wider the definition of usage, the better. No drug company wants to narrow its indication[s]. Everyone wants to widen the indication[s].

Indeed, biomarkers affect the efficacy of the drugs, but these markers are not present in everyone. This fact poses a dilemma for pharmaceutical companies because the potential market size of the drug will be much smaller. Considering that pharmaceutical companies have to spend significant resources in research and development before a drug is approved, this could mean that the unit price of the drug will have to be increased in order to still make a significant return against a lower demand.

Not surprisingly, costs of cancer medications have steadily increased over recent years as human genome science has entered the drug development process. According to Jackson and Sood (2011), in 1995 "the only widely used cancer drug that cost more than US$2,500 a month was paclitaxel. By contrast, many recently approved targeted drugs have entered the market priced at many times that amount, with more than 90 percent of anticancer agents approved by the FDA in the past four years costing more than US$20,000 for a twelve-week course." Similarly, Chiang and Million (2011:895) provide documentation that:

> Prices of novel agents in the oncology space have steadily risen in the past decades. . . .The launches of Yervoy (Bristol-Myers Squibb) and Provenge (Dendreon) have grabbed headlines with prices of around $100,000 per year per patient. The pricing of oral oncolytics such as Tarceva, Gleevec, Xeloda, Sutent and Nexavar shows an average increase in price of over 76 percent since 2006. Pfizer has recently announced a $9,600 cost per month for Xalkori, in line with Roche/Plexxicon's expected $9,400 cost per month for Zelboraf.

While drug companies are generally reluctant to produce racialized medicine because of the smaller market size noted above, there are commercial considerations under which doing so makes sense, as the following section shows.

Saving IRESSA

This chapter suggests that pharmaceutical companies seem particularly prone to racialize clinical trials (and, therefore, to produce racialized medicine) in the aftermath of poor or irregular drug performance in large-scale clinical trials. As noted above, IRESSA was originally found to be of low efficacy when the trial was run against a standard sample in the United States. When a further analysis revealed that the "Asian" population in the sample was more responsive to the drug, the IPASS was initiated.

Dr. Hsu explained:

You know the story of IRESSA? IRESSA was approved before 2005, right? And later on was withdrawn because the drug wasn't very effective. The drug was about to be buried, the company was suffering big-time. . . . So the only way to salvage it is the fact that they do see some occasional successes, and therefore they decided to explore the Oriental slant to this one. So it's not as if they willingly wanted to do the test. This test was needed to salvage a drug that was about to be buried, you see . . .

But for a drug that works very well, and [the] FDA fully approve[d], [the] company will resist testing it, because the more they test, the smaller . . . the market size. But this drug was condemned by the US. If they don't do the IPASS study, the drug usage will be zero. So the IPASS study . . . it's desperation, they have no other choice – they don't do the test, they're gone. Alright, so, they were lucky that the Asia study turned out positive. So they were given a second lease o[n] life. Therefore, *this strategy is very good, if you have a drug that is erratic in its outcome* [emphasis mine].

More importantly, Dr. Yeh pointed out that the IPASS did not select patients based on genetic profile:

I think [the] IPASS . . . in its own merit is the first study which compared in a population study of non-smokers, and heavy smokers and light smokers . . . now *they did not test for EGFR mutation prior to enrolling the patients onto the study*. In other words *they have no a priori knowledge of the genetic makeup of this group of patients*. . . . So I would say that [the] IPASS did not . . . in a sense, impact personalized medicine in a genomic manner. Because you did not test *a priori* ahead of time for the EGFR mutation and select the patients for therapy [emphasis mine].

The IPASS selected patients and grouped them according to phenotypes instead of genetic markers, and only later did IPASS researchers establish genetic connections to its results.

Dr. Yeh continued:

They didn't select [based on] genetic [makeup], they just selected based on clinical phenotype. But, when they went back, retrospectively, to analyze the data, they found that those with EGFR positive have much higher responses!

Dr. Hsu made a similar observation:

A good example is [the] IPASS for *Iressa*. It was done in 2009, they never prespecify everyone must have EGFR, they specify the clinical profile[8], knowing that within the profile, EGFR was common. That was already the perception then, but the [data] wasn't strong enough . . . to say they were confident to restrict to the only EGFR positive patient. But, fortunately, the trial analysis showed that most of the patient[s] happened to have [the] EGFR mutation anyway, so it kind of fulfilled the criteria.

Eventually, it was discovered that responsiveness to the drug was linked to the EGFR mutation, which can also be found in different racial and ethnic populations, albeit at varying frequencies.

Dr. Wu pointed out:

There was the pan Asian study . . . [that] only looked at Asian patients with adenocarcinoma, and female[s] who [were] non-smokers. But that was because,
in the earlier study, there was a hint that the benefit was only in this group.
That's why the trial did it in this group. After that they found that even
among this group, it was not the group that mattered, but because EGFR
mutations were more common among this group. So once you find the
genetic cause . . . then the genetic variant is the determinant. . . . So it may
be that, in Caucasians, this mutation is less common. But once you have it,
it doesn't matter that you're Caucasian or Chinese, you will benefit equally.
So *the new trials are based on the EGFR mutation status* [emphasis mine].

The underlying reason for the differences in drug efficacy should be explored
rather than simply stopping at an ethnicity-based explanation, as Dr. Deng
suggested:

We accept that there may be ethnic differences, but we need to find what is the
basis of th[ose] differences. So once you have that basis . . . be it a polymorphism from genetic testing . . . then that should be the subsequent strategy
in terms of ensuring that it can be extended to the broader population and
not just based on ethnicity.

Indeed, as Wilson et al. (2001) point out, "it is well known that there are
inter-ethnic differences in DME [Drug Metabolizing Enzyme] allele frequencies
and thus in drug response. . . . Not only can these [genetically inferred] clusters
be derived in the absence of knowledge about ethnicity (or geographic origin),
but they are also more informative than commonly used ethnic labels." With
respect to EGFR mutation status and targeted therapies, Saijo (2013:6) notes:
"all four of these trials [conducted in Japan, Korea, China, and Europe] produced similar results, suggesting that the biological character of EGFR mutated
NSCLC was similar in East Asians and Caucasians despite differences in mutation
frequencies."

If we are moving into an era of molecular biomarker-based drug development,
this would seem to mean that categories of race and ethnicity have decreasing
relevance. To what extent should one treat the IRESSA case as a single isolated
case, an exceptional misuse of race?

In the following section, I present interview data to suggest that IRESSA is not
an isolated case; rather, identifying somatic mutation patterns among racial and
ethnic groups has become embedded in the pharmaceutical industry's routine
practices. To begin with, the US FDA published the Demographic Rule (CFR
314.50 d(5)) in 1998 and a guidance document in 2005 on collection of race
and ethnicity data in clinical trials[9]. Standard ethnic categories, as recommended
by the Office of Management and Budget and followed by the FDA, are "His-
panic/Latino" and "Not Hispanic/Latino." For race, the minimum categories

recommended are American Indian/Alaska Native, Asian, black or African American, native Hawaiian or other Pacific Islander, and white.

At the same time, there has been rapid growth in international clinical trials. While the United States still has the largest proportion of clinical trials, it is facing slower growth. The largest proportion of non-US clinical trials is in Western Europe, and Asia has experienced the greatest absolute increase. Specifically, while previously confined to in and around the United States, as of 2008, according to Chin (2011): "80 percent of marketing application for drugs and biologicals approved by the US Food and Drug Administration contained data from US clinical trials conducted outside the USA."

According to yet another report cited above, "over the 2005–2012 period overall, 127,314 (67 percent) of 189,213 registered trials were conducted in the United States, Canada or Europe" (Drain et al, 2014:166). "The United States was the single largest country conducting clinical trials, with 58,980 (30 percent). The absolute increase was greatest for the Asian region (489 percent) and the Latin American/Caribbean region (112 percent); the smallest increase occurred in the North American region (9 percent)" (Drain et al, 2014:166).

Why has the Asian region experienced such a dramatic increase in its share of clinical trials? While the answer is certainly complex, part of it lies in the broader significance of the IRESSA case and the particular way in which the "Asian" category in the FDA regulations has been redefined and reified at the transnational level.

The larger significance of the story of IRESSA

While scholars have established and articulated the lengthy historical and political processes of racial formation in the United States (Omi and Winant, 2015), which include the creation and particular understanding of the "Asian" category, in this transnational setting, "Asian" is formulated as a geographically based concept. Drs. Yeh and Hu discussed this formulation in terms of IRESSA:

INTERVIEWER: Why is it important to conduct clinical trials in Asia?
DR. YEH: Even if the disease looks very similar, for example, lung cancer, in Asians, the percentage of EGFR mutation is about 30 percent. And in the West, it's three times less. . . . So, sometimes, if you study in the West, you may miss something. For example, [when] IRESSA [was] initially developed in the West, they did a phase III study, [and] found that [results were] negative. Didn't find it to be beneficial. So, [the] FDA actually reversed the approval, *but subsequently this drug [was] tested in [an] Asian population. Then found that . . . by selecting the appropriate characteristics . . . that time we still didn't know[whether] it's due to EGFR mutation. Those with Asian phenotype, non-smoker, Adenocarcinoma, this group of patients tend to benefit.* That subsequently led us to know [that] it's EGFR mutation. So, because of the different incidence of the tumour subtypes, treating it in one country

doesn't necessarily [indicate that] you'll get the same result in another country, so that's another reason why you need to do clinical trials in Asia.

DR. HSU: I must say that the IRESSA, probably is the landmark drug that change[d] the way the world views Asian trials. Because until the IPASS data came out in 2009, nobody believed our data, but the data is so convincing that now people understand – any time they talk about oral TKI [tyrosine kinase inhibitor] for lung [cancer], they better believe Eastern data, because we know what we're doing. Right, so there is a trend.

The interchangeability of the usage of "Asian" and "human subjects in Asia" is significant because it serves as an example of how the pharmaceutical industry is biologizing geographically based social groupings for the sake of protecting commercial interests. Moreover, drug development is a risky business. While it has almost always been the case that major pharmaceutical companies seek approval by the US FDA, there has been a noted divergence of research and development spending and new product approvals by the FDA in the genomic era. That is, since the human genome was sequenced a decade ago, the number of compounds in development has increased 62 percent, and total research and development expenditures have doubled. Yet, the average number of new drugs approved by the US FDA per year has declined since the 1990s. Hay et al. (2014:41) find that "approximately one in ten (10.4 percent, n = 5,820) of all indication development paths in phase I were approved by [the] FDA." When only the lead indication was used in the study, they found "nearly a one-in-six (15.3 percent) probability [that] a drug will advance from phase I to FDA."

It is in this context that the success of the IPASS study has been understood, as Drs. Wang and Zhao pointed out.

DR. WANG: . . . they [the drug companies] don't want to miss a situation like IRESSA again. Because it means a huge thing to them. It's either you get drug registered or drug not registered. So they're all here in Asia.

DR. ZHAO: There's two factors: one is that there's all [of these] EGFR results and so forth, showing that if you don't test in Asians, your drug may fail . . . so that's why a lot of the drug companies are coming down here, because they may be able to find successful drugs here, that they couldn't find in Western populations . . . because the Western population did not have the frequency that was suitable for having enough numbers for the drug to be successful.

Differentiating by disease types, Hay et al. (2014:43) found that oncology drugs had the lowest likelihood of approval. Specifically:

[U]nfortunately, in oncology, when all indications are considered, only around 1 in 15 drugs entering clinical development in phase I achieves FDA approval compared with close to 1 in 8 using the lead indication methodology . . . using the lead indication methodology to determine success rates, the scope of the challenge in oncology drug development would be dramatically underestimated.

By turning the concept of the "Asian" from a geographically based concept into a biomedically relevant object, drug companies are not only better positioned to win regulatory approval(s), but also stand a greater chance of gaining access to overseas markets. Indeed, the "Asian" market is perceived as a significant one, as Drs. Lin, Zhao, and Wang point out:

DR. LIN: If you're [a] pharmaceutical company, you develop a drug, [and] you want your drug to be widely used. And for years, they've not come to Asia. They don't care if you Asians have a different profile, okay? Because [the] big market is [the] US and Europe. Nowadays, they know where the market is.

DR. ZHAO: . . . now, cancer, for example, half the world's burden is actually in Asia, and you know, China and India [are] huge markets. So the pharmaceutical companies have got two big reasons to come down here. In fact, from what I hear . . . now, the major growth is in Asia, from Asia[n] markets, so they'll be very foolish not to engage in Asia.

DR. WANG: Why do you think they are all here in Asia? For several reasons. One, all the patients are here in Asia. Asia [ha]s a huge population. Like 3 billion people in Asia. So the patients are here.

Most certainly, it is not only the size of the market (understood in a racial and ethnic manner) but also the perceived consumption power of potential patients that matters in the decision-making of the pharmaceutical company. That is to say, the interest in developing drugs that are effective on biomarkers that are more prevalent in the "Asian" population is linked to the rising affluence of some people in Asia, as indicated by Dr. Hsu:

They [the pharmaceutical companies] think that Asian[s] [represent] a big population, so [for example] the Chinese . . . they [the companies] think of the 1.3 billion people, straightaway their eyes open big, because they think that, oh, suddenly you've got a big population to capture.

Dr. Tang made a similar observation:

INTERVIEWER: Why do pharmaceutical companies come all the way to Asia?

DR. TANG: The "Asian" population is still more in this part of the world. And the other thing is that that they would want the oncologist treating the patients to be familiar with the drugs. So by participating in clinical trials, you become familiar with the drugs so when the drugs get approved, they are more likely to continue to use the drug. So, it serves [a] dual purpose.

Conversely, when the biomarkers are present in populations that cannot afford the drug, the company may have less interest in developing the drugs for these populations.

Racializing clinical trials as a routine phenomenon

Even in the "new" biomarker-based drug development paradigm, it remains true that pharmaceutical companies have to channel their research and development efforts to areas where positive outcomes are likely. Moreover, one of the ways in which companies try to predict success is to rely on the frequency of a particular mutation "enriched" in certain racial and ethnic populations, as indicated by Dr. Tang:

> Drug companies when they plan their trials, they are given a budget. So they, at least, [at] the start of every budget year, they have to plan how are they going to use the budget, so having all the knowledge about demography and incidence is very helpful for them in planning their budgets and in allocating budget[s] to run clinical trials in particular parts of the world.
> . . . let's say a drug that is effective against a particular genomic alteration, it will go to the place where this problem is prevalent and it will approach the center where they see [the] most of such patients. Like for instance . . . they have been focusing on East Asians when they come to EGFR TKI.

Indeed, as Saijo (2013) points out: "70 percent of patients in the LUX-LUNG3 global trial for afatinib [an EGFR TKI drug] are East Asian." How do we understand the choice of centers – including those in Hong Kong, China, Indonesia, Japan, Malaysia, the Philippines, Singapore, Taiwan, and Thailand – in the IPASS? Dr. Tang continued:

> They [pharmaceutical companies] are picky. When they want to come to conduct the clinical trials, they want to make sure that the center can deliver because to conduct clinical trials is very expensive. So first of all they want to make sure that whatever research protocol they have, that the center is capable of being compliant with the protocol to the letter. [This] [m]eans that it must be conducted in accordance [with] GCP [Good Clinical Practice]. . . .
> Initially, there are only a few centers that are, that are of standard for phase I study, like in Korea, Taiwan, Hong Kong, Singapore, these are the four main ones. . . . And [for] any drug that is registered in Japan [the trials] must be done in Japan. So Japan is always considered separately. But Japan is also very advanced in doing phase I work. So these are the few Asian centers that drug companies will approach. . . . [For] phase III, they are usually a bit more lenient, [and] they will approach centers that will be able to just give the patients treatment, monitor for response, make sure [of] their survival, follow up. The patients are compliant to follow up. . . . [These] phase III trials usually, they can conduct in countries like Thailand, Philippines, maybe Indonesia, Malaysia.

However, the question remains, what boundaries are used to define East Asians? Are patients in these countries considered East Asians? For example, the

IPASS results suggest that "[g]efitinib [i.e. IRESSA] is superior to carboplatin-paclitaxel [i.e. chemotherapy] as an initial treatment for pulmonary adenocarcinoma [i.e. a type of lung cancer] among non-smokers or former light smokers in East Asia" (Mok et al., 2009:947). Dr. Tang clarified:

> East Asians [are] basically ethnic Chinese or Malay. Indian is not considered East Asian. [Interviewer: Why?] [P]eople tend to associate . . . Indians more with [the] Caucasian group. [Interviewer: Why?] I think . . . there is a[n] SNP consortium called the HapMap consortium. The HapMap, I think, will tell you the basis for defining the populations as such.

In other words, while the claim was made about the suitability of the drug for patients in a particular geographical area (i.e. East Asia), upon closer examination, the reference is to the ethnic, or non-Indian, patients.

Dr. Deng commented that, in general, certain ethnic groups may be left out of clinical trials:

> So in the drug development phase . . . [in which] your trial is very much in a fragile space and the successes and failures are determined by those trials, you want to maximize the chances of success. How you do that, you may have to resort to excluding certain ethnic populations that you know will actually dilute . . . your results.

More significantly, such racial and ethnic profiling of human genetic variation in the drug development process is unlikely to be explicit, as Dr. Zhao and Dr. Hsu pointed out:

> DR. ZHAO: There are so many people very sensitive about racial profiling and ethnicity that I think the smart way to approach it is to really say it's about molecular alteration that is more frequent in Asians, rather than, you know, designed specifically for Asians.
>
> DR. HSU: I find it politically a bit sensitive to really launch a trial to specify the ethnic group. I think that would be difficult. But so what they do is, they would report the ethnic distribution, in the results, and they will have a subset analysis based on the subgroup. But you can't exclude them from entering the trial in the first place.

Local transformations

As indicated above, to gain regulatory approval, a drug has to demonstrate a certain level of efficacy. If a drug's efficacy is linked to biomarkers that are prevalent only in certain populations, pharmaceutical companies will channel research resources to those populations in order to demonstrate higher efficacy. Thus far, we have tried to suggest that (re)formulations of racialized populations allow powerful pharmaceutical companies trying to win approval of regulatory agencies in developed countries to move their clinical trials seamlessly into developing countries and to enter markets there.

At the same time, the greater rate of increase for trials in Asia is about not only the strategies adopted by companies motivated by economic profits, but also the pursuit of genomic research in developing countries. Indeed, if developing countries do not have necessary infrastructure or credibility, pharmaceutical companies will not be able to set up clinical trials in those locations.

In leading countries like Singapore, infrastructure and technology for clinical trials, as well as the expertise of researchers, have vastly improved. Decades ago, there was minimal research in drug development in most, if not all, of Asia. As Dr. Zhang indicated, the research he conducted then was merely data collection, with little analysis:

> Twenty years ago, all [of this] research [was] done in the west. There was hardly any research done here, over this part of the world. When I was a trainee, when we [saw] research, research basically means that the drug companies come to you and say, "I need 30 patients in Singapore, can you get me 30 patients?" So, my function is no different from a vendor that suppl[ies] lab mice. I will just get patients and all I did was to collect data. The drug companies will come and analyze for me, and put it in a pool of 600 patients – a few from Hong Kong, a few from Malaysia, a few from Indonesia. My job and that is called research. That was those days.

However, the situation has changed. The Singapore government, for example, has invested millions in pharmaceuticals and biotechnology, including setting up infrastructure, training professionals, and even coordinating partnerships. In fact, according to the Singapore Economic Board, "Singapore has committed S\$16.1 billion in continued support of research, innovation and enterprise activities between 2011 and 2015[10]." Researchers themselves have noted vast improvements, as Dr. Zhang and Dr. Neo put it:

> DR. ZHANG: Today, it is different. They come to us and our lab will do all the genetic analysis. Our lab will tell them . . . , "there is this particular gene that we can target with that molecule." And then using that kind of basic knowledge, we translate that into clinical practice. So that is called translational medicine. So now . . . , drug companies are more interested in doing this. This is an untapped field. In the past, that w[ould] be done in the Caucasian population.
>
> DR. NEO: I don't think it is true that drug companies were not interested in us. I think you know it is by and large in a way where the infrastructure is for them to do the trials. . . . And now that you see that our infrastructure has improved, our science has improved to the level where they're confident that we're doing things the right way. . . . I actually think that they [we]re always interested; it is just that now . . . they can do those studies.
>
> DR. TANG: So Singapore, we do participate in all three phases. . . . If the center is deemed capable of participating in phase I, it means that the center has

advanced infrastructure. So if a country is labeled as up to phase I standard, the country should be proud of their country.

In addition to the ambitions and policies of local governments, there is an emerging sense of self-determination and assertion among scientists, as Drs. Hsu, Lin, and Teo described:

DR. HSU: So what the Western world like[s] to do is to do trial in the West, but ask . . . the Asian people to accept the trial data based on that. But Asian people now are stronger, they're becoming more self-assertive. So they will say why do I accept your data? I repeat the trial here to see how it goes, you see.

DR. LIN: Things have changed. Because China, Korea, Japan, they're getting more powerful, they also want to have their own results and trials.

DR. TEO: In fact, [the drug] Sorafenib came out from two very famous studies. One is the SHARP trial from Spain. And the other one is Professor Ann-Lii Cheng's study from Tai Da [i.e. the National Taiwan University] . . . the two big studies managed to convince the FDA that this is the drug for liver cancer. Okay?

The FDA said "Well, you know you did this Spanish trial [i.e. the SHARP trial], it's really cool and you showed that Sorafenib works better. But I don't buy that story in Asia. None of the Asian oncologists bought that story when we had our advisory board meeting. The reason is because we think Asian liver cancers are genetically different. . . .

So Bayer was very clever. Bayer is the company that basically has the drug Sorafenib. They say "let's do an Asian study." And Professor Ann-Li Cheng, was the Principal Investigator and so they ran it and it had exactly the same results. Because they had exactly the same results, they [i.e. the Asian oncologists] said "we think this's gonna be fine." The FDA approved it.

In sum, while the increase in clinical trials conducted in Asia is primarily a function of global pharmaceutical companies trying to earn more profits (Asia is a big market, and rising affluence of patients in Asia allows them to purchase drugs), other cultural, political, and social forces – such as improved infrastructure, technology, and expertise, coupled with a sense of emerging pride among scientists and observed phenotypes – are also contributing factors.

Pharmacogenomics, race, and post-marketing clinical trials

Given financial interests, the pharmaceutical companies are less driven to thoroughly examine potential adverse drug reactions than to establish drug efficacy, particularly during the post-marketing phase. However, they are required to do so. Phase IV studies are conducted after a drug or treatment has been marketed to gather information on its effectiveness and any side effects associated with long-term use. Those studies are mandated by the regulatory authority to be conducted in real world conditions – observational, non-interventional trials in a naturalistic setting (as opposed to pre-marketing randomized controlled trials [RCT] for Phase I–III) – are called post-marketing surveillance (PMS) studies. Results from such studies can possibly reveal rare adverse reactions that might not have been detected in earlier clinical trials. In turn, this informs decision-making on whether, for instance, there is a need to conduct further controlled studies; make labeling changes with a modified undesirable effects section, indications, and/or dosing schedules; and/or regulatory action (boxed warning, risk minimization action plan, withdrawal).

This section analyzes the ways in which categories of race and ethnicity penetrate pharmacogenomic studies of cancer drug toxicity, typically adopting comparisons between "Asians" and "Caucasians" in the context of Phase IV clinical trials.

To begin, in contrast to pharmacogenomic studies of drug efficacies that mostly rely on a better understanding of somatic mutations, pharmacogenomic studies of drug toxicities typically involve examining germline genetic variants for adverse drug reactions. Regardless of whether a study concerns somatic or germline mutations, pharmaceutical companies seem consistently interested in obtaining data on racialized differences. For example, in the public online database ClinicalTrials.gov, an ongoing trial is titled "Verification of a Pharmacogenetic Approach to Customizing Chemotherapy to Asians." There, we see the following (U.S. National Institutes of Health, 2013):

> Recently, based on meta-analysis of studies on germline pharmacogenetic variant frequencies and clinical trials, the investigators found that chemotherapy outcomes between Asian and Caucasian colorectal cancer (CRC) patients could potentially be inferred from the frequencies of variants between the ethnic groups and their respective biological functions. In this study, the investigators seek to further clarify the validity of using pharmacogenetic variants to customize chemotherapy between ethnicities through the following specific aims[:] (1) to verify the differences observed in the frequency of germline pharmacogenetic variants related to chemotherapy between Asian and Caucasian CRC patients and (2) to test whether variations in the frequency of somatic pharmacogenetic gene mutations between Asian and Caucasian CRC patients could be used to infer differences in clinical outcomes between the two ethnicities.

In the clinical trial cited above, it is noted that "samples will be obtained from the Tissue Repository, National University Hospital, St. John of God Hospital, Perth, Australia and Kanazawa University, Japan." Earlier, in collaboration with AstraZeneca, Lee et al. (2005) carried out a clinical study in Singapore to examine rosuvastatin pharmacokinetics and pharmacogenetics in white and Asian subjects, and the results were published in the journal *Clinical Pharmacology and Therapeutics.*

Drugs approved by the US FDA are routinely sold in countries other than the United States. Racial politics in the drug development phase – demonstrated to be highly problematic in medical sociologist Steven Epstein's *Inclusion: The*

Politics of Difference in Medical Research (2007) – have now migrated transnationally through racialized trials outside of the United States. Specifically, we found that studies of drug toxicities conducted outside of the United States are typically framed in relation to the lack of minority group participants in US biomedical research. For example, Ling and Lee (2011) note that "data is often extrapolated from landmark studies generated from Caucasian patients to Asian populations for clinical use, which may not be relevant for some drugs." Similarly, in a study of the cost-effectiveness of HLA-B*1502 genotyping in adult patients, the authors note that "the effectiveness data are from clinical trials in Caucasian populations" (Dong, Sung and Finkelstein., 2012:1259), thus uncritically adopting the existing racialized framework in justifying the need for further studies of the usage of carbamazepine and HLA-B*1502.

However, while a heightened awareness of a lack of minority group participants during the drug development phase may be the rhetorical frame through which the existence of racialized clinical trials is justified (i.e. by adopting the categories of "Caucasian" versus "non-Caucasian"), this is not the full story. The interview data also reveal that, sometimes, researchers emphasize the "Asian-ness" of their work in order to distinguish themselves from researchers in other parts of the world. Scientists and clinician-scientists need to show the uniqueness of their work in a highly competitive scientific community, as observed by Dr. Chong:

You know, you sort of have to invent for yourself, a niche, right? I mean, you can't be fighting with the big boys in researching colorectal cancer or breast cancer and everything. . . . You'll be trashed, instantly, you know. So what can you do that is very niche? [Something] no one else is interested [in doing], and yet seems to be potentially useful? So how do Singaporeans, or how do Southeast Asians, or Asians respond to a certain drug, and are their genotypes different? You know, so it's very common, it's very very common, but I think a lot of it just seems to be good for churning out papers, and getting grants, you know. . . .

Considering that Singapore is a small country, and as a way of capitalizing on its ethnic diversity, some researchers frame their Singapore-based studies as "Asian" in order to boost their significance. Dr. Paul Lin commented:

Sometimes when your paper says . . . "Asian Population Study," it sounds better than "Singapore Population Study."

Adopting an Asian-Caucasian frame in one's human genetics research agenda requires a definition of "Asians" and "Caucasians." As the interview data reveal, there are several ways in which such categorization and identification can be done.

Who is Asian?

Geographically, Asia (if it can be unambiguously defined at all) is such a broad region that it would be difficult, if not prohibitive, for a research project to take a randomized sample that would be truly representative. In practice, researchers may simply use the prevailing ethnic classification in their societies to make a claim about "Asians." For example, Singapore-based researchers place Chinese, Malays, and migrants from the Indian subcontinent in the Asian category, as Dr. Zhang succinctly pointed out:

DR. ZHANG: Okay, our "Asian" probably refers to Chinese, Indian, and Malay.
INTERVIEWER: So if a Caucasian lives in Singapore, which is part of Asia, he/she is not Asian?
DR. ZHANG: [He/she]'s not Asian.

At the same time, researchers have pointed out the difficulties of defining "Asia" or "Asian." For instance, Dr. Lin discussed this in relation to the definition of "Asian" in the IPASS:

Asia is so complex! I tried to write up this thing on Asian breast cancer patients. . . . [T]rying to define Asia is just a problem [including such matters as [w]hether you include India and Pakistan]. . . .
If we go and look at the study of, let's say, "Asian" patients, for example. Why do they call themselves Asian? [An] IPASS study says "Asian patient." So, [in the] IPASS report . . . did they self-report ethnicity? Were they tested for certain genes that made sure they are Asians? Or is it just because they happened to be living there?

Asia is also conveniently delineated by political boundaries (i.e. identifying an entire state to be in Asia or otherwise). But, even so, the category can become ambiguous and debatable when it comes to states at the edges of the region. As Dr. Huang put it:

. . . so anything that is 6 hours flight from here [Singapore] . . .
. . . I mean I think that the easy ones are easy. Thailand is Asia. South Korea is Asia, then you get . . .
. . . I would consider Japan Asia . . . maybe not South-East Asia. So . . . I would say anything that's not Western Europe or North America. . . .
Is Russia Asia or not? That becomes a bit of a blurry line. So it's a, it's a nice title to have [for a scientific paper presentation]? . . . But obviously, where does Asia end? Is Australia part of Asia, I don't know [laughs].

Moreover, diasporic communities create additional complexities for the definition, as Dr. Rajaratnam put it:

If you tell me [about] "American Asians," I am also very skeptical. Because Asians from the West, they may be mixed blood. They may have intermarriages with other ethnicities, Caucasians, Africans. . . . They may have so many different combinations of generations, belonging to different ethnic populations involved, so it is very difficult. That is one reason why when you look at the data, sometimes originating from the west, [for] just Asians, recruited in the west, [compared to] the pure Asians from our side, you can see [genetic] differences. Because they have a lot of intermarriages but they classify themselves as Asians.

Finally, inter-ethnic marriages are routinely seen as complicating the picture of who is Asian, as Dr. Lin pointed out:

[S]ome of the patients [have a] Chinese father, Caucasian mother, or vice versa. [In] what ethnic group do you place them?

INTERVIEWER: I don't know.

DR. LIN: Ya! Exactly! That's the problem! When you're trying to categorize like this, aren't you . . . it is frustrating! Because you are categorizing things that are not categorizable neatly, you see?

Who is Caucasian?

Turning our attention to the categorization of "Caucasian," we see that this term is demonstrably fluid and arbitrary. Figure 3.1 illustrates an advertisement call for "Caucasian" trial subjects in Singapore.

Sometimes, it can be geographically defined, other times it is preconceived racial thinking, and still other times it can be based on Singapore's National Registration Identity Card (NRIC), as garnered from interview data:

INTERVIEWER: The next question is, what's the definition of Caucasian?

DR. ZHAO: Well, I think in this sort of study done in Asia . . . I think it's just basically anybody from European heritage or American heritage.

INTERVIEWER: What about Europeans?

DR. TANG: Those that are in Europe. Australians are considered to be of European descent. . . . [U]sually, it's more of the racial thing rather than the geography.

INTERVIEWER: How [are] Western European[s] different?

DR. TANG: Caucasian appearance.

INTERVIEWER: Not location based?

DR. TANG: No. Like Chinese migrants who migrate to Europe or US will not be considered . . . Western European. They will still be called East Asian in [terms of] their ethnicity.

"Defining" Asians or Caucasians is different from "identifying" them as such. What are the ways in which identification may be done? In Singapore, it can be based on patients' self-identification, sometimes followed by the physician's checking it against their NRICs:

INTERVIEWER: So for this paper, the first paper, that's the latest, can you share with us how you identify a healthy individual as a Chinese, Indian, Malay, or Caucasian[?]

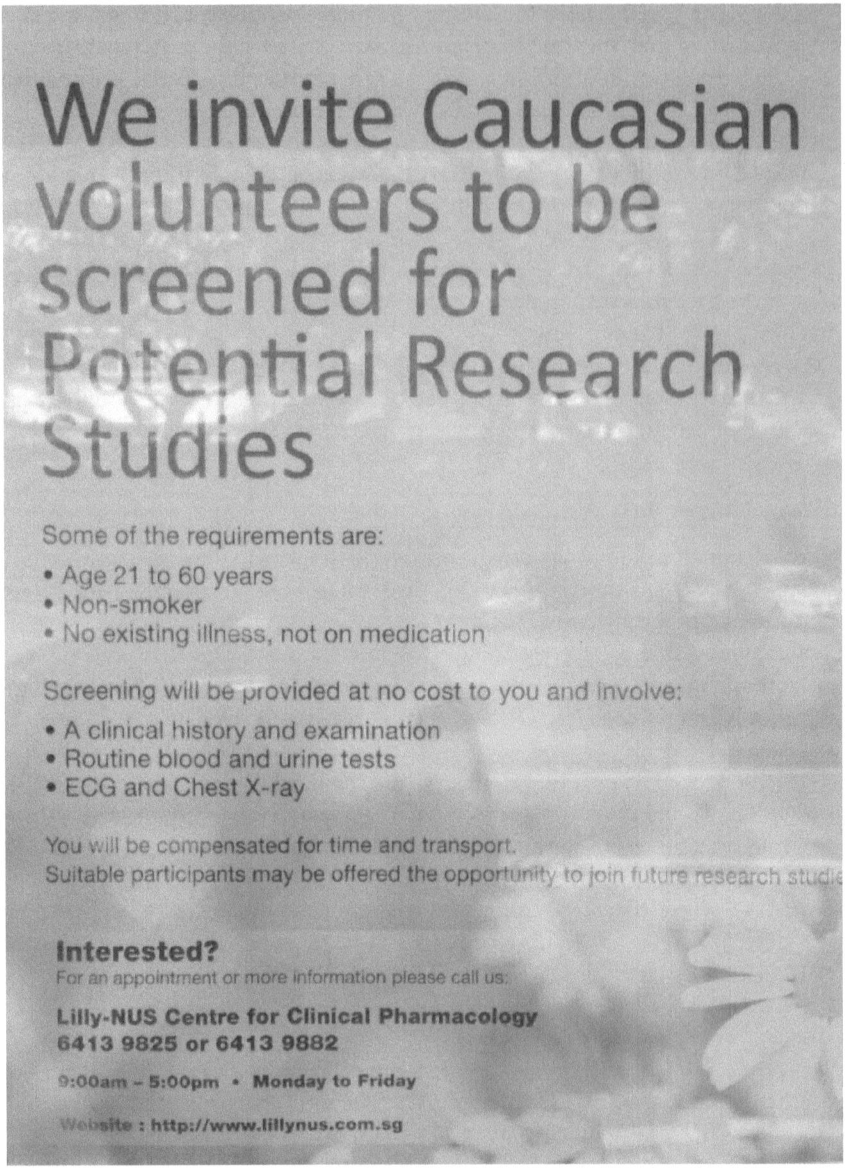

Figure 3.1 A poster revealing how clinical trials are sometimes racialized through seeking targeted participants by race.

DR. RAJARATNAM: By verbal. Verbally asking them, and by their IC [i.e. NRIC]. Because that is their national identification. So that's the only proof we have.
INTERVIEWER: When you say verbal, do you mean you ask the human subject to fill in a questionnaire?

DR. RAJARATNAM: Not really a questionnaire. We call it a "patient information and consent" form. We have . . . patient information telling them what . . . this study [is] about, [and] that will be followed by a consent form where the patients will sign and their clinician and the witness will sign. If the patient is unable to give consent, then normally his relative or next of kin will agree and will decide also.

INTERVIEWER: In other words it's already protocol; there is a protocol to follow?

DR. RAJARATNAM: Yes.

INTERVIEWER: And then you ask, just to confirm, two generations right? You ask the parents and grandparents?

DR. RAJARATNAM: Yes.

INTERVIEWER: What about patient? That was for healthy patients, right, [the] normal healthy population? How do you know . . . the ethnic background of patients?

DR. RAJARATNAM: Similar method.

INTERVIEWER: Why do you need to verify their self- reported ethnic identification with their IC card?

DR. RAJARATNAM: Because . . . the name, and I think the race is written there. Ya, because that's their national registry, that's what they are supposed to be. I mean . . . their ethnic identification is stated there. We presume that that's what they are.

However, ethnic identification on the NRIC is not limited to "Chinese," "Malay," "Indian," and "Eurasian." In total, there are currently 95 races (inclusive of the four mentioned) under which Singapore citizens can choose to be classified. Although the "Chinese," "Malays," and "Indians" constitute the majority (99 percent), the remaining one percent is constituted mostly of Eurasians and Arabs (0.6 percent in combination), followed by a distribution of the remaining 90 races (0.4 percent). Typically, a citizen's race follows that of his or her father, but can be registered differently if he or she is of mixed parentage (e.g. a child of Chinese and European descent can be registered "Chinese," "European," or "Eurasian").

In January 2010, it was announced in the Parliament that the registration of overlapping and mixed-race options for Singaporean children born to parents of different races would be implemented. For couples of inter-ethnic marriages, in addition to the existing options of choosing only one of the two different races for their children, they would now be able to choose to reflect both. For instance, if a child is of Chinese and Indian descent, his or her race can be recorded as "Chinese," "Indian," "Chinese-Indian," or "Indian-Chinese." This policy subsequently came into effect in January 2011. The government has explained that such added flexibility of registering race is consistent with the continual review of policies in order to recognize and respond to the evolving social landscape in Singapore.

Identifying a person as Asian or Caucasian can be arbitrary. As Dr. Rajaratnam suggests, for instance, in the Singapore context, a patient would self-report his or her race followed by a verification of this information against his or her ID card. The information provided would be assumed to be accurate. However, patients' identifications or races are not as straightforward as they seem, particularly for those of mixed parentage, as it is left to parents' arbitrary choosing of whether their child should be identified by their father's or mother's race.

If the study involves international collaboration, then the identification can become even more challenging. Dr. Rajaratnam explained:

> One thing I am very careful of is with Indonesians. Indonesians, they may have Malay names, but they can be Chinese, they can be Indians. But all of them, their names are Malay, you know. So I am very careful.
>
> I am very careful, unless I can get at least two people to verify for sure that that person, that Indonesian is a Chinese or Malay, [and same for verifying] Caucasians also. . . .

As the interview data indicate, such identification can also be based on the patient's physical appearance in the eyes of the physician or on other witness accounts based on local understanding. Other times, it can also be based on the words of an international collaborator:

INTERVIEWER: How do researchers know whether the person is Caucasian?
DR. POH: Because one of my colleges is from Germany . . . and he gave us samples. Normal German, Caucasians. . . . They tell us.

Thus far, we have highlighted the socially fluid definition and identification of "Asians" and "Caucasians." It is worth reiterating that such fluidity, in itself, is not a problem; it becomes problematic, however, because racial categories can be used to frame medical research and can potentially influence clinical practices, as the following comments by Dr. Yuan, regarding linking ethnicity to research on drug toxicity, illustrated:

> One of the key drugs in lung cancer treatment is . . . Docetaxel. And we in Singapore are the first group to show that Docetaxel stays in the system in Orientals much longer than [in] Caucasians. So, if I inject the same dose of Docetaxel in [an] Oriental versus a Caucasian, the Caucasian clears the drug much faster. . . . The bulk of the Caucasians of course came from Australia. We supplied the bulk of the Asians.

And Dr. Lin explained how ethnicity is related to clinical decisions:

DR. LIN: I generally would know [that] you are Asian, right? [Since] you speak with little bit of [an] American accent, but you are [of] Asian descent, if I were using Taxotere, I would be a bit careful with the dosing, check your blood count. Whereas if you are sitting here, Caucasian, then I generally would think that you might respond to a higher dose of the drug and so on. BUT, but this is not absolute. This is . . . generalized, so I suspect. But I can't be absolutely sure, just because you look Asian that you [are]. . . .

Both doctors illustrated that in clinical practice, their perceived identification of a patient's race would influence decisions on drugs they would prescribe to their patients. Moreover, these decisions are made based on results from race-based research on drug toxicity. If a particular drug is found to be less toxic to a patient perceived to be Caucasian and more toxic to a patient perceived to be Asian, a doctor might be tempted to adjust the dosage of the drug to be prescribed accordingly, even if he or she is not entirely sure of why and how its toxicity would affect the particular patient.

Conclusion

The overarching question with which this book is concerned is why categories of race and ethnicity have become dominant in interpreting and measuring human genomic diversity. We suggest that pharmaceutical companies often rely on information regarding the frequency of a particular genetic mutation or on an expanded panel of genes associated with drug responses in populations categorized by race and ethnicity in their decision-making about the kinds of medical interventions they will develop. This chapter makes a few key points. First, while IRESSA for non-small-cell lung cancer patients is publicly portrayed as an example of personalized medicine based on analysis of the EGFR-mutation status of a patient's tumor, it is revealed that the IPASS was a clinical trial that selected patients based on the Asian phenotype. Notions of Asian and East Asian are constructed based on geography (people in Asia) and ethnicity (i.e. non-Indian), respectively.

Second, while the success of the IPASS encouraged pharmaceutical companies to treat the "Asian" category as real, it was later proved that what mattered was the patient's EGFR-mutation status, not whether he or she was Asian or non-Asian. In this case, racialization of clinical trials was a matter of survival and reduction of attrition rates for a pharmaceutical company. As such, IRESSA may not be an isolated case of misappropriation of racial categories in the context of a globalized pharmaceutical industry.

Given the increasing affluence of the "Asian" market, increasing competence of medical professionals, and better research into infrastructure, governments in Asia also sometimes frame the continued monitoring of drug toxicity in racial terms – that is, testing them in "Asian" populations when drugs come to Asia. Moreover, there are now drugs that were first tested and developed in Asia, and the concern is that in order to sell the drug in the perceived core market, the "Caucasian" market, there has to be more monitoring and testing. Indeed, we present evidence for the usage of racially and ethnically labeled populations in all four phases of clinical trials, including Phase IV, post-marketing surveillance.

While previous studies have identified the role of the ethnic niche market in the medicalization of race (Duster 2007; Lee 2003), I argue that such a phenomenon cannot be fully explained without an understanding of the choices and rationale underlying the cooperation of participating clinical trial centers and doctors.

Finally, and perhaps most importantly, this chapter shows that definitions and identifications of Asians and Caucasians are based on fluctuating and often arbitrary criteria. One cannot be sure of how an individual is identified and categorized. For example, as noted, a doctor can place a person in a particular ethnic category based on his or her appearance or self-identity. If an individual has a "Chinese" mother and a "Caucasian" father, it is possible to self-report as "Chinese," "Caucasian," or both. Moreover, while it may appear to scientists and physicians that using NRIC is more "scientific," such census categories remain arbitrary and are, significantly, a colonial legacy.

To summarize, ethnic identities are shaped by social processes and individual choices. Parents may choose to identify a child who is of mixed parentage, whose mother is Chinese and whose father is French, for example, as "Chinese," "French," "Chinese-French," or "French-Chinese." If the child is perceived by a doctor as European because he/she looks more French than Chinese, but the child's parents chose "Chinese" as his/her registered ethnicity, what would the doctor use as the basis for a prescription, the seemingly more apparent "European" identity or what is registered on the child's ID? Likewise, if the child's parents had chosen the double-barreled race option to register their child, what should the doctor do in terms of providing prescriptions? In the case of, for example, ethnic quotas for state-subsidized public housing applications, the Singapore government's policy is that the first race stated in the double-barreled race option will be used. Would this be the case for drug prescriptions too?

There are currently 95 races that can be registered on an ID in Singapore. However, the list may not be exhaustive and can vary over time. In a Singaporean-Malay female friend's case, she is married to a citizen from Kazakhstan. Her son is a Singaporean citizen, but Kazakh is the declared ethnicity. What if the category "Kazakh" is new, bringing the total number of races on the list to 96? (There is no other Singaporean-born citizen registered as Kazakh, unless there are new naturalized citizens. Other local inter-ethnic Kazakh marriages are between Chinese men and Kazakh women, so therefore their children are likely registered as Chinese). She could have chosen "Malay" for her son, for practical reasons, such as to apply for tertiary tuition subsidies, even though the child hardly "looks" Malay (personal communication, Amalia Rahmat). What would doctors make out of such rare ethnic groups such as Kazakh?

Given the arbitrariness of how Asians and Caucasians are identified for clinical trials, the results are questionable. But such results can in reality constrain physicians' actions to prescribe drugs along racial or ethnic lines. In the end, patients may spend a lot of money for drugs that may not be effective or safe for them. Even more worrisome, we may be moving to a new platform in which producers and consumers of human genetic research are now more inclined to believe that racially and ethnically labeled groups are biologically meaningful categories because of the existence of racially or ethnically based medicine.

Notes

1 International Agency for Research on Cancer, World Health Organisation. 2012. "GLOBOCAN 2012: Estimated Cancer Incidence, Mortality and Prevalence Worldwide in 2012." Retrieved November 15, 2014 (http://globocan.iarc.fr/Pages/fact_sheets_cancer.aspx).
2 European Society for Medical Oncology. 2014. "Global Battle Against Cancer Won't Be Won With Treatment Alone." *World Cancer Report 2014.* Swiss: European Society for Medical Oncology. Retrieved November 16, 2014 (http://www.esmo.org/Oncology-News/World-Cancer-Report-2014).
3 Cancer Research UK. 2014. "Incidence Worldwide." Retrieved November 15, 2014 (http://www.cancerresearchuk.org/cancer-info/cancerstats/keyfacts/worldwide/).
4 American Cancer Society. 2014. "Lung and Bronchus" in *Cancer Facts and Figures 2014*:15. Atlanta: American Cancer Society. Retrieved November 16, 2014. (http://www.cancer.org/acs/groups/content/@research/documents/webcontent/acspc-042151.pdf).
5 International Agency for Research on Cancer, World Health Organisation. 2012. "GLOBOCAN 2012: Estimated Cancer Incidence, Mortality and Prevalence Worldwide in 2012." Retrieved November 15, 2014 (http://globocan.iarc.fr/Pages/fact_sheets_cancer.aspx).
6 Lee, Hui Chieh. 2010. "Good News for Lung Cancer Patients." *The Strait Times* (November 4). Retrieved November 16, 2014 (http://www.healthxchange.com.sg/News/Pages/Good-news-for-lung-cancer-patients.aspx).
7 American Cancer Society. 2014. "Lung and Bronchus" in *Cancer Facts and Figures 2014*:15. Atlanta: American Cancer Society; 2014. Retrieved November 16, 2014, (http://www.cancer.org/acs/groups/content/@research/documents/webcontent/acspc-042151.pdf).
8 Ethnicity was one of the characteristics in the clinical profile.
9 U.S. Food and Drug Administration. 2005. "Guidance for Industry: Collection of Race and Ethnicity Data in Clinical Trials." Retrieved January 18, 2015 (http://www.fda.gov/downloads/RegulatoryInformation/Guidances/ucm126396.pdf).
10 Singapore Economic Development Board. 2014. "Pharmaceuticals & Biotechnology" Retrieved September 12, 2014. (https://www.edb.gov.sg/content/edb/en/industries/industries/pharma-biotech.html).

References

American Cancer Society. 2014. "Lung and Bronchus." *Cancer Facts and Figures 2014*:15. Atlanta: American Cancer Society. Retrieved November 16, 2014. (http://www.cancer.org/acs/groups/content/@research/documents/webcontent/acspc-042151.pdf).

AstraZeneca. 2014. "About IRESSA." Retrieved January 16, 2015. (http://www.iressa.com/about-iressa.html).

Cancer Research UK. 2014. "Incidence Worldwide." Retrieved November 15, 2014 (http://www.cancerresearchuk.org/cancer-info/cancerstats/keyfacts/worldwide/).

Chiang, Alex and Ryan P. Million. 2011. "Personalized Medicine in Oncology: Next Generation." *Nature Reviews Drug Discovery* 10(12):895–896. doi: http://dx.doi.org/10.1038/nrd3603.

Chin, Richard. 2011. "Chapter 1 – Background." Pp. 3–17 in *Global Clinical Trials: Effective Implementation and Management*, edited by Richard Chin and Menghis Bairu. London: Elsevier Inc.

Daar, Abdallah S. and Peter A. Singer. 2005. "Pharmacogenetics and Geographical Ancestry: Implications for Drug Development and Global Health." *Nature Reviews Genetics* 6:241–246.

Dong, Di, Cynthia Sung and Eric Andrew Finkelstein. 2012. "Cost-Effectiveness of HLA-B*1502 Genotyping in Adult Patients with Newly Diagnosed Epilepsy in Singapore." *Neurology* 79(12):1259–1267.

Drain, Paul K., Marion Robine, King K. Holmes and Ingrid V. Bassett. 2014. "Trial Watch: Global Migration of Clinical Trials." *Nature Reviews Drug Discovery* 13(3):166–167. doi: 10.1038/nrd4260.

Duster, Troy. 2006. "The Molecular Reinscription of Race: Unanticipated Issues in Biotechnology and Forensic Science." *Patterns of Prejudice* 40(4):427–441.

Duster, Troy. 2007. "Medicalisation of Race." *The Lancet* 369(9562):702–704.

Epstein, Steven. 2007. *Inclusion: The Politics of Difference in Medical Research*. Chicago and London: The University of Chicago Press.

European Science Foundation. 2012. "Personalised Medicine for the European Citizen – Towards More Precise Medicine for the Diagnosis, Treatment and Prevention of Disease (iPM)." *ESF Forward Look* (November 2012):1–62. France: European Science Foundation. Retrieved January 18, 2015. (http://www.esf.org/file admin/Public_documents/Publications/Personalised_Medicine.pdf).

European Society for Medical Oncology. 2014. "Global Battle Against Cancer Won't Be Won with Treatment Alone." *World Cancer Report 2014*. Swiss: European Society for Medical Oncology. Retrieved November 16, 2014 (http://www.esmo.org/Oncology-News/World-Cancer-Report-2014).

Hay, Michael, David W. Thomas, John L. Craighead, Celia Economides and Jesse Rosenthal. 2014. "Clinical Development Success Rates for Investigational Drugs." *Nature biotechnology* 32(1):40–51.

Hughes, Bethan. 2009. "Lessons from the Lung for Targeted Anticancer Drugs." *Nature Reviews Drug Discovery* 8(10):758–759.

International Agency for Research on Cancer, World Health Organization. 2012. "GLOBOCAN 2012: Estimated Cancer Incidence, Mortality and Prevalence Worldwide in 2012." Retrieved November 15, 2014 (http://globocan.iarc.fr/Pages/fact_sheets_cancer.aspx).

Jackson, David B. and Anil K. Sood. 2011. "Personalized Cancer Medicine – Advances and Socio-Economic Challenges." *Nature Reviews Clinical Oncology* 8(12):735–741. doi: http://dx.doi.org/10.1038/nrclinonc.2011.151.

Kahn, Jonathan. 2004. "How a Drug Becomes 'Ethic': Law, Commerce, and the Production of Racial Categories in Medicine." *Yale Journal of Health Policy, Law & Ethics* 4(1):1–31.

Kahn, Jonathan. 2013. *Race in a Bottle: The Story of BiDil and Racilized Medicine in a Post-Genomic Age*. New York: Columbia University Press.

Lee, Edmund, Stephen Ryan, Bruce Birmingham, Julie Zalikowski, Ruth March, Helen Ambrose, Rachael Moore, Caroline Lee, Yusong Chen and Dennis Schneck. 2005. "Rosuvastatin Pharmacokinetics and Pharmacogenetics in White and Asian Subjects Residing in the Same Environment." *Clinical Pharmacology and Therapeutics* 78(4):330–341.

Lee, Sandra Soo-Jin. 2003. "Race, Distributive Justice and the Promise of Pharmacogenomics: Ethical Considerations." *American Journal of Pharmacogenomics* 3(6):385–392.

Ling, W.H. and S.C. Lee. 2011. "Inter-Ethnic Differences—How Important is It in Cancer Treatment?" *Ann Acad Med Singapore* 40(8):356–361.

Mok, Tony S., Yi-Long Wu, Sumitra Thongprasert, Chih-Hsin Yang, Da-Tong Chu, Nagahiro Saijo, Patrapim Sunpaweravong, Baohui Han, Benjamin Margono, Yukito Ichinose, Yutaka Nishiwaki, Yuichiro Ohe, Jin-Ji Yang, Busyamas Chewaskulyong, Haiyi Jiang, Emma L. Duffield, Claire L. Watkins, Alison A. Armour, F.R.C.R and Masahiro Fukuoka. 2009. "Gefitinib or Carboplatin-Paclitaxel in Pulmonary Adenocarcinoma." *New England Journal of Medicine* 361(10):947–957.

Omi, Michael and Howard Winant. 2015. *Racial Formation in the United States.* 3rd ed. New York and London: Routledge.

The Pharma Letter. "Japan High Court rules in favor of AstraZeneca over Iressa deaths." 30 May 2012.

Roberts, Dorothy E. 2011a. *Fatal Invention: How Science, Politics, and Big Business Re-Create Race in the Twenty-First Century.* New York and London: The New Press.

Roberts, Dorothy E. 2011b. "What's Wrong with Race-Based Medicine?: Genes, Drugs, and Health Disparities." *Minnesota Journal of Law, Science & Technology* 12(1):1–21.

Saijo, Nagahiro. 2013. "The Role of Pharmacoethnicity in the Development of Cytotoxic and Molecular Targeted Drugs in Oncology." *Yonsei Medical Journal* 54(1):1–14.

Sankar, Pamela and Jonathan Kahn. 2005. "BiDil: Race Medicine or Race Marketing?" *Health Affairs.* doi: 10.1377/hlthaff.w5.455.

Singapore Economic Development Board. 2014. *Pharmaceuticals & Biotechnology* Retrieved September 12, 2014 (https://www.edb.gov.sg/content/edb/en/industries/industries/pharma-biotech.html).

Suarez-Kurtz, Guilherme. 2008. "Ethnic Differences in Drug Therapy: A Pharmacogenomics Perspective." *Expert Review of Clinical Pharmacology* 1(3):337–339. doi:http://dx.doi.org/10.1586/17512433.1.3.337.

Tate, Sarah K. and David B Goldstein. 2008. "Will Tomorrow's Medicines Work for Everyone?" Pp. 102–128 in *Revisiting Race in a Genomic Age*, edited by B.A. Koenig, S.S. Lee and S.S. Richardson. New Brunswick, NJ: Rutgers University Press.

U.S. Food and Drug Administration. 2005. "Guidance for Industry: Collection of Race and Ethnicity Data in Clinical Trials." Retrieved January 18, 2015 (http://www.fda.gov/downloads/RegulatoryInformation/Guidances/ucm126396.pdf).

U.S. National Cancer Institute (NCI). 2011. "FDA Approval for Gefitinib." Retrieved January 16, 2015 (http://www.cancer.gov/cancertopics/druginfo/fda-gefitinib).

U.S. National Institutes of Health. 2013. "Verification of a Pharmacogenetic Approach to Customizing Chemotherapy to Asians." *ClinicalTrials.gov.* Retrieved November 19, 2015 (https://clinicaltrials.gov/ct2/show/NCT01596361?term=NCT01596361&rank=1) identifier: NCT01596361.

Wilson, James F., Michael E. Weale, Alice C. Smith, Fiona Gratrix, Benjamin Fletcher, Mark G. Thomas, Neil Bradman and David B. Goldstein. 2001. "Population Genetic Structure of Variable Drug Response." *Nature genetics* 29(3):265–269.

Zamiska, Nicholas and Jeanne Whalen. 2005. "Cancer Drug Helps Asians Even as It Fails in Other Groups." *The Wall Street Journal* May 4, B1. Retrieved April 1, 2016 (http://www.wsj.com/articles/SB111516441270323940).

4 Managing otherness

Genomics and public health policy in Singapore

Introduction

In contrast to the previous chapter, in which I focused on the interest of pharmaceutical companies in formulating and capturing the "Asian" and "Caucasian" markets in genomic medicine, this chapter explores how governments may incorporate genomic science in public health policy-making processes. The first section describes the ways in which medical researchers, doctors, and health economists have attempted to incorporate genomic data for the purposes of public health policies in Singapore. In particular, this chapter shows that, in the context of cost-effectiveness studies for managing public health resources, there is a tendency for social actors involved to think in terms of, and use, prevailing Chinese-Malay-Indian-Others (CMIO) census population categories as if these were biologically distinctive populations, thus providing a structural impetus for the implementation of "personalized medicine" that may be actually based on ethnic or racial categories.

I then move on to suggest how and why the pattern of using these ethnic categories, as if they were coherent, is problematic. First, interview data with medical doctors suggest that there is a tension between treatment decisions based on analysis of an individual's biomarkers versus his or her ethnic and racial identities. Second, using the formation of the "Malay" category as an example, I suggest that, in general, categorization by ethnicity is an ongoing process and one that is demonstrably shaped by social, political, and historical forces.

In sum, I argue that we need a better understanding of the evolution and continuing fluidity of these ethnic categories, which have become an integral part of the public health genomics rubric.

Population aggregate data, ethnicity, and post-market drug vigilance

Why is there a need to look at population groups when individual testing is possible and becoming increasingly affordable? Part of the answer lies in the area of public health resource management. Singapore has joined other nation-states in shaping the framework of genomic research. For instance, the authors of

"Interethnic Comparisons of Important Pharmacology Genes Using SNP Databases" note that:

> Drug-development programs of new molecular entities are becoming more global, with increasing clinical trial activity in Asia. However, at present, these programs still generally focus on *Caucasian* subjects. For regulatory authorities of countries with majority . . . *non-Caucasian* populations, a mandate for clinical trial data in the local population would delay the introduction of innovative medicines into clinical practice.
>
>   . . . We present the first steps in an effort to mine the wealth of pharmacogenetic data available from international [i.e. the International HapMap project] and local population genetic studies and databases [i.e. the Singapore Genome Variation Project] in order to help those in drug development and regulation quickly assess the magnitude of genetic differences between populations [emphasis mine].
>
> (Chen et al., 2010:1085)

Governments may be interested in pharmacogenomic studies of drug toxicity and adverse drug reactions because patients suffering from severe toxicity can drain public health resources. In the case of Singapore, when researchers attempt to answer questions including, but not limited to, who is at risk for developing toxicity and is it cost-effective to incorporate pharmacogenetic testing, we find that the "population" category used for their analysis is typically based on Singapore's contemporary ethnic categories.

Irinotecan and UGT1A1 genotyping

An example of this is the UGT1A1 gene and its variants, which are linked to drug toxicity with regard to Irinotecan. The authors of "Pharmacogenetic Risk for Adverse Reactions to Irinotecan in the Major Ethnic Populations of Singapore" state:

> [F]or genetic polymorphisms known to alter drug effect or safety, regulatory authorities can tap into population genomic databases and other sources of allele and genotype distribution data to make a more informed decision about the anticipated impact of such variants on the main ethnic groups in a country's population.
>
> (Sung et al., 2011:1167)

Indeed, a Health Science Authority advisory notes the prevalence of gene variants in the three main ethnic groups in Singapore: "The prevalence of double heterozygotes (*6/*28) in Singapore is 6.9 percent, 1.2 percent and 2.9 percent in Chinese, Malays and Indians, respectively" (Health Science Authority, 2010).

Dr. Rajaratnam explained that patients with two variants of the UGT1A1 gene, UGT1A1*6 and UGT1A1*28, are at increased risk of adverse reactions to

Irinotecan. The prevalence of these two gene variants are found to differ for different ethnic groups, and such difference has informed health authorities' decisions in terms of whether to introduce testing for these gene variations in their respective jurisdictions. Dr. Rajaratnam stated:

> Ethnicity matters; it does. So, for example, the UGT1A1; this is a very good model drug to study how pharmacogenomics is really important. This polymorphism is very common only in Indians and less common in Malay[s] and Chinese. But, comparing Asian[s] as a group, to Caucasian[s], if you compare *6, it is completely absent in a Caucasian and it is only present in an Asian. . . .
>
> [W]hat I meant was ethnic group matters . . . because this involves . . . regulatory bodies introducing the test. The FDA [in the USA] did not introduce *6 testing because it is totally absent in Caucasian[s]. Whereas [the] HSA introduced both *6 and *28 testing. That's where ethnicity matters.

However, doctors have different views concerning the usefulness of testing for UGT1A1 gene variants. The presence of the gene variants merely suggests increased risks of adverse reactions to Irinotecan, but is by no means definitive. Moreover, the severity of drug toxicities differs among patients. The doctors interviewed emphasize that clinical judgment is still required at the end of the day on whether to prescribe the drug and the dosage. According to Dr. Zhang:

> Toxicity . . . there are some tests but many people still think that [they] are not very specific nor . . . very sensitive. So, we can't use these genetic tests to see if a patient should or should not receive a particular drug. A lot of time it is still based on our clinical judgment.

Other than the current technical limitations of UGT1A1 genetic testing, the significance of test results is a concern. Dr. Koh assessed the utility of genetic testing in terms of its ability to influence clinical decisions, a criterion that he feels UGT1A1 genetic testing fails to meet because of the small difference in risk for severe toxicity between normal and variant alleles:

> [T]he norm, the normal allele, [is] maybe 20 percent, and the people . . . with the heterozygous, the heterozygous alleles . . . the variants, are maybe 30 percent. So it's not big enough for you to change your treatment. Let's say you get the result back, it doesn't change what we do. We wouldn't . . . not give those patients CPT11, we wouldn't reduce the dose of the CPT11, based on the results that we have right now, and we can't justify changing the schedule of the CPT11, so basically you get the result back, you're not sure what to do with it, that's why we don't get the test.

While Dr. Xie agreed that risk percentage is an important factor, he also pointed out individual variability as an additional point of consideration. Discussion between patients and doctors are thus necessary to ensure that patients understand the test results and what it means for them:

> I agree that the UGT1A1, with respect to certain drugs, [and this] means that you get much worse diarrhea and patients get toxic, very toxic and very unwell. But, then, the question is whether or not it applies to everyone and what is the option if you don't have it, and if you develop toxicities, is it manageable? I mean, how bad is the diarrhea? If you tell the patient . . . if I give you this drug, there is a risk that you might develop really bad diarrhea; but if you are willing to take that risk, we can see what happens and then you, if subsequently the patient does well, responds to treatment . . . they might accept that they are having diarrhea ten times a day – that it is worthwhile. . . . So it's really down to what that test actually means and then discussing it with the patients.

In sum, although UGT1A1 genetic testing can help to supplement the decision-making process, the limited sensitivity and specificity of the test, as well as the small differences in risk values between normal and variant alleles, do not instill confidence in changing clinical practices. Moreover, applying a sweeping assessment of an acceptable risk percentage may undermine some patients' access to treatment, as the determination of severity and the degree of tolerable toxic effects differs between individuals. Doctors are thereby reluctant to rely on UGT1A1 testing, emphasizing the importance of interaction between patients and doctors to facilitate clinical decisions.

Carbamazepine and HLA-B*1502 genotyping

Another example of a pharmacogenomic study of drug toxicity involves HLA-B*1502 genotyping and its relationship with the carbamazepine (CBZ)-induced toxicity known as Stevens-Johnson syndrome. The Ministry of Health (MOH) in Singapore announced in 2013 that genotyping for the HLA-B*1502 allele prior to the initiation of carbamazepine therapy is now considered the standard of care. That is, subsidized patients from MOH-funded restructured hospitals and institutions will qualify for a flat rate subsidy of 75 percent of the cost of the test. While 75 percent may seem like a surprisingly large subsidy for a genetic test, it only serves to emphasize the government's trust in the cost-effectiveness of this scheme. As explained by Dr. Huang, early identification of high risks of CBZ toxicity can help to circumvent the even larger expenditures incurred should the patient's sensitivity to CBZ only show up at a later stage in the form of severe side effects:

> Did anybody tell you about the carbamazepine test? . . . . [I]f you apply the test to every single patient . . . [y]ou can then avoid treating those patients [who test positive] . . . and you saved the costs of treating them if they wind up in the ICU [Intensive Care Unit]. So, from a global perspective, it becomes more cost-effective to measure everybody. Because the cost of

putting people in [the] ICU is very very high. So that's a situation where the Ministry of Health has deemed it on a national basis that this is a standard of care. But it, this certainly doesn't apply to all tests.

Dr. Huang's argument is not unfounded. According to Dong, Sung, and Finkelstein (2012), testing for CBZ toxicity before deciding on the course of CBZ therapy appears to be the superior choice even when presented with the alternative of simply prescribing drugs that will not induce CBZ-related toxicities to all patients regardless of risk profile. Moreover, Dong et al. (2012) suggest:

> To avoid one case of SJS/TEN [Stevens-Johnson Syndrome/Toxic Epidermal Necrolysis], 142 Chinese, 28 Malay, or 833 Indian patients would need to be genotyped. To avoid one death resulting from CBZ/PHT-induced SJS/TEN, 1,500 Chinese, 297 Malays, and 8,770 Indians would need to be genotyped.

As indicated, the cost-effectiveness analysis of incorporating pharmacogenetic testing in clinical practice is routinely based on population differences in terms of risk-allele frequency. Dr. Ballheimer, a health economist specializing in cost-effectiveness studies of genomic medicine, explained:

> Singapore increasingly is interested in understanding whether or not to promote or subsidize certain drugs, given their relative benefits and relative costs, compared to alternative treatments. . . . And if you're thinking about . . . interventions that target low or middle income countries that are more public-health-oriented, you have a fixed [amount] of money and a million things to fund, so cost-effectiveness is a way that helps you decide how to allocate resources from a public health perspective.
>
> INTERVIEWER: There are many ways in which a particular population can be divided. Why is ethnicity in this case very dominant?
> DR. BALLHEIMER: . . . The allele frequencies differ so the cost-effectiveness differs.
> INTERVIEWER: But why do you use ethnicity as a frame to find out allele differences because you can also use, for example, a patient's weight?
> DR. BALLHEIMER: I don't understand your question. 70 percent of Singaporeans are Chinese. We need to do a model that's representative of the population. . . . We just use allele frequencies based on what the government gives us. And they give us frequencies based on Chinese, Singaporean, Chinese, Malay, and Indian. So we just use it. If they gave it to us in a different way, we would analyze it in a different way. . . .

As alluded to in Dr. Ballheimer's remarks, researchers make use of genetic data calculated at the population-level not only for the purpose of controlling cases of adverse drug reactions, but also to engage in cost-benefit analysis of various genetic tests as part of the decision-making process. Typically, the distribution of risk allele among the population is a key component of such cost-effectiveness analyses.

Dr. Ballheimer's comments are very significant because they help us understand how health economists think about the national population. That is, while what constitutes a "population" can be conceptualized and analyzed in different ways, we found that ethnicity was adopted primarily because of the convenience of such categories for data collection and analysis. In other words, what Dr. Ballheimer said is that the primary reason that researchers are calculating allele frequencies using ethnicity is because these are the existing categories. If the data had been collected and arranged by weight differentials, the researchers would have used those.

Indeed, according to other medical genetic researchers, it is the internal ethnic differences among "Asians" in local contexts – Singapore in this case – that matter:

> [T]he category of "Asian" is very heterogeneous. [S]o . . . although we generally put down "Asian" . . . in our patient selection criteria, we would have to define [it] . . .
>
> . . . to the specific races. Whether we're talking about Chinese, we're talking about Malay, we're talking about Indian. We tend not to group them together. So, when we do an Asian study, that study may include Chinese, Malay or Indian, or sometimes just Chinese alone.
>
> So, I think "Asian" may be a quite misleading term because it's really very diverse. So it's important that each study, even though we use "Asian" as a heading, we specify the specific race that you are looking at. And then if you don't, when you analyze it, you may want to break them down into different races and see whether there're any differences.

Dr. Yuan and Dr. Wang discussed how researchers typically define and identify individuals as Chinese, Malays, or Indians:

DR. YUAN: When we do studies, if ethnicity is involved, we usually ask for three generations. So okay that's how we define. So . . . you know, how did your parents define themselves, how did your grandparents define themselves? So if the grandparents, parents and, and the patient, or the human subject, all declare themselves as Malay, then the person is classified as Malay.

DR. WANG: In these studies, the definition of Asian, definition of ethnic group is based on three generations. And what is written on the national registration identity card of these patients. So it's more or less a self-declared ethnic group. And of course we excluded those individuals that . . . we're a bit uncertain of. In other words if the patient were to say that my mom and my dad are Chinese and my grandparents are Chinese, we are okay. You're Chinese. If my mom and dad are Chinese, my grandparents one of them is not a Chinese . . . okay, you are not a Chinese.

Looking at three generations to define an individual's ethnicity in Singapore appears similar to the US-based Ancestry Informative Markers, which ideally take into account all four grandparents. However, it is unclear whether Singapore's regulations include both paternal and maternal grandparents or simply focus on paternal grandparents, as is the convention in defining one's ethnicity.

Researchers and health economists in Singapore are certainly not alone in relying on existing ethnically labeled population-level data. Our review of the eight studies quoted by Singapore's Health Science Authority in formulating its policy recommendations show that most studies have relatively small sample sizes (only one study included more than 300 individuals). The study population is usually defined based on medical conditions. However, the ethnic identities of subjects are consistently an area of focus for researchers. Nonetheless, only one in eight studies specified how it defined ethnicity – that is, in the journal article entitled "Carbamazepine and phenytoin induced Stevens-Johnson syndrome is associated with HLA-B*1502 allele in Thai population" (Locharernkul et al., 2008: 2089), one finds the following statement:

> Ethnicity of all subjects was elucidated by racial history identification from both parents, two generations back. The individual is considered a "pure" Thai if none of the four biological grandparents came from other races. Individuals having at least one grandparent of non-Thai race were classified as mixed Thai.

As we saw in Chapter 2, however, the "Thai" category *emerged* in a specific time and place – indeed, no one can be called or identified as a "Thai" prior to 1932!

Dr. Ballheimer's comments, noted above, together with those of Drs. Yuan and Wang, highlighted what I will discuss in great length in the section on the formation of the "Malay" category. As will be shown, while such ethnic categories – Chinese, Malay, Indian – may appear coherent to these contemporary researchers, once we look into their recent social histories, we see the complexities inherent in their formations.

Analysis of the prevailing practices noted above

When health economists and researchers accept predefined and seemingly static ethnic groups in their analyses, what is at stake?

First of all, there is a tension between the promise of "personalized/targeted medicine" and the practical usage of information based on "population-related" genetic markers and regions. Personalized drugs are, typically, expensive. The main question for a government responsible for delivering public health is whether it should subsidize these drugs. For cheaper drugs, whether to subsidize the genetic testing becomes a relevant issue. As Dr. Wu pointed out, in deciding how to allocate public health care resources, public policy makers analyze the aggregate data (i.e. what proportion of a population will benefit if a particular type of "personalized" medicine or screening is funded):

> [Y]ou're doing that because of a cost model, because it's more prevalent in that population, and thus screening the population. So, for example, it could be that you have to screen one hundred Indians, and you will find seven people to intervene [i.e. treat]. Seven versus [having] to screen ten thousand Chinese to find one, in order to intervene that one, then, although

that one person would have benefited had you screened everybody, it just isn't practically feasible. So it's actually focusing your efforts where you're most likely to get the benefit. . . . [I]t's more for a pragmatic purpose. . . .

In sharp contrast to this, for many doctors, it is the individual case that matters, even if that case happens to be in the minority or even exceptional in the general profile of the population. Dr. Hsu explained:

[T]he differences here essentially relate to who is the person wanting the data, right? If it's the Ministry of Health, a bureaucratic organization of any sort, they want a whole population-based [study], because that is to make policy, to decide who should be tested, who should be funded for the testing, and so on and so forth. . . . So [this is the] information wanted by organizations, that look at people in a faceless manner, right? Basically, for all Chinese I would do this, for all Indians, I would do this. But at the individual condition level, the person sitting in front of me is a human being, *Homo sapiens*, I don't care [about] anything else.

In the following section, I draw on the social science literature to suggest that, in addition, these ethnic categories were significantly generated by the historical colonial encounters – that is, they are not biologically coherent categories. A paper published in the *American Journal of Human Genetics* titled "Deep Whole-genome Sequencing of 100 Southeast Asian Malays" (Wong et al., 2013) displays the special attention that has been paid to this group – as opposed to the Chinese or the Indian categories – by geneticists. Thus, for illustrative purposes of the argument, I focus on the example of the "Malay."

The historical emergence of "Malay" as a group during the precolonial era

In searching for an understanding of the emergence of the "Malay" group, Andaya (2001) provides a narrative for the historical environment that birthed the conditions for a specifically Melayu[1] ethnic awareness. He asserted, "in asking where and how Melayu ethnicity may have evolved, the issue is not to pinpoint the exact time and place of the origins of the group, but to reveal the process of ethnic formation" (Andaya, 2001:316).

Linguists have claimed that proto-Malay was spoken in western Borneo by at least 1,000 BCE, and speakers of this language then spread to southeast Sumatra and the Malay Peninsula. In southeast Sumatra, Malayic speakers spread along the Musi and the Batang Hari and their tributaries and into the interior highlands. The name "Melayu" appeared for the first time in a seventh-century Chinese document in reference to a settlement in southeast Sumatra (present-day Jambi). In the thirteenth and fourteenth centuries, Melayu was the name of a kingdom in the Jambi area. The conventional practice of naming people based on a settled area would suggest that the inhabitants of lands identified as Melayu, wherever and however this word was defined, would be known as *orang Melayu*, or "the people of Melayu" (Andaya, 2001).

Settlements on the Malay Peninsula, on the other hand, were not associated with "Melayu" until the foundation of Melaka in the fifteenth century following the arrival of Melayu immigrants from Palembang. Melaka then sought to assert its leadership in the Melayu world, inheriting the lifestyle and methods of governance of southeastern Sumatra and Western Borneo. The influential literary document *Sejarah Melayu* (History/Story of the Melayu) reaffirmed Melaka's central position in Melayu and facilitated the reinforcement and export of Melaka values to other parts of Southeast Asia. The Melaka's claims regarding Melayu leadership were, however, disputed by Sumatran contenders such as Aceh and Minangkabau; however, the identification of Melayu with the peninsula became increasingly rooted (Andaya, 2001).

Andaya (2001:330) further expounds:

> With the division of the Melayu world into Dutch and British spheres by the Anglo-Dutch treaty of 1824 and the subsequent creation of independent nation-states in the mid-twentieth century, Melayu finally became identified politically and in the popular mind with the peninsula. Although to this day Melayu groups elsewhere, particularly in the Indonesian provinces of Jambi and Riau, claim to be the original and pure Melayu, their story is rarely heard. The political struggle for the right to claim to be the center of the Melayu has been won by Malaysia. It continues to monopolize the study of Melayuness, with the kingdom of Melaka made to represent the 'core values' of the Melayu.

"Malayness" during the colonial era

Before and during the early days of British colonial rule, a person's identity was based on the sultan of whom the person was a subject, rather than membership in a particular race group (Manickam, 2009:596). Reid (2001:300) explains, "in the sixteenth and seventeenth centuries, Malayness in maritime Southeast Asia retained these two associations – a line of kingship acknowledging descent from Srivijaya and Melaka or Pagarruyung (Minangkabau), and a commercial diaspora that retained some of the customs, language and trade practices developed in the emporium of Melaka."

The application of race gained momentum in the Malay Peninsula during the late nineteenth and early twentieth centuries, due in part because the printing press provided opportunities to voice allegiances to entities other than the royal courts and due to the cosmopolitan environment in which printing took place (Manickam, 2009). Competition for readership was stiff, as most printed material, being expensive and scarce, only reached the elite. According to Manickam (2009:597–598):

> Under such circumstances, ideas of what constitutes a 'Malay' were used by some writers to build identities and to guard against perceived infringements on their place in Malaya. . . . To present oneself as Malay and to discredit the Malay-ness of others played a role in furthering the interests of those

newspapers. Being Malay was imbued with a variety of characteristics involving changeable boundaries depending on who was speaking.

Discourse in the vernacular press about Malayness in the archipelago contrasts sharply with British colonial scholars' discourse of race during the same period. Manickam (2009:598) points out, "knowledge production by British authors was closely tied to territorial acquisitions in the Malay Peninsula during the nineteenth interplay century which saw the British government and Malay polities begin more extensive political relations than had hitherto been known." Initially, the British were relatively unfamiliar with the peoples of Southeast Asia, even though they had been present in the region for some time (the British had been in Singapore for 50 years and in Penang for 85) (Hirschman, 1987). Manickam (2009:598) suggests that:

> [M]any British authors had initially regarded all inhabitants of the Malay Archipelago as Malays, and considered only those east of the archipelago as a different group, the Papuans . . . arguably due to the fact that Malay was the lingua franca of the peninsula and its neighboring islands; it was thus the language commonly encountered by the British in the region, who then erroneously associated language usage with race.

In a similar vein, Reid (2001:305) adds:

> [I]n the urban world of the nineteenth-century Straits Settlements, which from 1824 comprised Penang, Melaka and Singapore, modern European ideas of nationality (and later race) carried much weight. . . . In the Straits Settlements there were undoubtedly many Abdullahs, for whom Malayness was a new identity acquired in the ethnically competitive world of these port-states. Austronesian Muslims seemed to be outnumbered and outcompeted by Chinese, Europeans and Indians in these ports. Although of various origins, they were too small a minority to carry much weight separately as Bugis, Aceh, Java or Mandailing, and in any case they intermarried with each other in the ports. The English rulers of the Straits used "Malay" as the collective term to refer to them, and to a considerable extent it became internalized. . . .

However, toward the end of the nineteenth century and in the first decades of the twentieth, the British had consolidated their control over the entire Malay Peninsula (Hirschman, 1987; Manickam, 2009). The expansion of their position of power influenced their "attitudes towards the kind of investigations that were deemed important and also towards the rhetoric surrounding Malays" (Manickam, 2009:599). An influx of European, Chinese, and Indian migrants, who were encouraged to develop Malaya's resources, led to the creation of a plural society (Reid, 2001; Shamsul, 2001a, 2001b), "in which the concept of Malay as race was there to stay" (Shamsul, 2001b:76). By the 1920s, Malaya had become one of the most affluent economies in Asia, and such lucrative development had been legitimized by the Malay rulers, thus prompting the colonial statesmen to quickly develop a colonial discourse about "protecting" them and their people, while having a clear idea of what sort of Malay they should protect (Reid, 2001).

According to Reid (2001:306), "the 'real Malay' of colonial discourse was rural, loyal to his ruler, conservative and relaxed to the point of laziness." Indeed, it seems that such a racial construction of the Malays by the British was used by the British to legitimize their rule in the Malay Peninsula (Hirschman, 1987; Shamsul, 2001a; Manickam, 2009; Ong, 2010). The Malays, being supposedly inherently incompetent, were seen as in need of assistance from the British to guide them lest they were left to falter, as Manickam and Hirschman describe:

> The stereotype of lazy Malays and hardworking Chinese served the purposes of the British who wanted to develop Malaya's economy using Chinese labor and at the same time, preserve Malays as they supposedly were. This position of stewardship was upheld by promoting the perceptions that Malays and Chinese could not coexist peacefully, and that Malays would be swamped economically and numerically by the Chinese if left to their own devices. The effect of this approach was the entrenchment of the position of the British as stewards over the Malays, and the rationale that it was Britain's duty to develop the economy and the natural resources of the country on behalf of the Malays, who were unable to do so themselves. Furthermore, the British continued to pose indigenousness as a racial issue. Being part of the Malay racial group (and their associated groups such as those from the archipelago) meant being indigenous to Malaya. By this formulation, other racial groups were unable to gain access to indigenousness and the rights that were associated with that state of being.
>
> (Manickam, 2009:600)

> The new theory of race was founded on the idea that peoples were different not only in appearance and culture but also in inherent capacities or potential. According to this perspective, societal differences in technological advancement were measures in the evolutionary march toward civilization. . . . Racism provided a rationale for the "white man's burden" of leading, ruling, or conquering peoples at "lower evolutionary stages" throughout the world. This ideology fitted well with the British need to justify its empire. . . . I suggest that British attitudes toward the Malay community changed during the late nineteenth century in the direction of a more unquestioned belief in the weaknesses of the Malay character and the need for a strong paternalistic role for the colonial government. The problem was no longer the resistance of Malay rulers to British intervention but the British need for a justification for imperialism. Paternalism, the protection and guidance of the Malays, was the ideological justification for most of the colonial era.
>
> (Hirschman, 1987:568)

Vernacular Malay-language schools were set up following the establishment of English and Chinese schools (Reid, 2001; Shamsul, 2001a, 2001b). The ostensible function of such schools was to acquaint Malay schoolchildren with their histori-cal identity. For instance, Shamsul and Reid pointed out, "in the textbooks for the 'Malay' schools, the British constructed a distinctly 'Malay' historiography and 'Malay' literature in which 'Malay' *hikayats* were used to create or implant a certain sense of historical identity and literary taste" (Shamsul, 2001b:76); "to rediscover the first of the nineteenth-century meanings of Malayness . . . a tradi-tion of Malay kingship descended from Melaka – and impose it on the varied Muslim immigrants to the Peninsula" (Reid, 2001:307). The underlying logic of the schools' function, that is, was to preserve the stereotyped Malay identity rather than to change it. Reid (2001:306–307) explains:

> Despite its greater wealth, Malaya spent a smaller proportion of public money on education than did other Southeast Asian colonies. In 1920 only 12 per cent of the Malay population aged 5–15 was in school, and virtually all of these were in the vernacular Malay-language schools the government believed best equipped to keep the Malays in their stereotyped place: "It will not only be a disaster to, but a violation of the whole spirit and tradition of, the Malay race if the result of our vernacular education is to lure the whole of the youth from the kampung to the town."

Indeed, part of the "spirit and tradition" of Malays in the kampung was to par-ticipate in agricultural peasantry, supposedly crucial in forming the backbone of the nation. In 1913, the Malay Reservation Act was introduced, an act "in which agricultural land could only be alienated to people defined as racially Malay, irre-spective of their place of birth" (Reid, 2001:306). This further strengthened the definition of "Malay" and "Malayness," as Ong (2010:20) points out:

> This setting aside of special areas for Malay cultivations required a colonial legal definition of who constituted a "Malay". In 1913, the Malay Reser-vations Enactment Committee defined "Malay" as "a person belonging to any Malayan race who habitually speaks the Malay language or any Malay language and professes the Muslim religion" (FMS Enactment no. 15, 1913). . . . Thus, in the name of "the continuation of the Malay race," the reservations act was passed.

However, it is worth noting that as the enactment was instituted in the state constitution of each of the 11 provinces separately, the definition "Malay" varied slightly from one constitution to another. For example, someone of Arab descent might be identified (as a Malay) in Kedah but not in Johor, and someone of Sia-mese descent might be considered Malay in Kelantan but not in Negeri Sembilan (Shamsul, 2001b).

The word "race" first appeared in official documents in the 1891 census, which delineated three racial categories: Chinese, "Tamils and other natives of India," and 'Malays and other Natives of the Archipelago' (Hirschman, 1987). Since then, the list of subcategories under the Malay (Malaysian) category has evolved over time (see Table 4.1). Hirschman (1987:570) suggests that while

Table 4.1 Classification of the Malays in Censuses from 1871–1980

Ethnic Classifications in the Censuses of the Straits Settlements and the Federated Malay States, 1871–1911

1871	1881	1891	1901	1901	1911	1911
Straits Settlements	Straits Settlements	Straits Settlements	Straits Settlements	Federated Malay States	Straits Settlements	Federated Malay States
The Malays and other groups listed below were not classified under a particular category		IV. Malays & other Natives of the Archipelago	IV. Malays & other Natives of the Archipelago	IV. Malays & other Natives of the Archipelago	Malays & Allied Races	Malay Pop. by Race
Boyanese	Achinese	Aborigines	Aborigines	Aborigines	Achehnese	Malay
Bugis	Boyanese	Achinese	Achinese	Achinese	Amboinese	Javanese
Dyaks	Bugis	Boyanese	Boyanese	Boyanese	Balinese	Sakai
Javanese	Dyaks	Bugis	Bugis	Bugis	Bandong	Banjarese
Jawee-pekans	Javanese	Dyaks	Javanese	Dyaks	Bahjarese	Boyanese
Malays	Jawi Pekans	Jawi Pekans	Jawi-Pekan	Javanese	Bantamese	Mendeling
Manila-men	Malays	Malays	Malays	Jawi-Pekan	Batak	Krinchi
	Manila-men	Manilamen	Manilamen	Malays	Borneo Races, misc.	Jambi
			Sam Sam (Malay-Siamese)	Manilamen	Boyanese	Achinese
					Bugis	Bugis
					Bundu	Others
					Dayak	
					Dusun	
					Javanese	
					Jawi Pekan	
					Kadayan	
					Korinchi	
					Malay	
					Rawanese	
					Sulu	
					Sundanese	
					Totong	

Note: Adapted from Appendix A and Appendix B in Hirschman, C. 1987. "The Meaning and Measurement of Ethnicity in Malaysia: An Analysis of Census Classifications." *The Journal of Asian Studies* 46(3):555–582. Exact headings, category spellings, and order of categories found in the original source were followed.

Ethnic Classifications in the Census of British Malay, Malaya, and Malaysia, 1921–1980

1921	1931	1947	1957	1970	1980
The Malay Pop. by Race	Malaysians by Race	Malaysians by Specific Community	Malaysians	Malay	Malay
Malays	Malays	*Malays*	Malays	Malay	Malay
Javanese	Javanese	*(Indigenous*	Indonesian	Indonesian	Indonesian
Banjarese	Boyanese	*Malaysians)*	All	Negrito	Negrito
Boyanese	Achinese	Malays Proper	Aborigines	Jakun	Jakun
Bugis	Batak	Aborigines	Negrito	Semai	Semai
Achinese	Menangkabau	Biduanda, Mantera,	Semai	Semelai	Semelai
Korinchi	Korinchi	and other Jakun	Semelai	Temiar	Temiar
Mendeling	Jambi	Negrito	Temiar	Other	Other
Bornean	Palembang	Other and	Jakun	Orang Asli	Indigenous
Races	Other	unidenti-fiable	Other	Other Malay	Other Malay
Sakai	Sumatra	aboriginal stocks	Aborigines	Commu-	race
Other	Riau Lingga	*Other*		nity	
Races	Banjarese	*Malaysians*			
	Other	Sundanese			
	Dutch	Javanese			
	Borneo	Boyanese			
	Bugis	Achinese			
	Other	Menangkabau			
	N. E. I	Korinchi			
	Dayak	Jambi			
	Sakai	Palembangan			
	Others	Other unspecified			
		or indeterminate			
		Sumatra peoples			
		Riau Lingga Malays			
		Banjarese			
		Dyak			
		Other unspecified			
		or indeterminate			
		Borneo peoples			
		Bugis			
		Other unspecified			
		or indeterminate			
		"Indonesians"			
		peoples			

the links between broader social currents and census classifications are unclear (since records describing the reasoning behind the formulation of ethnic classifications by census administrators are unavailable), he nonetheless concludes that:

> [C]hanges in racial ideology had clear effects on ethnic classifications in censuses. Given the limitations of other forms of historical records . . . the census classifications provide important evidence on the development of European racism in colonial Malaya. Although many of the outward forms of racist thinking have been eliminated from census classification in the post-Independence era, the residue of racial ideology continues to haunt contemporary Malaysia.

Importantly, the conceptualization of the Malay race, Manickam (2009:601) argues, came not only from the British colonial perspective but also from Malay intellectuals:

> [T]his knowledge of race among Malays coincided with some elements of British racial construction, but there were also key differences due to diverging strategies of race used by the Malays. Strategies are just that, courses of thought and action taken at particular times and places and ways of employing and deploying the discourses of race by some among the Malay intelligentsia.

First, in contrast to the British discourse on the disempowerment of the Malays economically and politically, the Malays' strategy of race was not fatalistic. Manickam (2009:604) points out:

> Taking on racialized groupings instead of state-bounded or smaller group loyalties made it possible to talk of a unified Malay subject within the breadth of territory under British protection and rule. . . . The radicalizing of a segment of the population enabled these writers to talk of Malays in relation to other groups less favored by the writers, such as Chinese and Indians, and sometimes even the British. This could arguably be called a "positive" use of racialization, as opposed to the negative use by the British. The radicalizing of Malays . . . produced knowledge that could be useful for the colonization of Malaya and everyday governance. . . . By turning these oftentimes stereotypical portrayals into elements which bound Malays together, the conceptual power of that knowledge entrenched them as the privileged race in the Malay Peninsula. . . . This is in contrast to the effects of writing histories of Malaya by the British, who instead took away questions of ownership.

Second, although the British and Malay authors appeared similar in that they positioned the Orang Asli (indigenous peoples of the peninsula) as lower in the civilizational scale compared to Malays and most other races, the perception of the Malay authors that the Orang Asli are primitive by nature served, in Manickam's (2009:607) words, "to deprive Orang Asli of autonomy in their dealings with Malays and put them out of the running for the right to govern the peninsula at least in their own affairs, again positioning Malays as the only true heirs to governance," whereas British marginalization of Orang Asli "stemmed from wanting to claim that forest land inhabited by them was undeveloped and uninhabited" (Manickam, 2009:611).

Lastly, another divergence from British race knowledge involved the manner in which race was presented so that it would have enough currency to be seen as a nation. Calling a group of people a nation entails a trajectory as a separate state if they are under colonial rule, and, conversely, asserting that a group of people is a "race" sometimes means downplaying the status of that group as undeserving of self-government, as in the case of the Malays in Malaya. Yet, the Malay authors were undeterred, as Manickam (2009:609–610) describes:

> Rather, references to Malays were used in the histories as a way to entrench the authors in Malaya and to argue for certain rights against other groups under the umbrella of British power in the peninsula. The elevation of Malays from a race category to that of a nation, which also entitled them to more rights, is most blatantly seen in Abdul Majid's *The Malays in Malaya*, by one of them. . . . This raced nation, based on a population purportedly sharing similar racial characteristics, was used to bring up the issue of rights of Malays in Malaya, as well as the appropriateness of participation in government by groups other than Malays such as Chinese and Indians.

In summary, with the consolidation of power by the British over the entire Malay Peninsula, developing a colonial discourse to justify colonization became crucial. The racial construction of the Malays was used by the British to legitimize their rule in the Malay Peninsula. The logic followed that Malays, though loyal to their rulers, were "lazy natives" in need of assistance in developing their homeland, thus compelling the British to take on a paternalistic stance and ruling role over the peninsula. Malays seemingly had a privileged status, however, as self-respecting agricultural peasants, and the idea was promoted among Malays that it was risky to leave such a livelihood in search of other opportunities. The condition of the Malays was maintained in part through vernacular schools. The Malays were also explicitly defined in the Malay Reservation Act in 1913. However, censuses collated over the colonial and postcolonial years show that defining the Malays as one essential race was a difficult task. The conceptualization of the Malay race should also not be seen as limited to discourse by the British colonialists, but should be seen from the point of view of the Malay intelligentsia as well, whose construction of the Malay race diverged from that of the British to serve different ends.

"Malayness" in the Malay Peninsula in the postcolonial era

In the first few decades of the twentieth century, "Malay" nationalism was invigorated, taking on, in Shamsul's (2001a:364) words, "a cultural, rather than a political character; the discussions that made the 'Malay race' into a 'Malay nation' focused primarily on questions of identity and distinction in terms of customs, religion, and language, rather than politics." Nah (2006) explains that "Malay intellectuals began to talk about themselves as 'a Malay race' (*bangsa*). . . . The 'Chinese' groups – who were economically successful in a number of industries – were seen as a 'danger' to them. It was felt that the Malay *bangsa* had to unite together . . . to defend their position in 'their land.'" For instance, as Reid (2001) explains, for the young graduates of the Malay teachers colleges who wrote in the Malay press of the 1930s, the "Malay race" (*bangsa Melayu*) "was defined by what they perceived as two overwhelming facts – they were the 'natives with primary claim on the country, and they were the weakest group in it. They concluded that the *bangsa* required unity and solidarity to make stronger demands of the British" (Reid, 2001:308).

"Malay" nationalism seemed most pronounced when the British proposed a new form of government following the World War II, the Malayan Union, in their own vision of a "united nation" whereby plural communities would have a shared Malayan outlook and purpose (Shamsul, 2001a, 2001b; Nah, 2006). Part of the proposal stipulated equal citizenship rights to most residents of British Malaya (including non-Malays such as the Chinese and Indians) and further reduced the political authority of the sultans, consequently spurring the Malays to political action (Siddique and Suryadinata, 1981). The British were then compelled to replace the proposal with the 1948 Federation of Malaya, "in which the centrality of Malayness was explicitly expressed" (Reid, 2001:308). That is, according to Shamsul (2001a:364), "the 'Chinese' and the 'Indians' effectively became citizens of the independent state but they had to acknowledge *ketuanan Melayu*, or Malay dominance, which implied they had to accept 'special Malay privileges' in education and government services, and 'Malay' royalty as their rulers, Islam as the official religion, and the 'Malay' language as the official language of the new nation-state." Lian (1997:71) describes this as such:

> [T]he Federation of Malaya Agreement, which laid the foundation for the creation of an independent state in 1957, served to formalize the status of Malays relative to non-Malays. While citizenship was unconditionally conferred on Malays, it was only given to non-Malays if they fulfilled certain conditions – including birth, duration of residence, and reasonable knowledge of the Malay or English language. The special position of the Malays was also constitutionally recognized; this concerned land reservations and reservation of quotas in public service appointments, licenses and educational benefits.

The Federation eventually achieved independence in August 1957. In the Federal Constitution (first introduced as the Constitution of the Federation of Malaya in 1957), the Malay was defined in Article 160(2) (Malaysia Constitution, Article 160, Section 2):

> "Malay" means a person who professes the religion of Islam, habitually speaks the Malay language, conforms to Malay custom and – (a) was before Merdeka Day born in the Federation or in Singapore or born of parents one of whom was born in the Federation or in Singapore, or is on that day domiciled in the Federation or in Singapore; or (b) is the issue of such a person.

Yet, the formation of the Federation of Malaysia in 1963 (when Sabah, Sarawak, and Singapore joined Malaya) gave rise to a new dimension to understanding the definition of "Malay" and "Malayness," due to the inclusion of Muslim groups in Sabah and Sarawak, who, however, were minorities in their states, whereas the majority of the populations there consisted of non-Muslim natives and Chinese (Shamsul, 2001a, 2001b). This presented a political problem, as it meant that the Malay-dominated federal government in Kuala Lumpur "had to cooperate with, and attempt to co-opt, non-Malay Muslims as their political partners" (Shamsul, 2001a:364).

Bumiputera (son of the soil) is a term used by the federal government to refer to the indigenous status of the Malays (Shamsul, 2001b) and is commonly used interchangeably with "Malay" (Siddique and Suryadinata, 1981). The *bumiputera* (the "Malays" and their Muslim counterparts in Sarawak and Sabah) had political dominance throughout Malaysia, except in Sabah, which was ruled by its own opposition party, which was Christian Kadazan. In order to win Sabah over, in the 1980s, UMNO (the United Malays Nationalist Organization, the leading party in the federal government) "opened itself to non-Muslim *bumiputera* so that eventually the UMNO-led Barisan National ('National Front') could regain control over Sabah" (Shamsul, 2001a:365), as explained:

> [T]hese developments show that the need to define the borders and margins of a concept can have far-reaching effects on its central content: "Malayness" as defined by the Malay nationalist movement in the 1920s and 1930s and implemented and redefined by UMNO, had to be reformulated in Sabah once again, illustrating how flexible the concept or category of "Malay" is. It also shows that the ongoing discussions about "Malayness" are at once both important and irrelevant: the concept can easily shift in meaning, adapting itself time and again to new situations and making clear-cut statements impossible or incredible.

Economically, according to Lian (1997:71), the New Economic Policy (NEP) "was launched in 1971 for the specific purpose of propelling the Malays to a position where they would enjoy economic parity with the other ethnic communities." One important consequence of the NEP was the radical restructuring of Malay society, whereby many Malays had moved from agricultural to urban settings, were occupying more middle-class jobs, and were more highly educated. This restructuring led to disengagement from the traditional patronage structure (Sultan-centered loyalty) of the rural environment (Lian, 1997). This initiated a metamorphosis of a new Malay identity, from *bumiputera* to *Melayu baru* (new Malay), as Lian (1997:74) explains:

> With the emergence of a middle class, the continued presence of a rural proletariat – and now an urban proletariat, and a traditional royalty under siege and fighting to maintain its privileges, it has become a more obviously class-differentiated society. This has manifested itself in the considerable political acrimony generated within UMNO since the late 1970s. As if to articulate a new identity to make sense of these changes and to disengage it from the "old UMNO," Dr. Mahathir at the UMNO general assembly of 1991, coined the term *Melayu baru* (new Malay) – which he defined as someone who possesses a culture in keeping with the times, prepared to face challenges, educated and knowledgeable, disciplined and efficient, honest and trustworthy. [That is,] the new Malays should not only be involved in a modern economy but also be able to compete internationally; in short, they should adopt the ethos of the immigrant community in the country.

In the long run, the concept of *bumiputera* may be phased out if the term *Melayu baru* gains wide acceptance, though this will depend on whether the Malays continue to make economic progress (Lian, 1997). This may be more acceptable, and according to Lian (1997:75), "because *bumiputera* is an exclusive status defined with an ethnic preferential bias, it may act as a disincentive to further overseas investments in the economic development of Malaysia."

The case of the Malay in Singapore

Singapore achieved independence in August 1965 following its expulsion from the Federation of Malaya. The Malays in Singapore, once part of the majority in Malaya, suddenly became a minority rather than a privileged group that had preferential treatment, as Singapore became governed by the principle of equal opportunity for all Singaporeans (Zuber, 2010). In the Constitution of the Republic of Singapore, the only reference to "Malay" is found in Article 152(2): "Malays . . . are the indigenous people of Singapore." It provides no explanation on what attributes and traits make up a "Malay" individual (Constitution of the Republic of Singapore, Part XIII General Provisions, Article 152, Section 2).

In 1988, however, the state attempted to provide a more solid definition of "Malay." Aljunied (2010) discusses the processes involved in the creation of the definition of Malay, through analyzing a public debate on Singaporean Malay identity, which occurred in November 1987 during the passing of two bills in the Singapore Parliament that resulted in the implementation of the General Representation Constituency (GRC) scheme. Aljunied's analysis demonstrates that the Malay identity in Singapore has been a source of continuous controversy and contention.

Aljunied (2010) argues that the establishment of a single official definition of the Malay identity by the Singapore state resulted from "the emergence of a network society that was shaped by global and regional developments and the rise of Malay ethnic resurgence on the island in reaction to state policies and the perceived threats of modernization and deculturation." It was intended "to steer the minority community toward a more inclusive outlook, while recognizing the supreme authority of the state" (Aljunied, 2010:308). This was especially crucial for the government, which perceived that such an ethnic resurgence within the Malay community would cause the popularity of the ruling party (the People's Action Party [PAP]) to wane.

Several social forces combined to create conditions to define the Malay identity in Singapore. One was "to lay emphasis on the notion that Malays in Singapore were different from Malays in Malaysia, as well as Muslims in other neighboring countries, due largely to many decades of shared experiences among Singapore Malays that developed their sense of rootedness and belonging" (Aljunied, 2010:316). Practically, "Muslims in Singapore were instructed to yield their conception of a global imagined community (the *Ummah*) to the territorial edifice and unifying myths of the nation" (Aljunied, 2010:316). Another strategy involved directing state rhetoric toward "imbibing the success of multi-racialism in Singapore, and assuring the Malay community that Malay rights were protected by the state" (Aljunied, 2010:316), through public dialogues organized by Malay Members of Parliament. Lastly, findings on the spread of deviant Islamic teachings formed a public perception that the Malay community had been influenced by fundamentalist and extremist ideologies founded abroad. Together with extensive media coverage of social problems plaguing the Malay community, such as high rates of drug abuse and divorce, this strategy created the sense that much effort was needed to instill a strong consciousness of Singaporean nationhood among the Malays (Aljunied, 2010).

Two bills pertaining to the GRC scheme, introduced in November 1987 and passed in May 1988, were aimed at legally ensuring minority representation in Parliament, thereby seeming to strengthen the foundations of a multiracial society (Aljunied, 2010). They established the criteria for a Malay candidate to be eligible for election as a Member of Parliament (MP) as "any person, whether Malay race or otherwise, who considers himself to be a member of the Malay community and who is generally accepted as a member of the Malay community by that community" (Aljunied, 2010:322).

Upon close scrutiny, this definition poses several problems and possibilities. First, it assumes that prior knowledge of *the* Malay community, with set boundaries differentiating Malays and non-Malays, exists. Second, self-identification as a Malay is effectively ruled out, as the definition entails the authority of the "community" in determining a person's identity. Finally, the phrase "Malay race or otherwise" implies that Malay identity is tied to both a hereditary and non-hereditary criteria, as in the case of, for instance, a Singaporean citizen with

Chinese ancestry who is accepted by the Malay community as a Malay and is registered as one, who would then qualify to stand for election as a "Malay" MP (Aljunied, 2010).

The state's attempt to define Malay identity through the strategies discussed above had a generally negative effect on its popularity among Singapore Malays. This was manifest in the 1988 general elections results, where a large number of Malays swung their votes to the opposition parties. Far from achieving its intended aims, "the long-term objective of forging a sense of nationhood through the introduction of a new interpretation of the Malay identity heightened the transnational sway of resurgent Islam and sub-ethnic particularisms in Singapore. Ethnic resurgence remained an entrenched feature of the Malay community in Singapore throughout the 1980s" (Aljunied, 2010:323).

On the other hand, Zuber (2010:35) argues that the definition provided has its strengths:

> [S]ince a group's identity is part of the group's consciousness, it is accept- able that the group's identity will be understood by all within that group, either implicitly or explicitly and that the group has some form of common understanding of what is basic to the group's identity. . . . [T]he Singapore Malays have long existed as part of a group. . . . [I]t can be expected that the Malays in Singapore intuitively know who they are. . . .

However, Zuber also points out that this legalistic definition "created a situ- ation where the Singapore Malays had to expressively articulate the meaning of a Malay. . . . It was in light of this need that the Malay community had to con- sciously put forth an expression of being Malay in Singapore, and articulate the traits of Malay" (2010:35). This task was undertaken by the Malay elite, whose expression of the Malay identity is steeped in the core identifiers of the Malay language, customs, and traditions and the Islamic religion (Zuber, 2010).

Over the years, conscious efforts have been made in Singapore to promote and iterate the consciousness of these identifiers. For instance, to promote and sustain the Malay language, events such as the bi-yearly Malay Language Cultural Month are held. When the 2010 Census Survey revealed that the use of the Malay language has declined, the Malay Language Council began to look into initiatives to improve the teaching of the language in schools. Also, in an effort to increase awareness of Malay customs and religions, the Malay Heritage Centre was established in late 2004.

Conclusion

Why are ethnicity and race used in Singapore's public health genomic policy- making? In the first part of this chapter, I suggest that the answer has to do with the Health Science Authority's (HSA) concern with determining "who to give the drug to" in a cost-effective manner. I delineate the ways in which medical researchers and health economists typically think about "population" categories in the context of public health genomic policy-making – for example, whether (or not) to subsidize certain drugs or testing – in the context of cost management concerns. For example, to restate some of the key remarks:

DR. RAJARATNAM: The prevalence of double heterozygotes (*6/*28) in Singapore is 6.9 percent, 1.2 percent and 2.9 percent in Chinese, Malays and Indians, respectively. . . . [W]hat I meant was ethnic group matters . . . because this involves . . . regulatory bodies introducing the test. The FDA [in the USA] did not introduce *6 testing because it is totally absent in Caucasian[s]. Whereas [the] HSA introduced both *6 and *28 testing. That's where ethnicity matters.

DR. BALLHEIMER: . . . The allele frequencies differ so the cost-effectiveness differs. . . . We need to do a model that's representative of the population . . . We just use allele frequencies based on what the government gives us. And they give us frequencies based on Chinese, Singaporean, Chinese, Malay, and Indian. So we just use it. If they gave it to us in a different way, we would analyze it in a different way. . . .

As such, it was shown that the social actors involved in decision-making take the current ethnic composition of the nation as given. While factors other than ethnicity can be used to sort data, existing routines for collection and easy availability of data categorized along ethnic lines make ethnicity a convenient choice.

Duster (2006:435) points out that "some African Americans have cystic fibrosis even though the likelihood of that is far greater among Americans of North European descent and, in a parallel if not symmetrical way, some American Whites have sickle cell anemia even though the likelihood of that is far greater among Americans of West African descent. But in the world of cost-effective decision-making, genetic screening for these disorders is routinely based on commonsense versions of the phenotype."

This chapter indicates that it is vital to identify limitations when researchers use ethnicity or race as a proxy in formulating public health genomics policies. I suggest that there are at least two types of potential harm with respect to the typical calculation of allelic frequencies or other genotype information along ethnic lines. At the very least, the interview data provide evidence that there is the conflict between public health policy guidelines couched in the ethnic distribution of genetic variants and medical doctors' clinical ideal of delivering medicine based on an individual's DNA analysis.

More significantly, as we see by examining a detailed history of the formation of the Malay category, the nature and character of ethnic identity formation is an ongoing project shaped by complex historical, political, and social forces. As such, when scientists, health economists, or public health officials use race or ethnicity as a surrogate for personal genetic information, there is an almost unavoidable risk of giving a false appearance of biological coherence to ethnic identities, which are actually fluid and historically contingent.

Note

1 Manickam (2009) provided a detailed example of a documented argument between three newspapers to illustrate her point on the Malay "race" being used for the writers' own ends. In summary, one of the newspapers, *Jawi Peranakan*, was not appreciative of the analysis of Malays found in *Bintang Timor*, a Chinese Peranakan-run newspaper, and responded from the position of one part of a Malay community reluctant to let "non-Malays" comment on its state of affairs. The issue was complicated further by an earlier exchange between *Jawi Peranakan* and *Sekola Melayu*, in which the latter newspaper addressed the authors of the former as non-Malays. Yet, the "Malayness" of Sekola Melayu's writers was, itself, questionable; one was of Indian origin and had previously written for *Jawi Peranakan*.

References

Aljunied, Syed M.K. 2010. "Ethnic Resurgence, Minority Communities, and State Policies in a Network Society: The Dynamics of Malay Identity Formation in Postcolonial Singapore." *Identities: Global Studies in Culture and Power* 17(2–3): 304–326.

Andaya, Leonard Y. 2001. "The Search for the 'Origins' of Melayu." *Journal of Southeast Asian Studies* 32(3):315–330.

Chen, Jieming, Yik Ying Teo, Dorothy SL Toh and Cynthia Sung. 2010. "Interethnic Comparisons of Important Pharmacology Genes Using SNP Databases: Potential Application to Drug Regulatory Assessments." *Pharmacogenomics* 11(8):1077–1094. doi:10.2217/pgs.10.79.

Constitution of the Republic of Singapore. Part XIII General Provisions, Article 152: Minorities and special position of Malays, Section 2. Retrieved March 30, 2016 (http://statutes.agc.gov.sg/aol/search/display/view.w3p;ident=03407ef6-c5fc-4c65-9f31-0053b02e1145;page=0;query=DocId%3A%22cf2412ff-fca5-4a64-a8ef-b95b8987728e%22%20Status%3Ainforce%20Depth%3A0;rec=0#pr152-he-)

Dong, Di, Cynthia Sung and Eric Andrew Finkelstein. 2012. "Cost-effectiveness of HLA-B*1502 Genotyping in Adult Patients with Newly Diagnosed Epilepsy in Singapore." *Neurology* 79(12):1259–1267.

Duster, Troy. 2006. "The Molecular Reinscription of Race: Unanticipated Issues in Biotechnology and Forensic Science." *Patterns of Prejudice* 40(4–5):427–441. doi: 10.1080/00313220601020148.

Health Science Authority. 2010. "19 Apr 2010: Association Between UGT1A1 Variant Alleles and Irinotecan-Induced Severe Neutropenia." Singapore: Health Science Authority. Retrieved November 26, 2015 (http://www.hsa.gov.sg/content/hsa/en/Health_Products_Regulation/Safety_Information_and_Product_Recalls/Product_Safety_Alerts/2010/association_between.html).

Hirschman, Charles. 1987. "The Meaning and Measurement of Ethnicity in Malaysia: An Analysis of Census Classifications." *The Journal of Asian Studies* 46(3):555–582.

Lian, Kwen Fee. 1997. "Between Kingdom and Nation: The Metamorphosis of Malay Identity in Malaysia." *Southeast Asian Journal of Social Science* 25(2):59–78.

Locharernkul, Chaichon, Jakrin Loplumlert, Chusak Limotai, Wiwat Korkij, Tayard Desudchit, Siraprapa Tongkobpetch, Oratai Kangwanshiratada, Nattiya Hirankarn, Kanya Suphapeetiporn and Vorasuk Shotelersuk. 2008. "Carbamazepine and

Phenytoin Induced Stevens-Johnson Syndrome Is Associated with HLA-B*1502 Allele in Thai Population" *Epilepsia* 49(12):2087–2091.

Malaysia Federal Constitution. Part XII GENERAL AND MISCELLANEOUS, Article 160: Interpretation, Section 2. Retrieved March 30, 2016 (http://www.wipo.int/edocs/lexdocs/laws/en/my/my063en.pdf).

Manickam, Sandra K. 2009. "Common Ground: Race and the Colonial Universe in British Malaya." *Journal of Southeast Asian Studies* 40(3):593–612.

Nah, Alice M. 2006. "(Re)Mapping Indigenous 'Race'/Place in Postcolonial Peninsular Malaysia." *Geografiska Annaler: Series B, Human Geography* 88(3):285–297.

Ong, Aihwa. 2010. *Spirits of Resistance and Capitalist Discipline: Factory Women in Malaysia*. Albany, NY: State University of New York Press.

Reid, Anthony. 2001. "Understanding Melayu (Malay) as a Source of Diverse Modern Identities." *Journal of Southeast Asian Studies* 32(3):295–313.

Shamsul, A.B. 2001a. "A History of an Identity, an Identity of a History: The Idea and Practice of 'Malayness' in Malaysia Reconsidered." *Journal of Southeast Asian Studies* 32(3):355–366.

Shamsul, A.B. 2001b. "'Malay' and 'Malayness' in Malaysia Reconsidered: A Critical Review." *Communal/Plural: Journal of Transnational & Cross-Cultural Studies* 9(1):69–80.

Siddique, Sharon and Leo Suryadinata. 1981. "Bumiputra and Pribumi: Economic Nationalism (Indiginism) in Malaysia and Indonesia." *Pacific Affairs* 54(4): 662–687.

Sung, Cynthia, Pui Ling Lee, Liesbet L. Tan and Dorothy S.L. Toh. 2011. "Pharmacogenetic Risk for Adverse Reactions to Irinotecan in the Major Ethnic Populations of Singapore: Regulatory Evaluation by the Health Sciences Authority." *Drug Safety* 34(12):1167–1175.

Wong, Lai-Ping, Rick Twee-Hee Ong, Wan-Ting Poh, Xuanyao Liu, Peng Chen, Ruoying Li, Kevin Koi-Yau Lam, Nisha Esakimuthu Pillai, Kar-Seng Sim, Haiyan Xu, Ngak-Leng Sim, Shu-Mei Teo, Jia-Nee Foo, Linda Wei-Lin Tan, Yenly Lim, Seok-Hwee Koo, Linda Seo-Hwee Gan, Ching-Yu Cheng, Sharon Wee, Eric Peng-Huat Yap, Pauline Crystal Ng, Wei-Yen Lim, Richie Soong, Markus Rene Wenk, Tin Aung, Tien-Yin Wong, Chiea-Chuen Khor, Peter Little, Kee-Seng Chia and Yik-Ying Teo. 2013. "Deep Whole-Genome Sequencing of 100 Southeast Asian Malays." *American Journal of Human Genetics* 92(1):52–66.

Zuber, Noraslinda M. 2010. "Singapore Malay Identity: A Study of Dominant Perceptions of Islam in Post-Independence Singapore." PhD dissertation, Department of Malay Studies, National University of Singapore, Singapore.

5 Cancer genomics in clinics

> *For most complex problems, the pursuit of perfect knowledge is asymptotic. Uncertainty, ignorance and indeterminacy are always present.*
>
> *– Jasanoff, 2007*

Introduction

Genomic medicine is concerned not only with the acquisition and understanding of knowledge regarding the human genome, but also judgments concerning whether and how to translate knowledge into practice. In previous chapters, I have focused on how populations are constructed in the broader contexts of knowledge production concerning human genome variations and illustrated the ways in which populations become racially and ethnically labeled in various settings – transnational genomic science, the global pharmaceutical industry, and national genomic public health policies. Moreover, I have tried to problematize the relatively routine practice of using ethnicity/race as a proxy by pointing out that these ethnic and racial categories are intrinsically a function of the social dynamic known as "othering." In this chapter, I turn to the clinical setting to describe the ideal of personalized medicine that most medical oncologists in Singapore hold, which involves using the molecular characteristics of individuals to improve prevention, detection, and treatment of cancer. These doctors, who are delivering health care on the front lines, articulated their serious concerns about using the ethnic or racial identities of patients as proxies in making decisions concerning drug efficacy, drug toxicity, and preventive medicine for individual cancer patients. In other words, we suggest that there are limitations to racially and ethnically framed knowledge of human genome variation not only at the conceptual level but also at the practical level. This chapter identifies some of the social and economic conditions, which are seen as suboptimal by most, if not all, clinicians, under which the racial and ethnic identities of patients shape treatment decisions.

Using ethnicity or race as a basis of clinical decision-making

The oncologists interviewed were not explicitly critical of researchers using ethnic or racial categories in studying the human genetic or genomic structure; however, they articulated problems in using ethnicity or race as a basis for clinical decision-making. Specifically, ethnicity cannot be a substitute for genotype information in deciding how to treat a patient. In fact, once the relationship between genotype and the medical outcome has been identified, ethnicity is no longer relevant, as explained by Dr. Wang:

> [C]ertain geographical regions and certain ethnic populations are more prone to certain diseases than others. Whether this is because of a genomic interaction, or is it because of an environmental interaction, because of certain diets and practices. That is what we want to find out. But the ultimate [goal] should not be to use ethnicity as the means to deny or allow access to healthcare or certain treatment because of your race or because of your ethnic group.

In other words, researchers create proxies based on observations already framed in terms of popular, *a priori* taxonomies, such as geographic regions and ethnicity, and assume that there exist possible genotypic similarities that contribute to an ethnic group's vulnerability to a particular disease. Ethnicity serves as an intermediate step for further research to identify the assumed underlying genetic factors. Once the genetic variants are known, ethnicity ceases to be of value, Dr. Wang continued:

> . . . if you were to say it's more common in Chinese, therefore Chinese patients with lung cancer should be treated with IRESSA, then you'll be missing the patients who are Indians and Malays who have the EGFR mutation, you see? That's what I mean. So you have to use the ethnic group, to, as the basis of drilling down, what is the cause of this difference, and then based on that EGFR mutation, you treat every ethnic group the same.
>
> If you have a particular genotype, does it behave [in a] similar manner in different groups? Yes. It should. And all the examples point towards this. So a Caucasian, Spanish, who has a EGFR mutant will respond [to] the same quantum and the same way compared to an Asian who has got the EGFR mutant lung cancer, when treated with IRESSA.

Thus, Dr. Wang presented the example of IRESSA being effective for patients with EGFR mutations regardless of race, despite the fact that IRESSA was initially discovered to work best in Asians, especially Chinese, female nonsmokers.

In a similar manner, Dr. Yuan reinforced the argument that ethnicity is used only as a transitional classification in order to move toward identifying specific genetics to improve treatment:

> I was in Boston, presenting [on] our CTRG trials and ethnicity [i.e. clinical trials for prospective cancer drugs using ethnicity as a frame], when I was called a racist. This lady said, "in America, we'd never allow you to do this research, 'Cause it's racial profiling." And I said "Look, we're just looking for signals, and once we find the [genetic/genomic] signature, ethnicity becomes redundant."

In other words, ethnicity is no longer of concern once specific genetics are known. Doctors do not administer medicine based on ethnicity, but on genomic status, such as EGFR mutation status. While it is understood that racial classification is sensitive and deemed as discriminatory, Dr. Yuan shared his observation that researchers in such cases see racial profiling as a necessary short-term strategic measure for further investigation.

Likewise, Dr. Wu discussed the difference between research and medicine: that ethnicity might be useful to stimulate further research, but should not be used once the specific genotype information is established:

> One must distinguish between what is research-based and what is medicine . . . you have to use the best knowledge that you have, and race and ethnicity is just one layer of information that is of less precision. If you do know what the variant is, and it's been proven through research that it matters, then you should clinically adopt the variants and not the ethnicity. Ethnicity is when you don't know [the genetic variant], and it just gives you something to consider.

A lung cancer medicine, for example, would benefit a patient of any ethnicity, as it targets the genetic variant, which remains the same across ethnic groups. Dr. Wu continued:

> . . . EGFR mutant lung cancer is only ten percent of all adenocarcinomas in the Western world, but forty to fifty percent of all (such patients) in Singapore . . . or in Asia. But if you carry the mutation, whether you're a Westerner or you're Asian, you benefit fairly similarly from the drug. So there may be different frequencies of the alteration, but the meaning of the alteration, once it's present, is probably similar.

This view is echoed by Dr. Deng, who stated that:

> [W]hen it comes to molecular profiling, you move beyond ethnic and racial profiles because it doesn't matter what race you come from, it is the tumor that is important. We believe that the tumors may have common characteristics regardless [of] whether you are Chinese, Malay, Indian or Caucasian.

Moreover, the physicians explained that there is no perfect correlation between ethnicity and genotype. That is, there is no gene variant that is present in only one ethnic group, nor is there an ethnic group whose members all carry the same gene variant. Hence, ethnicity should not be used as a proxy for the presence or absence of a gene variant. These points were articulated by Dr. Koh:

> Based on all the data that we've seen so far . . . in terms of the distribution and frequency [of the genetic variant]? It's very unlikely that you're [going

to] find a population with an allele frequency of 99 percent. I mean, we've never seen anything like that.

Even if it's 50 percent, if it's 50 percent, you're [going to] be wrong 50 percent of the time! You can't do that. You can't be wrong 50 percent of the time, that's unacceptable.

To these doctors, race/ethnicity as a proxy is acceptable only in research – but even then, it is used as a temporary category, which can only hint at the presence/absence of specific genetic variants involved. Drugs do not become effective because of a patient's ethnicity; rather, it is the specific genetic mutations that cause a drug to work, as explained by Dr. Hsu:

The ethnic groups simply provide a pre-test surrogate of what the result would be. So if I see a Chinese, Asian, woman, non-smoker, I would say, before I test you, I know that you are 55 percent chance of being an EGFR mutant. But, after the test result comes out, the results speak for itself, right? Because at the end of the day, the drug recognize the [genetic/genomic] target. So it doesn't quite matter, whatever color you are, whatever ethnic background, as long as the mutation is present. And this is proven, so . . . Italian patients with EGFR mutation respond very well to Iressa, just as Singapore Chinese women do. Same. So it's the target that matter, I think drug is ethnic-blind.

In short, genetics are what matter in the end, rather than racial or ethnic categories. As Dr. Yeh emphasized:

So as long as you carry the EGFR mutation, regardless if you're Korean or Japanese, Taiwanese, Singaporean, Indian, U.S . . . If you carry the EGFR mutation . . . you would treat with the drug! Absolutely. It is the driving mutation. It does not respect ethnic boundaries.

In other words, while the genotype may be presented in varying frequencies in different ethnic or racial groups, the doctors were against using ethnicity or race as a basis to preferentially select or exclude certain patients from genetic testing or medical treatment. Indeed, for the EGFR mutation, while it is prevalent in "Chinese" or "Asian" lung cancer patients, the doctors stressed that patients of other ethnicities should also be tested for it. As Dr. Poh put it:

Because it [i.e. the presence of the EGFR mutation] is [in] about 50 percent of our patients with NSCLC here. In Western Europe, in European populations, Caucasian populations, it is about 10–15 percent. You will still test it and the reason is because it makes such a dramatic difference so you don't want to miss it.

If you don't [conduct EGFR mutation testing], you will get sued. And you don't want to miss it [the mutation status].

Clinicians are legally bound and have a sense of duty to administer treatment according to a patient's individual diagnosis, especially in prescribing genome-based medicine. As Dr. Deng put it:

> . . . you know EGFR mutations, more common in Chinese, less common in Caucasians, 10 percent in Caucasians, 40 percent in Chinese, but does that mean if you are Caucasian, you got lung cancer, you are not going to screen for it? You still are. Because for the individual patient, it is really really important because it makes such a big difference in the outcome.
>
> Just like having the EGFR mutation, just because it is more common in Asians, it doesn't mean you can't prescribe it to a Caucasian who's got the mutation.

Likewise, Dr. Tang pointed out that assumptions about mutation statuses in patients should *not* be made on the basis of general observations and statistics reflected by populations:

> . . . going to the genetic basis of it should be the criteria, because certain genetic changes found more commonly in [Asians] doesn't mean it is excluded in other races. Because it is less common, but that doesn't mean that you don't do the test. You understand what I am saying? Like EGFR mutant lung cancer is found in Asians; but if it is found in Caucasians, they also respond to the drug.

Other shortcomings of using race and ethnicity as a proxy in clinical practices exist, including, but not limited to, the phenomenon of intermarriage, the contemporariness of such categories, and the uniformity of genetic structure within groups, as these doctors described:

DR. WEE: . . . My medic will help me call Mr. Chong Ah Kow. The person that enters my room is an Indian, looks exactly like an Indian, but (his name) is Mr. Chong Ah Kow.
[INTERVIEWER: You would have presumed that Mr. Chong was Chinese?]
"So your father is Mr. Chong?" [Dr. Wee asked the patient.]
"Ya, correct, (and) my mum is an Indian." [The patient replied.]
So, so I guess . . . ethnicity is some kind of genetic information, but we realize that it has limitations.
DR. LIN: There are some patients with a Chinese father and a Caucasian mother, vice-versa.
DR. HSU: I think in medicine . . . races don't really matter, right? Whether you're Chinese, Indian or Malay, you will treat a heart attack the same way; likewise, for diabetes. There is no major need to treat one race differently.
The second thing about this is, how uniform is your group? How uniform is the (genetic structure) of the Chinese ethnic group? So when people say that Asians are more likely to have EGFR mutation for lung cancer, what does "Asian" mean, right?

In the past the Indians were Asians; now we consider them as South Asian. So the definition of an ethnic group's uniformity is always evolving. So if I tell you that Americans respond better to this drug than the Chinese, (you'd think,) "Americans what?" Jewish? Irish? Spaniard [*sic*]? You know, the world's been highly globalized, and people are moving left and right of the geographical boundary, which may not correspond to the political boundary – which, in turn, may not correspond to the genomic boundary.

DR. LIANG: . . . the matter is not so straightforward, because of mixed marriages, alright? A person who looks like a Malay might be Chinese . . . so it is not so simple to look at the declared race. In fact, if you have read the newspapers not too long ago, some people don't know what race to give themselves.

So – there's Malay-Chinese, Chinese-Malay, [but] what if you have got some European blood, is it Eurasian or . . . ? [Race] is no longer reliable anymore, because people are intermarrying across races.

Sometimes, doctors may be forced to use the ethnic or racial profile of a patient to make clinical decisions under suboptimal circumstances. These include times when genetic testing is unavailable, or when the relationship between genotype and medical outcome has not been discovered. For instance, Dr. Yuan said:

[I]f we were a poor country, okay? I mean, to do these tests is a few hundred dollars. So let's say I'm in a country where I don't have the ability to do the test.

And I have a white patient and an Oriental patient with lung cancer. I can tell the white patient, look if I give you this drug, there's a 10 percent chance it's going to work, and I can tell the Oriental patient there's a 50–70 percent chance this drug is going to work. That's using ethnicity. But I would rather be a 100 percent certain, I'd rather do the test.

The doctors interviewed also made clinical observations of inter-ethnic differences in toxicities of the chemotherapy drug docetaxel (Taxotere) and have used ethnic background to guide the dosing of docetaxel, while no clear genetic explanation has been offered in such scenarios. Dr. Hsu shared his observations:

Chemotherapy is also known to differ between ethnic groups. For example a drug called Taxotere. Taxotere is a very famous drug that is used for breast cancer and all kind of cancer. A common dosage in the West is 75 milligram per meter square, every three weeks, but we know that 75 milligram is not something that many Asian patients can take. So, as a result, NUH did the study I think four five years ago, that showed that a Chinese woman getting breast cancer treatment at 16 milligram per meter square achieved as good an outcome as Caucasian woman getting 75. So that knowledge of the ethnic background immediately allows you to adjust the first dose, straightaway. And in fact, if you give 75 milligram to Chinese woman first dose, some of them will die, because of the side effect, and also, it's quite customary for all Asians to use a lower starting dose. In fact, Japan, the same drug, for the same indication, the official labeling is never 75, it's 60. They already have imputed into their drug approval system that every time you see Taxotere, we drop by twenty percent. So in Japan, and maybe to some degree the Chinese in Singapore, we are quite in favor of reducing the dosage of certain chemotherapy drug, based on purely ethnic background.

Patients with dihydropyrimidine dehydrogenase (DPD) deficiency are more likely to have severe side effects from the chemotherapy drug 5-fluorouracil (5-FU). According to Dr. Teo, if DPD deficiency testing cannot be done, doctors may be compelled to use ethnicity as a factor to guide the dosing of 5-FU:

> [Administering] 5FU . . . I am a little bit more nervous with Malay and Indian patients. Because the DPD deficiency test is not currently available routinely. It is only available in laboratory setting, in a very sophisticated lab, and we can't do that routinely. So what we do is that when we see patients from Malay or Indian origins, I may reduce the dose a little bit by 10 percent. But that's based on intuition. It's not based on science. It's not based on protocol. It's not based on any algorithm. It's just based on intuition, cause that's all I have available today. But there are no drugs that you can say "Oh Indian, take this drug. Chinese, take this drug. Malay, take this drug." There isn't anything like that. There isn't.

Finally, there may be clinical situations in which a patient cannot afford the luxury of time. As Dr. Lin clarified:

> The thing about lung cancer is you may not have a second chance. Sometimes the patients are very breathless with lung cancer. And by the time you realize takes weeks later that it doesn't work or few weeks later, they're dead, you know. . . . Non-trial situations are very complicated. Sometimes the patients don't want [to have this particular treatment]. Sometimes it's cost issues, sometimes it's too breathless to wait. Sometimes we give both chemotherapy and IRESSA at the same time. Because there's not much time to wait, to wait for one or the other to work.

To sum up this section, physicians are clear about using ethnicity: yes for scientific research – but only with strict terms and conditions – and a resounding no for clinical practice. The use of ethnicity in research is acceptable only when it is used as a surrogate category that is assumed to lead to the discovery of concrete genetic characteristics. In clinical practice, race and ethnicity should only be considered as a last resort, if genetic test results are unavailable. In any event, all doctors interviewed unanimously agreed that it is the presence/absence of genetic mutations that influences the drug efficacy of personalized medicine.

Personalized medicine in clinical practice: drug efficacy

Scientific research and clinical trials seek to establish whether, in subjects under study, there is a relationship between the independent variable (e.g. presence of a genetic marker) and the dependent variable (e.g. responsiveness to a drug treatment). In a clinical setting, the doctor is making an assessment about an individual patient. A statistically significant relationship observed within a study population may not be applicable to the individual patient. As Dr. Lin explained, that is a major challenge for doctors in applying personalized medicine in a clinical setting:

> [W]hen you talk about personalized medicine, you are assuming that it has to be 100 percent accurate. It's not a 100 percent accurate. Obviously, it can't be. It's just maybe more accurate in your selection versus other criteria!
>
> It's the same with this test. . . . Look, this is a graph. It divides the score, the recurrence. They don't even give you right and left, yes and no. . . . They give you a continuous range! And they say this is low-risk, intermediate risk, high risk! That day I just tested this woman, is right in the middle here. So genomics, they can be informative, they can be helpful. It's again how you use the information. In some situation, your clinical judgment and assessment can be as good and can still supplant without your genetic tests!

Doctors were interviewed about three key areas in which genetic testing could be applied to personalized medicine: drug efficacy, drug toxicities, and preventive medicine. Drug efficacy involves assessing the effectiveness of a particular drug therapy for an individual patient. Drug toxicity involves assessing the likelihood of an individual patient developing adverse drug reactions (ADRs) from a drug therapy. Preventive medicine involves assessing an individual's susceptibility to a particular disease with a view of possible preventive measures or early treatment.

The doctors generally had positive views about applying genetic testing to assess drug efficacy, while pointing out limitations. Genetic testing has been helpful in formulating more treatments that are differentiated for patients and for avoiding costly drug treatment prescribed to patients who are unlikely to respond to it. One of the doctors, Dr. Wu, also noted that personalized medicine has made great advances in certain fields such as the treatment of colorectal cancer and lung cancer:

> . . . in colorectal cancer for example, only patients who are, do not carry a particular mutation in KRAS or NRAS will benefit from a particular drug. So if you carry the mutation, there're biological reasons, which have been shown in clinical studies, to show that you will not benefit from the drug, and you will save the cost, which is expensive – the drug is seven thousand dollars. To put this in context, the test for that is less than a thousand, often less than three hundred dollars, so it's a dramatic difference.

Genetic tests also shed light on a patient's biological composition, such as the presence/absence of mutation; this is crucial to the decision-making process, as a suitable, cost-effective treatment can then be tailored for each patient, as Dr. Deng pointed out. Without this genetic test, the patient will undergo a general treatment, which may see the patient taking several drugs to find a suitable one that is responsive. This process could be costly, and risky, if the drug(s) has side effects that could complicate matters. As Dr. Deng described:

> I think lung cancer has been . . . it has really changed dramatically in the last five years. We previously used to very much just apply certain treatment to patients with lung cancer, all non-small cell lung cancer would [be] group[ed] together, and now we actually wait for specific genetic test to be done and for the results that, before we actually decide which is the best initial treatment and at the moment we test for three common markers, EGFR, ALK, and ROS1, and each of these have got specific implications on the type of treatments that would be deemed most effective. So we actually wait, sometimes two weeks, for these results to come out before we start treatment.

Similarly, for Dr. Koh, advances in genomic medicine facilitate targeted treatments that maximize the benefits patients may receive from a particular drug and minimize potential adverse drug reactions:

> [I]t's good for the patient, because they're subjected to potentially more effective treatment by sub-selecting the groups that are most likely to benefit from a particular treatment, and they're less likely to be subjected to toxicity of the treatment that doesn't work for them, so it's good for them. It's good for society, because it reduces healthcare costs and improves outcomes.

Genetic testing was thus perceived by these doctors as a beneficial development that serves patients and society well, including its economic impact. Dr. Yeh shared his view:

> So prior to the EGFR testing, we would put patients who fit the clinical phenotype, nonsmokers, adenocarcinoma, Chinese, or Asian. Into . . . to treat! But they would have to treat for maybe about a month or . . . 6 weeks. And pay maybe [over] 3000 . . . dollars? For that core amount of drug before you see whether there's a response. Whereas now, you test ahead of time, you are going to spend 300 dollars, a tenth of that amount . . . and be able to decide whether you're going to expose the patient to this drug or not.

According to scientist Dr. Huang, genetic testing can help a patient who is in the early stages of breast cancer assess whether he/she requires chemotherapy after undergoing surgery. This helps the patient to save costs and avoid the side effects of chemotherapy:

> We know that from retrospective studies, that 40 percent of patients with early stage breast cancer after surgery actually will not require chemotherapy. Meaning that, meaning that if you don't treat them with chemotherapy after surgery, these patients will have very good 5 year survival. But 60 percent of patients after surgery will relapse. So those people require chemotherapy. What happens if you were a clinician? And you had a female patient . . . after surgery. Would you treat or not treat?
>
> You treat! So the reality is that everybody gets treated. Which means that 40 percent of patients actually get overtreated. So they incur the toxicity of the chemotherapy, they incur the costs. So there is actually a test that measures the expression levels of 70 genes. It's called MammaPrint. This is not an Asian-specific test. This was developed in Europe. That you can send your patient to and they can analyze the breast cancer, and they can tell pretty accurately that, does it follow the 40 percent or does it follow the 60 percent. And on the basis of that, you can synthesize that information as the doctor and you can decide if you still want to proceed [with] the treatment or not.

Fundamentally, however, the relationship between genotype and drug efficacy is still not completely understood. As Dr. Zhang pointed out, even with a gene variant that is established to be linked to drug efficacy, doctors have always encountered exceptions in their clinical practice:

> There are many other factors that affect the outcome of the treatment or how a gene behaves in the body. We cannot say just because two patients have the same genetic mutation, they should behave and they should react similarly to the same drug. . . . There are many other things that affect the patient and the functioning or interaction of these drugs and genes. I don't think we know enough to predict for sure how this will react. We can at best tell you 70 percent, 80 percent of patients will react to a certain degree.

The results of genetic testing offer important insights, helping doctors and patients to better evaluate a situation and relevant treatment options. However, these genetic test results are still probabilities. There is no certainty that a targeted treatment will definitely work in all patients with specific mutations, nor is there a definite duration for which the drugs remain effective against a patient's mutations. As Dr. Tang explained:

> About 70 percent of the patients will carry that EGFR mutation. Of those patients who are EGFR mutation, you do expect that 80 percent of them

will respond to the drug so 20 percent that will not respond – meaning that they either remain the same or they may even grow with the treatment. And of those patients who respond, not all will respond in a durable manner to the drug; meaning that some of them will develop resistance to the drug within 6 months, some will have the disease controlled for much, much longer [than] that 2 years, 3 years; the longest I had is like 10 years. So the spectrum is really wide. Although majority of them will relapse within a year, so the main thing that we need to know is that why this variability in terms of response? . . . And if the patient develops resistance, is there a reason for that?

The doctors recognized not only the benefits of genetic testing, but also its limitations. Furthermore, as Dr. Xie pointed out, in clinical practice, there is no guarantee in any situation – even when a specific mutation is present, that does not mean that the drug will definitely work:

> [J]ust because you have a EGFR mutation, you got a high chance of respond-ing to it, but not all patients respond to it.

Moreover, new knowledge about the interactions between genes and drug effi-cacy is constantly being developed. Hence, underlying genetic links for some pre-viously unexplained cases may surface with further advances in medical research. Dr. Hsu shared his clinical experience:

> I just tell you the latest development – for colon cancer, you know we do it for KRAS testing right? We do this testing because the KRAS is showing no mutation, we will use a drug called Erbitux, right? So if the tumor KRAS, which is a proto-oncogene, if the KRAS gene is mutated, we cannot use this drug. Quite the opposite from lung cancer. Before 2008, we don't even test, we just give this drug. After 2008, we test this drug, KRAS, as a matter of routine, standard – every colon cancer Stage 4 we test, alright? So if they have mutation, can't use the drug; no mutation, we use the drug. Every-body's happy right? Until last month. Last month's data have shown that even the KRAS no mutation, inside, 18 percent of them have a separate type of mutation that's not captured by the KRAS. So now we're doing NRAS, so now, it's very complicated, from six years ago, we don't test; last six year we do KRAS, everybody's so happy – then they found that 18 percent of the KRAS is not truly sensitive to the drug. Why? Because there's a second-ary mutation, it's called NRAS. And after they found NRAS, they go to a third one called BRAF. So nowadays for colon cancer we're doing so many molecular profile, until the big colon cancer group is now split into five or six different subtype. So this movement is moving at a rapid pace.

In summary, physicians generally did not see any ethical problem with genetic testing to assess drug efficacy. The testing is for somatic mutation in the cells in the tumor area. Somatic mutation is nonhereditary, and, hence, there is no concern about how the genetic information would implicate a patient's biological descendants. By contrast, genetic testing for preventive medicine (to be discussed later in this chapter) could pose concerns, as it typically involves testing for germline mutations, which could be passed on to descendants. As Dr. Wu pointed out:

> Somatic alterations [are] in the tumor, whilst germline are something that's inherited, which is inherited in your genome from your parents. For somatic, I don't think there's much ethical considerations, because it's very clear-cut that you get the benefit from the treatment and you therefore reduce the expense and side-effects of unnecessary treatment that wouldn't have benefited you.

There is, thus, little or no ethical concern about genetic testing for somatic mutations as the results from the tests concern only the individual patient involved, unlike germline mutations, which affect future generations. Furthermore, genetic tests for somatic mutations will facilitate better decision-making for the most suitable treatment for the individual at that point in time. According to Dr. Deng:

> . . . I think, the community is generally comfortable with somatic testing, because that's the cancer genome, it's very specific thing that we're testing for, with a very targeted objective, which is to try to see what therapies a patient may be eligible for.

Hence, it is broadly agreed that genetic testing for somatic mutations is morally and medically acceptable. However, the same cannot be said for genetic testing for germline mutations, whereby future generations would be genetically at risk, as well. Thus, genetic testing for somatic mutations is largely supported by the doctors. As Dr. Xia put it:

> [F]rom the medical viewpoint . . . because these are somatic mutations. They are not inherited. So there is no implication for the next generation. These are just random mutations that happen in the lifetime of someone. There is no risk involved [in] testing for these things.

With respect to somatic mutations, these doctors agreed that genetic tests assist them in advising on treatment options for individual patients, based on the individual's genotype information, facilitating personalized medicine. At the same time, they recognized that the genetic mutations being tested are only strongly correlated – not definitively causative – with the efficacy of the drugs. However, genetic tests for preventive purposes seemed to be less welcomed by these doctors. This will be discussed in greater length in a later section, "Personalized medicine in clinical practice: preventive medicine."

Personalized medicine in clinical practice: drug toxicities

In contrast to their attitudes concerning drug efficacy, doctors had more reservations about the usefulness of genetic testing in assessing drug toxicities. For Dr. Xie, the vast amount of data necessary to verify claims and difficulties in offering a clear definition of toxicity present huge obstacles in using genetic tests:

> I think the problem is that you need huge amounts of data to validate any marker you think may be predictive of toxicity because you've got to ask yourself, how do you define your toxicity, there is a whole spectrum of toxicity. Is it very bad diarrhea, moderate diarrhea?
>
> There may be very subtle differences in one particular polymorphism in the gene that predicts for this particular toxicity versus the other one that predicts a less toxicity. And then you got to study a thousand patients to give you a validated perspective, so it is very difficult to validate.

There is no single, unanimous definition of toxicity. There are shades of toxicity intensity, as discussed previously – ranging from mild to detrimental. These terms are subjective not only to doctors but also to patients as well. Hence, evaluation of genetic testing to reduce toxicities would be vague. Moreover, doctors can directly adjust dosage based on patient feedback, as shared by Dr. Hsu:

> The data [on toxicity] is somewhat immature, so the immaturity of the scientific translation, is the barrier for the SNPs testing. And, some of the clinicians will say that why do you need the SNP test? You just give the drug, any side effect you just adjust the dose. So this skepticism will make SNPs a somewhat a nice concept, but it won't be widely adopted.

Moreover, according to Dr. Chong, some existing genetic tests of drug toxicities suffer from a lack of specificity and sensitivity:

> [F]or predicting drug toxicity, I know there are tests out there to predict for toxicity to Irinotecan [and] to 5-flurouracil . . . none of it has been robustly replicated and proven to be highly specific and sensitive, so it's not in common use.

The clinicians that were interviewed remained, thus, somewhat unconvinced about toxicity tests. These tests are, for the moment, not as scientifically rigorous and statistically meaningful as drug efficacy tests; not many clinicians use them today. As Dr. Koh said:

> There are lots of patients who have that certain polymorphism, but don't have toxicities. . . . So the predictive power is not as strong as we would like for it to be. We're definitely doing the genetic testing for efficacy . . . but for toxicity, because it's still somewhat controversial, and the utility is still limited, we're not using it. It's not standard of care right now.

Because the tests are not as useful and are open to diverse interpretations, they are largely put aside. Therefore, for Dr. Zhang, many of the decisions made in clinical practice are based on the doctor's judgment:

> Toxicity . . . yes there are some tests but many people, some tests, many people still think that it is not very specific nor is very sensitive. So, we can't use these genetic tests to see if a patient should or should not receive a particular drug. A lot of time it is still based on our clinical judgment.

Drug toxicities, similar to drug efficacy, are also affected by nongenetic factors. Warfarin is an anticoagulant that is used in the prevention and treatment of thrombotic disorders. Two genes, CYP2C9 and VKORC1, are known to influence the body's metabolism and sensitivity to Warfarin. Excessive dosage of Warfarin can cause fatal bleeding. It is suggested that the profiles of these two genes could potentially guide doctors in determining the dosage of Warfarin to administer to a patient. However, Dr. Zhang pointed out that an adverse reaction (i.e. bleeding) to Warfarin could be caused by many nongenetic factors. Thus, Dr. Zhang described clinical vigilance and patient management as more important than genetic testing in mitigating the adverse effects of Warfarin:

> For example, a certain kind of herbal tea, even simple like chamomile tea, will affect the coagulation of warfarin. So we can't tell patients that you must not eat this and that . . . there are 1000 of things (to avoid). If patient has cough and cold, and went to see a GP (General Practitioner) and get some medicine. That interferes with Warfarin, and you run into trouble.
> So one way is to do that [genetic] test and use it to assess how much Warfarin to give. But even with that test . . . we still have to monitor the Warfarin, titrate the dose by looking at the clotting duration or the clotting time. . . . So without Warfarin, maybe 12 seconds, with Warfarin, maybe 24 seconds. So this is our target. Anybody who is on Warfarin will do the clotting test and make sure that their blood clot within 24 seconds. If it takes longer than that, it is considered high dose . . . excessive. If it is too fast, we increase the dose. Now you have this genetic test, does that mean that you don't have to do the clotting test? You still need to! So with or without this genetic test, we still need to do the observation test. But this [genetic information] helps you predict which patient, when you start Warfarin, [is] more likely to run into trouble.

Even if genetic testing suggests that a patient might potentially have adverse reactions to a drug, clinicians like Dr. Xie pointed out that sometimes the drug may be the only treatment option available. In such cases, it might be better for the patient to tolerate the drug toxicities than to have no treatment. A case in point is Irinotecan, a chemotherapy drug used to treat colorectal cancer. Studies have shown that patients with certain variants of the UGT1A1 gene are more likely to develop adverse effects such as diarrhea from Irinotecan treatment. However, doctors may still prescribe Irinotecan if this is the best (or only) treatment option and then try to manage the side effects by adjusting the dosage. As Dr. Xie put it:

> I agree that [patients with variants in] the UGT1A1, who take certain drugs will get much worse diarrhea, get very toxic and very unwell. But the question is whether or not it applies to everyone, what is the option [if not taking the drug]. If you then develop toxicities, is it manageable? I mean, how bad is the diarrhea? If you tell the patient, "if I give you this drug, there is a risk that you might develop really bad diarrhea; but if you are willing to take that risk, we can see what happens." If subsequently the patient does well, responds to treatment, they might accept that they are having diarrhea ten times a day – that it is worthwhile.

Even though Irinotecan results in toxicities, the doctors would still prescribe it if it is deemed the most suitable treatment option for a patient at a given point in time. To deal with the toxicities, genetic testing is not really necessary as the dosage can be adjusted based on the patient's feedback along the way. As Dr. Chong described it:

> We just sort of bite the bullet and use it [anyway]. This chemotherapy, Irinotecan, is not used that commonly, but sometimes . . . we need to use it, because it's the only option. You know what I mean? So sometimes we use a bit of clinical discretion; we start off at a bit of a lower dose and see if it goes well. . .

The example of Irinotecan illustrates that genetic testing for toxicities is thus not really helpful, as, in reality, patients can be in trying circumstances with limited treatment options. Even if they are going to suffer from toxicities, the doctors would advise the treatment if it is the only viable attempt to help them. As Dr. Xia pointed out:

> In actual fact, Irinotecan can be given in several ways, can be given once every 3 week or can be given on [a] weekly basis and if given on a weekly basis, you have an even better handle on the toxicities. And also, in a context of nothing else to offer for that particular patient, for whatever reason, you know you have exhausted everything else, you are going to try, anyway.

Another example is carbamazepine (CBZ), which is used to treat epilepsy and other conditions, including diabetic neuropathy, trigeminal neuralgia, and bipolar disorders. The Singaporean Ministry of Health has issued an advisory that the use of CBZ should be avoided in patients who are found to be positive for the HLA-B*1502 gene allele due to the risk of adverse side effects. Nonetheless, according to Dr. Liang, doctors may still have to use the drug for such patients if there is no other treatment available:

> [T]he problem [of CBZ's adverse side effects] was thought to be significant enough that the study was done. Some economic projections suggest that it may be worthwhile doing the screening, so Ministry accepted it and sent out the circulars to all doctors. But it is not mandated, in the sense that the doctors still have the freedom to decide whether he thinks it should be done or not, because sometimes, we may have no other choice, meaning besides this medicine, you don't have any other choices.

Though some genetic tests for toxicities are highly recommended, as in the case of CBZ, whose adverse side effects are widely recognized as significantly harmful, in most cases such tests are not as useful as those for efficacy. Two common reasons for this stand out among all of the doctors interviewed: (1) the degree of toxicity is subjective for both doctor and patient, and (2) in clinical practice, patients sometimes do not have another choice than to use the drug anyway because of limited options or because it is the only treatment option. Hence, even if the toxicity test discourages the use of a drug (citing a patient's vulnerability to side effects), the treatment has to be given, albeit at a lower dosage if necessary, for the patient's benefit.

Personalized medicine in clinical practice: preventive medicine

The application of genetic testing in preventive medicine is a double-edged sword. On the one hand, early identification of susceptibility to certain diseases enables early intervention to manage the disease or even prevent it from occurring at all. On the other hand, unlike drug efficacy testing, which is for somatic mutations (and nonhereditary), preventive medicine involves testing for germline mutation. As germline mutation is hereditary, the information affects not only the individuals being tested but also other people related to them by blood.

To begin with, the doctors generally agreed that genetic screening is more appropriate when the subject already has a family history of the disease in question, as Dr. Chong described:

> [S]o genetic testing on healthy subjects . . . I think the common ones would be like breast cancer, if you have strong family history of breast cancer, you check for BRCA, you can do just a check for Lynch Syndrome, so I would say healthy subjects only if there's strong family history.

At present, there are a few genetic tests that can be done for preventive screening. However, as Dr. Koh explained, such tests are only encouraged if an individual has a family history of certain cancers, suggesting that the relevant hereditable mutations might be present, putting the individual at risk:

> There has to be a reason to do the testing, it has to be a good reason. So for example, I mean, patients who have very heavy family history of breast cancer that span across generations, affect multiple family members, well, of course we're concerned that they have certain mutations that increase the risk for breast cancer.
>
>   . . . there are patient who'd come in and ask us to do genetic testing for this cancer or that cancer. I say, look, your history doesn't warrant that because you have no history of this in your family, or you have a history of another cancer, which is not relevant to this test at all.

The link between genetic profile and disease propensity is only a probabilistic relationship and not a definitive one. In some cases, as Dr. Wu explained, such as between a BRCA gene and the risk of breast cancer, the statistical relationship is perceived as strong. But, in other cases, scientific research has only established a weak relationship, which would have limited value for clinical purposes:

> [F]or very specific, well-described phenomenon, where the penetrance of the disease is very high, such as BRCA, and cancer. . . . But not . . . when you're looking at the GWAS result, where it tells you that the risk is 1.3 times, or 1.2 times, I mean, how does that actually impact human health?
>
>   I guess it's a matter of effect size. . . . [T]he number of genes where the odds ratio is more than five, or whatever, is really limited. . . . [M]ost of these variants are at less than odds ratio of 2. So how does a 1.8 times or 1.7 times risk matter?
>
>   There's . . . I mean, there are very clear causative variants that . . . such as BRCA and all that, where the odds, the penetrance is like 80 percent or so, and that is very clear. Those are clear-cut causative.

Unless the causative relationship between the incidence of the disease and the specific gene mutation is proven to be significantly conclusive, the test results would not have practical concerns for the doctors interviewed. After all, according to Dr. Xie, given that the human genome is huge, such findings can be common and clinically insignificant:

> There are some genes where the penetrance is very high, where you know that if you got this underlying mutation, you are very likely then to develop this cancer, like the BRCA mutations for example. . . . [T]hese patients then go ahead and have their prophylactic mastectomy and oophorectomy. The problem is that there are probably a whole host of other genes that people have done these big studies on what we call SNP studies, single nucleotide polymorphisms studies. So they found that this particular polymorphism in a particular amino acid, in a particular exon, or promoter region or even a non-coding region of the gene, predisposes you to a risk! So how do you

resolve that biologically and the thing is we don't understand that much at the moment.

The doctors interviewed pointed out that the public may not understand the full picture – that gene mutations only suggest probabilities of developing cancer and do not precisely determine the emergence of cancer. Dr. Liang pointed out that, without proper counseling by medical professionals, genetic testing runs the risk of creating unnecessary anxieties:

[E]ven Angelina Jolie – doesn't mean she will get breast cancer. She has a very high chance, that's all. There is a chance that she might not even get it. You know, but the public, some of them don't understand this thing about probability and chances.

The problem with genetic counselors is that they can only counsel from a very statistical viewpoint. They don't know the disease. They cannot know so many diseases. He may know in terms of understanding from the probability perspective, what it means and the risks of inheritance.

Quoting the prominent case of Angelina Jolie who underwent mastectomy and oophorectomy because of the presence of the BRCA1 gene mutation, Dr. Koh explained that the presence of the specific gene mutation implies only a high probability of suffering from the cancers in the future, but nothing is definite. Healthy subjects might be subjected to health scares, with statistically significant predisposed genetic risk shown, especially if genetic counselors provide guidance mainly based on statistics reflected in the reports, with minimal or no knowledge of the diseases in question. Dr. Koh continued:

You can tell someone, [taking the genetic test] will help you to understand that your chance of developing a disease is twenty percent higher than a person who is negative for that polymorphism, or even twice – but the problem is that, they don't explain to people, before they are tested, that the frequency of this problem is one in ten thousand, and so your risk of having this if you test positive is two in ten thousand. I mean, that's not really meaningful, right?

That's not really meaningful to people, because, people will be walking around thinking, oh, I have twice the risk of developing Parkinson's disease. Well, yes, but Parkinson's disease is not that common!

The risks reflected are not always clinically meaningful, as the probabilities of getting the disease might not be as high as the statistics appear to show, especially after taking into account population statistics. As Dr. Wu noted, these results could lead to unnecessary apprehension and would not serve anyone well, as there is no guarantee that the subject will suffer from the disease:

I think there are two things to balance, the sin of omission and the sin of commission, which is, the patient knowing it will allow them to go for screening, or go for certain risk-reduction strategies, and that will benefit them and potentially save lives. But if you tell them the wrong information, it will cause unnecessary anxiety and possibly in certain rare cases, overtreatment.

The results of the genetic tests for preventive purposes can be highly detrimental to a healthy subject's psychological health. He/she could become highly insecure and paranoid, and if there is a family history, other family members could be affected as well. As Dr. Hsu pointed out:

> . . . you may actually get results that impose psychological stress to the patient. Once they know that they're a carrier of the gene, every time you have a stomach pain, you think that cancer is back; every time you feel a lump in the breast, you think that cancer has come. So the psychological cloud over you is very devastating. And more importantly, you're also transferring that psychological pressure, to all your blood relations. Every woman in your family, every sister gets the same stress (with breast cancer as an example), so that's very devastating.

Doctors like Dr. Koh emphasized the necessity of support mechanisms to help subjects understand the implications of their genetic profiles and also manage anxieties that may arise:

> . . . so we ask them to do testing, but we explain to them why we think that they're likely to have the mutation, we explain to them what the mutation testing involves, we explain to them what the possible implications are, including, loss of privacy, potential loss of employment, insurance, if that data were to become available to third parties, all those things you really have to explain to patients.

The data from genetic testing are sensitive, highly personal, and require relevant professionals and experts to provide an explanation of the results. Individual patients without the necessary knowledge might not understand the outcome properly and may not be able to deal with the situations that could arise. As Dr. Xie put it:

> I think we need to agree that they should at least understand what is being tested, what are the implications to them if something positive is found, especially if it is a germline mutation that predisposes . . . them [to] a high risk of developing of a particular condition and how to deal [with] that condition. So suddenly you do a test and you got an 80 percent [chance of] Alzheimer's disease, or you got Huntington disease. How are you going to deal with all that? So I think . . . there will need to be healthcare professionals that are trained specifically to deal with these issues of molecular testing and, and sequencing in order to de-convolute the complexities of these issues for the patients.

On top of the need to have health care professionals to assist individuals in understanding their test results and consequent decision-making, Dr. Xia warned that other general issues, such as health insurance concerns and data privacy, should be considered, as information on predisposed biological risks might prove to be too much of a liability:

> There are other implications, you know such as insurance. . . . Because if let's say her daughter [i.e. the patient's daughter] were to buy health insurance in the future, the family history is often asked about. Then she would have to say that her mother has breast cancer and of course the question on whether you should then offer and volunteer the information that your mother has a BRCA mutation. I mean the mother could choose not to tell the daughter right? Okay, then in which case, that's the point the daughter is not burdened with this information . . . should you or should you not tell your relatives that you are a carrier.

Thus, for subjects who are found to have gene variants that are associated with increased risk of a certain disease, there is then the difficult question of what the clinical response should be. Apart from more frequent screenings, which in themselves could generate anxieties, should highly invasive medical procedures be considered to further reduce risk? For example, if a subject has a mutation in the BRCA1 and BRCA2 genes, should she undergo a mastectomy to eliminate the risk of developing breast cancer? Dr. Hsu shared his clinical observation:

> . . . once you know the results of the test, it leads to two adverse outcomes. Number one, you need to do mutilating surgery to yourself – if you have BRCA1 and BRCA2, you need to remove both breasts, both ovaries. If you're found to have FAP gene, you need to take out the entire large intestine, at the age of below twenty-five. So, we're talking about doing mutilating surgery, to people who haven't got the cancer, but they have a high-risk of getting the cancer. So you're doing mutilating surgery to young people before they even get the disease. Very hard to accept.

Consequent actions that individuals have to consider or act upon after being informed of their predisposed genetic risks are usually surgeries to remove relevant body parts where the diseases in question might develop. The effects of these surgeries are permanent, and, hence, such preventive measures require much consideration by both the doctors and individuals. Dr. Zhang wondered how doctors should advise patients on preventive measures based on genetic test results that reveal the probability of developing a particular disease:

> As for susceptibility, yes we know it predicts susceptibility but the level of prediction is still not very high. In other words, the person who has a particular mutation, the chance of them developing cancer is still not 100 percent. So,

we probably can't use that to guide us in our treatment. We can at best tell patients to be more careful and to do more frequent screenings.

Genetic testing for preventive purposes seems to have more adverse implications than benefits based on these doctors' accounts. First of all, such data are not easily comprehensible. Second, these tests only indicate the likelihood of disease but provide no definitive answers. This could potentially cause much distress for individuals, and even for family members, particularly since the germline mutations in question are heritable and would affect future generations. Lastly, there are limited measures that individuals can adopt to reduce biological risks and prevent the diseases in question. Thus, doctors generally agreed that these genetic tests in relation to preventive medicine should be done in the context of a strong family history.

Conclusion

This chapter highlights the tensions between racial and ethnic categories constructed in the contexts of global genomic science and the pharmaceutical industry, and national public health policies and practice at the clinical level. The physicians interviewed explained that these endeavors are not helpful in their daily practice of personalized medicine. The reservations from the physicians were not so much concerned with research methodologies and the deployment of racial/ethnic categories in genome science and medical research, but the usefulness of such information because there is no perfect corrleation between ethnicity and genotype. For example, even though the prevalence rate or the frequency of the EGFR mutation may be higher in the "Asian" or "Chinese" population, this does not mean that doctors do not offer genetic testing to an "Indian" or "Caucasian" patient. Indeed, they emphasized that EGFR mutation testing should be done for each lung cancer patient, irrespective of ethnic identity. This chapter lends support to what Cooper, Kaufman, and Ward (2003:1167) point out: "if you really need to know whether a patient has a particular genotype, you will have to do the test to find out."

Moreover, the applicability of such racially/ethnically framed knowledge about human genetic structure seems weakest in the case of preventive medicine, as compared to treatment decisions related to either therapeutic efficacy or toxicity. That is, even if the penetrance rate of the BRCA gene, associated with breast cancer, may be particularly high in a given population, the doctors still think that such genetic testing for disease susceptibility should only be recommended when the individual has a strong family history of suffering from the disease. There are complicating factors such as the fact that there is no consensus regarding the definition of high penetrance, the context of each disease might be different, and the percentages and/or effect size of a particular genetic variant changes as a function of shifting boundaries of ethnically and racially labeled populations. Ultimately, what the research studies and genetic tests offer are probability statements. Through genetic tests, and being informed about whether a specific mutation is present or absent, certain treatment options will be preferred, as these treatments are "probably" going to work better than others.

Genetic tests are not available for all types of mutations or all diseases. Thus, given the availability of selected tests, clinicians have to balance treatment options and discuss them with patients. If the desired treatment against one particular mutation does not work in sync with another treatment for other mutations or diseases, clinicians have to restrategize. Additionally, drugs may not have been developed to work against particular mutations. As genetic testing is becoming more prevalent in the clinical setting, and more and more genetic tests can be developed at a faster pace than drugs can be developed, clinicians may find increasing numbers of "orphan patients" without medical treatment.

Last but not least, given the limitations noted in this chapter – such as limited or lack of access to genetic tests, the immaturity of scientific research on genetics and disease causality or drug response – clinicians might still rely on existing racial/ethnic categories of patients to prescribe medicine, a practice that they criticize. To put it differently, the overwhelming consensus among the practicing clinicians interviewed is that race/ethnicity is a specious proxy for individual genotype. Given this, we need to be wary of the increasing bifurcation of the clinical care where race and ethnicity is used, unfortunately, as the poor man's genomic test. In other words, the overwhelming consensus among the practicing clinicians interviewed is that race/ethnicity is a specious proxy for individual genotype. Given this, we need to be wary of the increasing bifurcation of the clinical care where race and ethnicity is used, unfortunately, as the poor man's genomic test.

In line with this discussion, I will also suggest that this production and utilization of genetic knowledge involves an ethical dilemma, which will be further explored in the next chapter.

References

Cooper, Richard S., Jay S. Kaufman and Ryk Ward. 2003. "Race and Genomics." *New England Journal of Medicine* 348(12):1166–1169.

Jasanoff, Sheila. 2007. "Science & Politics Technologies of Humility." *Nature* 450:33. doi: 10.1038/450033a.

6 Socio-economic factors and ethical dilemmas in personalized medicine provision

"If living were a thing that money could buy, you know the rich would live, and the poor would die . . ." All My Trials (traditional folk song)

Introduction

This chapter highlights lessons learned, primarily from medical oncology, in terms of challenges and limitations of interventions at the molecular, as opposed to the environmental, level when addressing the complex disease of cancer. Interview data suggest that the unique feature of genome-based personalized medicine is that it is expensive but not curative. Given this characteristic, we focus on various ethical dilemmas of personalized medicine provision from the perspectives of physicians. For example, doctors struggle with questions of whether to recommend genetic testing and, after testing, whether to recommend certain kinds of genome-based personalized medicine. Given that socio-economic resources are finite, should a doctor provide all available information or only information as needed by the patient? This chapter describes the different ways oncologists handle these ethical dilemmas and potential challenges to their resolutions. Finally, some medical researchers and oncologists raise the question of whether personalized medicine should be the primary way to fight cancer, particularly when "estimates based on a range of scientific evidence indicate that more than 50 percent of cancers can be prevented" by interventions at the environmental level (Colditz, Wolin and Gehlert, 2012).

Genome-based personalized medicine is effective but not curative; moreover, it can be prohibitively expensive

Concerted efforts to promote personalized medicine could lead to patients and the general public having unrealistically high expectations, thinking that many previously incurable diseases could now be treated with personalized drugs. Dr. Zhang (public hospital) noted the need to manage the expectations of patients and the public:

> I think one of the things that we have to be careful [about] is the patient's expectation, the expectation of the society, of the community. There are actually very few blockbusters, very few real big breakthroughs in the last

thirty years. Things like Penicillin is one breakthrough. Beyond Penicillin . . . there's hardly any new breakthrough in medicine. Because all these new molecular [therapies], they are not curing the patient.

Oncology is the field of medicine that has seen the most extensive application of personalized medicine. However, personalized drugs rarely cure cancer – even if they have the promise and potential to prolong the lifespan of the patients by several months and perhaps also to improve quality of life during those months. Dr. Zhang said:

> Just prolonging, so in the past it's maybe from 6 to 9 months, now from 9 months to 12 months and later on from 12 months to 18 months. So it's longer. So we tell patients, say, this drug helps to . . . reduce the risk of death by one third, prolong the life by double. To patients, of course, reduce one third, very good. Double, of course it's very good but the absolute difference is actually minimal.
>
> Effective but it is not curative. We don't cure the patient. If we use this effective drug, patient live longer. The conventional chemotherapy with a lot of side effects . . . patients live shorter. The difference is probably 6–12 months . . . many more thousand dollars per month.
>
> . . . It is effective because it is targeted therapy; it only hits the cancer cells, and sparing the normal healthy cells. There [is] a lot of chemotherapy that ends with NIB or NAB. NAB is all the antibodies, all these costs probably $5000–8000 a month, this one more expensive. The outcome of patients treated with this therapy [referring to NAB] is a lot better – they live longer than patients who just received treatment using conventional, old-days chemotherapy. But, unfortunately, most of these patients are still not cured. So using all these expensive NIB and NAB, maybe they live one and a half year, two years, three years; whereas those who use the conventional therapy maybe live one year, 14 months. So there is a difference.

Indeed, Dr. Zhang went so far as to say that, if he had cancer, he would not want to undergo expensive personalized medicine treatment just for the sake of prolonging his life by a few months.

> I believe that if I have cancer, I will not want to waste my money to using such expensive (Cetuximab) chemotherapy to prolong my life for just one year. I will be happy just with conventional chemotherapy – whether type B or type C are good enough, just control my cancer and let me live 6 months longer – 1 year longer to do what I need to do.

Dr. Tang shared a similar observation that genome-based personalized medicine is not a cure:

> At this point in time, the majority of the patients, their response is not durable.

Genomic medicine, as a representation of progress and advancement in scientific knowledge, also has its limitations. A recurring theme discussed by multiple doctors is the myth that personalized medicine "cures," while, in fact, most of the time it offers only temporary relief. Moreover, doctors are voicing serious concerns about the high and growing costs of personalized medicine for cancer patients (Pfister, 2013). As Aronson (2015) explains:

> If precision medicine can distinguish patients who will benefit from a treatment from those who will not, in principle, care should become more efficient and less costly. But the converse can also be true: treatments become more expensive as the costs of development must be distributed across smaller populations.

Furthermore, while drug development and related research are costly, Pfister (2013) suggests that "what the market will bear" seems to be a central pricing consideration and priority among pharmaceutical companies. The high prices of such drugs inevitably call affordability for patients into question.

Should the cost of a cancer drug be part of the treatment decisions?

Personalized medicine is a nascent field and is at different levels of maturity for different diseases. Nonetheless, as personalized medicine represents a "new frontier," some doctors may be pressured to employ its techniques, especially in terms of ordering genetic testing, even though clinical benefits may be uncertain. Dr. Xia argued:

> We must order FoundationOne[1] for all our patients. Because we have talked about this in this meeting . . . and such [organizations] have already endorsed this, so sometimes the squeakiest wheel gets the most grease, right. But it's like advertising. . . . Do you really understand what is being said and on what basis? You have to think critically . . . and you must have the knowledge of science to actually judge and interpret yourself, whether it is all fluff, and just another way for companies to make money or it really does make an impact on your clinical practice. And *I actually suspect that there are a whole lot of clinicians that don't understand it . . . [and] therefore they are very taken, they are very easy to get swept off their feet, with brilliant pictures, full of colors . . .* [emphasis mine]

Genetic testing is currently, to some extent, a medical trend. However, looking beneath the surface, the test results might not be useful for clinical practice. As implied above, what is the relevance of a genetic test if the patient cannot afford the specific drug afterward? Dr. Zhang illustrated this point:

> Once upon a time, I told our colleague, if you have a patient who has colon cancer after operation, just to do that test, is $400. So if I think I don't want to use this drug, no need to test, don't waste my money. Now EGFR is also

very expensive. All these are expensive. But my colleagues looked at me and laughed. They said, "you are an old dinosaur. In this era, everybody must have that test." So now it becomes a standard test . . . anybody who has gone for the operation will have that test, whether you want to use that drug or not, it doesn't really matter. Some patients are so frail and weak that they didn't have the chance to take even simple chemotherapy, but they have that [genetic] test done.

Because science has moved to a new era that everybody will have that test. So that we can tell our foreign colleagues, we can tell other countries that in Singapore, we have X percent of patients who have this test done and X percent who have this positive, X patients who have [been] treated [with] this [targeted therapy]. . . . This is [a] standard test, nobody has a choice. You don't have a choice.

Indeed, even if the genetic test sheds light on a specific treatment to maximize patient outcomes, such results are of no value if the patients cannot afford the specific drugs. However, genetic tests are still often advised, or may even be binding, as the first step forward in cancer treatment. Patients sometimes unknowingly have their choices restricted by a medical trend that has increasingly engulfed their trusted doctors. Dr. Zhang pointed out:

A good example is . . . a patient being offered a treatment that cost $6000 a month. Now, this patient is a recent migrant; she didn't have much of savings. This is a tailored personalized treatment because the cancer has a certain mutation that can be treated with this new drug. . . . But this patient cannot afford [it]. Are you going to tell her, "sorry, we have a medicine but since you can't afford [it], we can't treat you"? [pause] On the other hand, we also have other drugs for this kind of cancer. The result is not as good as the new molecular targeted therapy, which cost[s] $6000 a month. Our standard, basic chemotherapy for these patients probably cost[s] about $1500/$1200 per cycle or for a month. In terms of outcome, yes, the targeted therapy has less side effects, they live a little bit longer. The cheaper therapy . . . more side effects and the survival is a little bit shorter. But [considering a] patient's [difficult] social and financial situation, probably the basic old treatment is more applicable. But because of the emphasis and the need to brand our targeted personalized therapy, patients were very often given only one choice [of the $6000 a month treatment].

Having said that, while the "new norm" in cancer treatment may be to order genetic tests and to prescribe genome-based therapies, doctors also pointed out that most genetic tests are not mandatory. In principle, doctors and patients have the liberty to decide whether to perform genetic testing, as Drs. Xia and Hsu pointed out:

DR. XIA (PRIVATE CLINIC): Testing for BRCA mutation in a patient with breast cancer is not a problem. You know that, of course, patient herself, make the decision as to whether she wants to test it or not.

DR. HSU (PRIVATE CLINIC): So for the tumor profiling, in fact, all the profiling the patient will pay, insurance company will pay, and they are not very expensive because each test of the tumor profiling is about a few hundred dollars. They are only specific, commercially-provided tests, the Oncotype DX, these two tests, one for breast, one for colon, they cost about four thousand dollars each. That one is quite hefty, I'm not sure whether all insurance [companies] will pay. But for the other tests, which are only two hundred dollars, three hundred dollars, the patient will pay out of pocket without difficulty. So the payment is not much an issue, therefore adoption is widespread, because the data is very important to the therapeutic, and the cost is only two three hundred dollars, most patients are willing to do the test.

In other words, compared to the therapeutic (drug) aspect of personalized medicine, the diagnostic (genetic testing) aspect may appear less costly and is probably not much of an issue for patients who can afford private health care in the first place.

However, for poorer patients, a genetic test costing hundreds or even thousands of dollars is still a significant financial burden, as Dr. Xie noted:

Some patients [would say] . . . if you are telling me that . . . I should get this drug, but only if this test is positive, but I can't afford the drug, so why waste my time? I'm not going to have the test. The test itself is expensive.

Similarly, Dr. Hsu was concerned about the accumulated costs, and he added the problem of "orphan patients":

Even a research assistant can find a new gene, you know, very easy to find, and very easy to translate that into a test. The cost is very low. The genomic testing nowadays, molecular or immunohistochemistry, very easy to do. So, truly, the laboratory advances, there is no barrier, there is no barrier, they can move very fast. Every few months you have a new gene that comes out, and, nowadays, all the clinical trials store specimen, so they're able to go back to the archive to take out a specimen to test, so they can correlate between what is in the lab, and what is in the specimen. So, this movement is very quick.

The problem is, who is going to pay for all these additional tests? Each test is about three four hundred dollars, so to put things in perspective – previously, we do KRAS number 2, now we know there's KRAS 3 and 4. And then now we do NRAS 2,3,4. So, in other words, previously we do one test, which cost two hundred and twenty-five dollars. Now there are six tests. That becomes a thousand plus dollars. And if we see this we're not happy, we can do the BRAF, which is 11 and 15. So there are eight tests to do. So this rapid explosion, there's no limit for it, because people feel that being able to be more targeted allows less wastage of drugs. So as a result of that, there is insatiable desire to keep taking out [a] new gene, and try to narrow [it] down. But this makes therapeutic[s] a bit complicated, because for those groups of patients that don't fulfill the very narrow group, what do you treat them with? So, more and more patients are excluded from drugs which previously they would receive. So the complexity of such an approach is that, number one, a lot of costs will go into the testing; number two, some delay, in terms of treatment; number three, more and more people are disqualified, from treatment, because the treatment is becoming more and more targeted, you see. So you have a lot of orphan patient. Orphan without parents right? So orphan patient. Because there [is] no drug to treat them, because oh, by this criteria, excluded, by this criteria, excluded. By the time you split everything, all the good drugs cannot be used anymore.

In the context of limited economic resources (such as public hospitals), oncologists sometimes assess the financial background of their patients and recommend treatment that is affordable rather than the most cutting edge. This is partly to save patients and their families from having to confront face-to-face the morally difficult question of how much an extra few months of life are worth. Dr. Zhang pointed out:

Here, when I see a patient in [a] public hospital, we don't tell them "look, this drug is $10,000. You can have Drug A. Or, otherwise, you can choose Drug B, $3000. Or, you can have Drug C at $1000." If I say this in front of patient's children, "Here are 3 drugs for your mother, you can have $10000, $5000, $1000, which one do you want?" How do you expect the daughter to answer this question?

So here, we roughly assess and look at the patient's and family's financial background, and we make our own decision: "look, I think that 6 months extra life is not worth putting in all this money. Don't sell your house. Don't borrow money from relatives." If I think using this drug is good enough, I will treat this patient with this drug and I will not escalate . . . if necessary, we will keep it around that level.

In Singapore, the Standard Drug List (SDL) is based on the World Health Organization's (WHO) Essential Drug List, but is ultimately determined by the Drug Advisory Committee (DAC) and MOH (Ministry of Health, 2011). As Appendix E indicates, in Singapore, many of the PM drugs are not on the Ministry of Health's Standard Drug List and hence not subsidized by the government. The SDL has been split into two components, SDL I and SDL II (Khalik, 2011). The former covers an array of cheaper generic drugs, while the latter covers *some* more expensive targeted and branded therapies (Khalik, 2011). The SDL lists, I and II, appear to be collectively compiled on the MOH website (Ministry of Health, 2015). The state's decision to publish this list is relatively new as well. As recently as 2011, in Singapore's Parliament, the Worker's Party (WP) asked if the SDL was public record, as even health care professionals appeared unsure of what drugs were actually on the lists (Ministry of Health, 2011). The state's justification for not publishing them, as was reported in Today Online, rested in the fear that "Big Pharmacy" would exploit the lists and lobby for their products to be included (Lim, 2013).

Drugs on the SDL II list are subsidized at a rate between 50 and 75 percent of their retail cost (Ministry of Health, 2012). To qualify for the higher 75 percent subsidy, however, patients must come from a low-income family, earning no more than a monthly SGD$1,500 household per capita income (Ministry of Health, 2012). Of the 18 personalized drugs listed in HSA's database, only two are on the SDL. They are trastuzumab (known as Herceptin) and letrozole (known as Femara) (Ministry of Health, 2015). The remaining 16 drugs, however, may be covered under the Medication Assistant Fund (MAF). The MAF subsidizes expensive drugs that have not been included on the SDL, but are deemed necessary to treat patients (Ministry of Health, 2012). Indeed, in response to a query made concerning the availability and cost of afatinib, a personalized drug used to treat non-small-cell lung cancer with an EGFR mutation, the National Cancer Centre noted that, though the drug is not currently on the SDL, the MAF could be extended to cover it (Toh, 2014).

Even with state subsidies, however, doctors interviewed pointed out that for patients who are of fewer means and who are also not covered by private health insurance, personalized medicine drugs are simply out of reach, or they would involve depleting savings, borrowing, or selling property to raise funds. Dr. Xie pointed out that:

> [I]n this economy . . . everyone is a paying patient, the cost of health-care is quite an issue that we don't tend to consider, in terms of genomic medicine – even if the patient has got [an] EGFR mutation, and you say that look you've got to spend $3000 a month, to pay for this drug, and you got 18 months of expectancy, it means that you survive for 18 months versus six months, the guy might say, okay, so for the extra year, I'm [going to] spend a heck of a lot of money for something that is ultimately going to kill me. So why don't I save the money and give it to my kids for their education? Okay, so there's, at the end of the day itself, there is the opportunity cost as well, for individual patients. And, in the end, it is beyond genetics, it is also a social issue, alright? Socio-economic issues. I mean the guy who can afford anything, it doesn't matter what they're doing, $3000 a month is like a job promotion, but for the average uncle, he can't afford to pay for his rent. . . . I am sorry, your genetic test or not, I am still not being able to afford my treatment.
>
> But, the other question is . . . an overall survival benefit is not that huge . . . so the question is how much are you willing to pay for an extra year of life? How much are you willing to pay for extra two years of life? [I]t looks like in the country where there is no national health service, health provision is primarily provided by patients, then it very much depends on whether you

have insurance or not. If you don't have insurance, then unfortunately that a lot of these things are beyond your means.

The accessibility of PM drugs being closely linked to socio-economic circumstances can be especially disturbing in cases where the PM drug is the only treatment option available, as Dr. Teo described:

> [I]f a cancer patient comes to us; we don't want to deny care to them. So [you] can imagine a person with liver cancer, and he lives in a two room flat, Jurong West, and he's a low cost labourer, for example, and he has liver cancer. And [the doctors] say "Uncle, it's going to cost you $8000 a month to get sorafenib." You know what I mean? It's crazy. And that's the only approved drug for liver cancer.

Doctors have found themselves caught in a dilemma. On the one hand, they feel compelled to prescribe genomic medicine as it is deemed as the "new norm" of medical advancement. On the other hand, they have to confront situations in which patients are unable to afford the cost of such medical acceleration.

As oncologists grapple with the issue of whether to order genetic testing and prescribe genomic medicine for the general public, they have pointed out the necessity of opening up a difficult discussion regarding priorities in allocating finite resources for public health care deliveries. More specifically, this entails intensive deliberations on moral and social dilemmas. When asked to allocate limited resources (thus involving valuing one population group over the other), doctors found themselves torn between making a financially sensible decision or an emotional one. Dr. Zhang asked:

> How do I tell patients that the difference is about a year, or a year plus and do you think this is affordable? If I have money, I pay $8000 a month and I live 3 years. If I can't afford, I use cheap chemotherapy, I live 1.5 years. The patient says how can you measure lifespan, human's life with money? That's why, last week, there was a complaint letter in *Straits Times* column about patients. The starting statement is "My mother is 84 years old" and the last statement is: "This drug cost $4500 a month, how come [the] government doesn't subsidize [it]?"[2] You are the tax payer, you [have got to] ask do I want to use my money to subsidize the care of a patient at 84 years old, who has an incurable cancer using something [for] $4500 a month? Can I use this money to help children get better nutrition and education?

Although uncomfortable, an open discussion and debate regarding the priorities of allocating public resources is vital in answering important questions: who are the stakeholders, and how are they affected? It appears that, in response to these questions, one is made aware that eventually the cost may have to be passed on to the citizens, either in terms of higher insurance premiums or higher taxes. With this awareness of sharing costs, what other repercussions will arise? Dr. Zhang answered "wastage":

> So in America, everybody gets Cetuximab upfront. Anybody [who is a colon cancer patient] who has Kras wildtype will get Cetuximab upfront. Here, I do not give Cetuximab. We use conventional chemotherapy. In [a] private hospital, in [the] U.S., everyone gets Cetuximab upfront. Here, no. So if you have money/savings, that's fine, carry on. But if [the] health insurance [company] knows that everybody who has colon cancer gets Cetuximab, next time they will jack up the premium for everyone. So in the U.S., everyone is paying $400–800 a month for health insurance. . . . But if I buy health insurance, am I going to spend money on [a] premium to subsidize other people so that they can get Cetuximab – something that I myself will not want to waste my money on? [pause] And if [the] government steps in and say that we will fund everyone, then my income tax will be used to pay for other people's Cetuximab treatment when I myself will not want. And when you go into health insurance and government full subsidy, it is okay if you use the money to pay for effective treatments wisely. But the trouble is that once you get into that mode, people become very wasteful. . . . [E]verything I want, I bring home first, whether I use it or not, never mind . . . since it is free. So if everybody takes everything, premiums have to go up and taxes have to go up.

Nonetheless, doctors have noted the health care expenditures borne by patients are disproportionately high in Singapore compared to other jurisdictions in Asia at a comparable stage of economic development, such as Hong Kong and Taiwan. Dr. Teo said:

> I think there is still a lot of out of pocket payment for patients. . . . I just came back from Hong Kong and a Singaporean spends 58 cents of every dollar on healthcare . . . and that includes Medisave. In Hong Kong, it is less than 10 cents. If I am not wrong, it is about 10 cents. Can you imagine? A Hong Kong citizen who falls sick only spends 10 cents for every dollar of healthcare. But here they spend 58 cents. I think the government knows that and is rolling out more and more healthcare subsidies for this year's budget. But we felt that for the longest time, it was just too low. Some of us see it that way. And . . . in Taiwan, it is national health insurance.

Doctors pointed out that Singapore government policies restricting the use of Medisave to cover expenses for genetic testing and counseling are obstacles to using PM not only in therapeutics but also in preventive medicine. For instance, if a patient tests positive for a gene variant that predisposes him or her to a particular type of cancer, then the patient would need regular screening (such as MRIs) to monitor whether he or she actually develops the cancer. Such preventive screening, however, cannot be reimbursed under Medisave. Therefore, for a patient with an average income, this begs the question of, what is the true purpose of developing or bringing in PM when the patient's hands are tied by the steep cost of treatment and the inability to get any subsidies for it? Dr. Liang (public hospital) asked:

> If [the] government sends me for this test, and I can prevent these illnesses, why can't I pay Medisave for it? These questions will come, you see? . . . . [T]hen the next thing is that now that I have the test done, when I go and consult a geneticist, do I get subsidies when I consult?

The issue of state subsidies also surfaces in the area of recommending genetic testing as a preventive measure. Chieng and Lee (2006) note that, since 2003, patients could qualify for a 100 percent subsidy for the BRCA1/2 mutation screening if they were clinically deemed to have a 30 percent chance of having the mutation. But the extent to which state subsidies cover other types of predictive genetic testing is not clear. As Dr. Neo (public hospital) pointed out:

> We have no insurance reimbursement, we have no Medisave revenue; let's say we have a mutation, and you need time to [have an MRI screening]. . . . So, if you can imagine, if I talk to a patient, and I tell them, based on your family history, you have a very high chance of having a mutation. I am going to offer you screening. Screening is $4000. It has to come out of your pocket. And sometimes, they will think about it and they will say okay, fine, because of my family history, I would like to know. They do the testing but even if they're positive, subsequent to that, there is still no reimbursement for the screening measures to keep them free from disease. So that's something that I am hoping to change.

In summary, several challenges were raised in discussing the cost of prevention and treatment using PM. First, the introduction of PM left doctors running on a medical treadmill. Yet, this cutting-edge development (i.e. genetic testing) is limited in both long-term benefits and value, particularly for patients unable to afford follow-up genomic therapies. Doctors thus found themselves caught in a difficult situation: since a reasonable conclusion would be that adoption of such genomic medicine corresponds to economic resources, should they even create the awareness of the availability of costly drugs for lower income patients? Eventually, we may observe a scenario in which PM serves only a small, privileged group of people who can afford it. Second, the adoption of PM inevitably implicates a wider population beyond the patients and their family members. Ideally, insurance and/or government subsidies should assist in making PM affordable for those in need. Realistically, such practices will encounter an uphill battle in convincing the general public to contribute higher premiums/taxes, particularly when the pricing of PM is unlikely to come down in the near future. Ultimately, we may see that the high costs of PM may serve as a negative factor in effectively (re)distributing health care resources.

Who should be expected to interpret genetic tests when cancer is a "context-dependent manifestation"?

In addition to the matter of high costs of personalized medicine, there is also marked concern about knowledge gaps. That is, the question arises of whether doctors are sufficiently knowledgeable about genetics to be able to competently interpret test results in order to inform their clinical decisions. Dr. Xia described this situation as follows:

> I think that a lot of clinicians, not that I'm trying [to make them look good] or to blacken their names. But I think they don't truly understand the science behind all [this] molecular testing. They take a lot on trust. What I kind of fear, is the formulation of treatment recommendations, that [are] based on what their scientist friends tell them. You know what I mean? Because they may not have the capacity to actually delve into the scientific data and to truly understand, what it all means but rather they are taking it on the basis or on the recommendation of their scientist colleagues. I actually fear that.
>
> [T]his edges upon the age old thing about how much of a clinician should you be and how much of a scientist should you be. Of course, in an ideal world, you understand everything, but that's not the case. *In reality, there are actually a lot of clinicians who don't understand the scientific basis of a lot of the stuff.*

Existing studies have found that nongeneticist physicians are not well equipped with the knowledge to interpret complex clinical sequencing reports and communicate results to patients (for example, see McGowan et al., 2014). This observation is likely to be relevant to Singapore's context due to the very nature of medical specialization. Dr. Liang, who specializes in palliative care and does not practice in the field of oncology, admitted that he does not have in-depth knowledge about genetics:

> Honestly, sometimes the doctors themselves do not know the exact information. Just ask me about [the] BRCA gene, I really don't know very much about it. I know it is a source of cancer but I can't tell you what is the probability, and I can't tell you what are the other factors that may affect it. . . . So, it becomes more and more difficult for the doctor to have that amount of knowledge with them.

Due to the hype about personalized medicine and the enormous amount of information available on the Internet, better educated patients could investigate on their own. They could ask their doctors questions that the latter may not have up-to-date knowledge of to answer competently. This could put doctors in a dilemma: appear ignorant in front of patients or risk providing incomplete or inaccurate information. This concern was addressed in a candid manner by Dr. Liang:

> For example, if let's say you have an interest in [the] BRCA gene, after reading an article, you may have read up more. But let's say I am working with the elderly, I don't care about [BRCA] genes, then suddenly if you ask me, I really

don't know. I must go and check. . . . And sometimes, the doctor can be caught unaware about some things and doctors don't like to look stupid, that they don't know about it. . . . And that's the danger because it's better to say I don't know than to say something that you think is right but actually you are wrong, without knowing it. And the patient thinks that you told them the right thing.

Since most physicians receive limited training in genetics, could the knowledge gap be filled by genetic counselors? Dr. Liang expressed reservations about this idea because genetic counselors, who are not trained as physicians, would not have sufficient knowledge about different medical conditions:

The problem with genetic counselors is that they can only counsel from a very statistical viewpoint. They don't know the disease, they cannot know so many diseases. It's like I can advise you on elderly-related diseases, even if it is genetic. [But] I cannot advise you on pediatrics conditions. I cannot advise you on cancers. So very much it is still the expertise of the individual groups, I can't see a geneticist, knowing all the conditions. He may know in terms of understanding from the probability perspective, what it means and the risks of inheritance. That, the geneticist will be quite good at. So, it's a bit complex.

To further complicate matters, personalized medicine is developing at a rapid pace with new drugs and new diagnostics being regularly launched by pharmaceutical companies. It is difficult for doctors to individually digest the plethora of information (including clinical research findings) about these products and then to decide which ones should be applied in a clinical setting. Dr. Liang suggested that greater professional support from within the medical community would be helpful in bridging the knowledge gaps of individual doctors:

To my mind, there should be some panel of experts to advise. So, I would expect, say, in Singapore, the Chapter of Oncologists. [Which] will then advise what drugs might be suitable for what, and give their position statements. . . . These are [also] international guidelines. This cancer should be treated this way. I am following the guidelines. It's when I veer away from the guidelines, I got to justify. . . . So that's helpful because there's some international experts coming to say this is the way to go, then the doctor won't be faulted.

The logical conclusion from the above discussion seems to be that there is an urgent need to incorporate genomics into the training of new doctors as well as into the curriculum of medical education. In response to this need, medical schools are starting to address personalized medicine, in particular pharmacogenomics, in their curricula (Cornetta and Brown, 2013). However, as Dr. Wee pointed out, cancers are "context-dependent manifestations," and scientists need to know that genetics is not everything:

I suspect that the medical school kind of training that we go through, is often not geared towards equipping us to interpret genetics results. So I guess then there may be people who sub-specialise, become medical geneticists, perhaps certain not so straightforward types of results and interpretations will need to be handled by the medical geneticists. But on the other hand it is true that . . . the scientist needs to probably also appreciate the other side of the world, [which] is that genetic[s] is not destiny. It is not destiny because there are always modifiers. . . . That's why I start off by defining what is penetrance, it is the probability of getting the disease given the genotype. So this probability can be, is a continuous scale, can be 0 to 100. And it is very rarely at the extremes, it is often somewhere in the middle and there are modifiers. We have known of people who have mutations – you thought sure to have certain [disease] conditions but they don't have. I mean, there is context dependent manifestations.

(The Swiss Academy of Medical Sciences (SAMS), 2012:7)

In short, due to medical specialization, physicians normally lack the breadth and depth in genomics whereas genetic counselors lack sufficient knowledge of various medical conditions.

Direct-to-consumer genetic testing

To further complicate the issue of knowledge gaps and correct readings of genetic testing results, there are now many commercial offerings of genetic testing for clinical purposes. Many of these are widely publicized. Questions have been raised about the benefits of such testing, especially direct-to-consumer (DTC) testing. DTC testing refers to genomic analyses that are marketed directly to consumers without involving health care professionals. Such tests usually claim to identify an increased or decreased risk of certain diseases. Regulators and medical professionals are critical of DTC testing. For instance, the Swiss Academy of Medical Sciences (SAMS, 2012:7) expresses strong criticisms:

The availability of "predictive" tests of this kind *is apt to discredit PM in its entirety.* Such genetic tests are offered on a direct-to-consumer (DTC) basis by well-known companies, operating internationally. . . . The real problem revealed by these unscientific offerings is that, in the PM sector, a market has become established which cannot be controlled or regulated. In Switzerland, DTC tests of this kind – not ordered by a physician – are essentially prohibited. . . . [H]owever, prohibitions are of little use, as they are so easy to circumvent in a globalized world. . . . A number of national and international professional bodies have already adopted clear positions, issuing warnings about these services [emphasis mine].

Dr. Liang expressed similar objections:

There are companies, internationally, that do that [offering DTC testing]. They send your blood, they come and tell you you have this, this, this, this, this. Your risk is this, this, this, this, this. Okay? Should that be done or not?

Should the public be given that or not? Should the public have access to all their own information or not? So that's now a new challenge. . . . Recently, [the] FDA, just a few months ago, ordered one of their companies, . . . to stop offering those free cheap kits for genetic testing. . . .

What Dr. Liang was referring to was the US FDA ruling, in November 2013, that a company called 23andMe stop selling its DTC product "The Saliva Collection Kit and Personal Genome Service" until it obtained FDA "marketing clearance or approval."

One of the key concerns with DTC testing is that, without the advice of medical professionals, the general public is not equipped with sufficient knowledge about medicine and genetics to be able to comprehend the implications of the test results. Dr. Liang, who was comfortable undergoing one of these DTC tests himself because he was knowledgeable about it, cautioned that it would create anxiety for a layperson:

> So I sent in a kit to them, they sent it back, I just went to [the] website . . . they tell me that, I have a higher risk of these kinds of conditions. . . . Some I already know, so it's okay. . . . And based on probability, they say these are my risks. They also try to explain why, what's the background behind these risks. Because I think I am knowledgeable enough, I am not worried about what I see. Some things they say I'm at risk, but I am not worried, no big deal, can wait and see. . . . But a lay person sees it, what happens? [Interviewer: He brings to the doctor.] Correct. Then the doctor also doesn't know what's happening, or the doctor might know. [In any case] [h]e creates a lot of anxiety and problems as well.

Scientists and medical professionals have "expressed concern about the inability of many patients with cancer to adequately comprehend the purposes and complexities of pharmacogenomics testing, especially the potential psychosocial implications of germline and somatic genetic testing" (McGowan et al., 2014:189). Dr. Liang pointed out, in particular, that the public, in general, does not understand that genetic testing merely reveals a probabilistic indication of disease likelihood. He felt that the story of the actress Angelina Jolie undergoing a mastectomy because she had the BRCA gene mutation presented an overly deterministic message about genetic testing:

> It's a probability thing. And this is where it can be very complicated because if a patient goes for genetic testing, he is likely to want to know an answer that is yes or no. Will I get cancer or not? But the doctor actually says you have a higher chance of getting cancer. Does it mean you will? Even Angelina Jolie – doesn't mean she will get breast cancer. She has a very high chance, that's all. There is a chance that she might not even get it. You know, but the public, some of them don't understand this thing about probability and chances. . . . So the problem is the message to the general public is that you

got this gene, you better go and get your breasts operated. And commercial people . . . plastic surgeons . . . will be very keen.

The same concern of lack of genetic counseling was expressed by the SAMS (2012:7):

> Some DTC services are certainly valid, such as the detection of mutations in genetic disorders with a dominant or recessive pattern of inheritance (e.g. Huntington's chorea). But users receive the results in a direct, unfiltered form, without the necessary additional information or appropriate counselling. This practice cannot legitimately be defended by invoking people's . . . right of freedom to obtain information. In fact, what is involved is an ethically unacceptable omission, since the "information" in question concerns complex medical matters which require careful interpretation.

Indeed, even for genetic testing that has to be ordered through doctors, the same question of benefits has to be raised. While such costly testing will reveal a whole wealth of information about mutations present in the patient, the information itself does not indicate any treatment. As noted by Dr. Xia:

> Actually there are plenty of companies that will offer to investigate your tumor and they will interrogate like a whole genome worth of mutations. . . . You pay a lot of money. You pay a lot of money for information that is for what? I mean what is the purpose? I mean there isn't a matching treatment to go with that particular mutation. Then what is the point?

Many companies offering genetic testing may be based overseas and not subject to the regulation of local health authorities. According to Dr. Liang, there are also potential concerns about the quality of their services:

> And the first question would be, how reliable is that data? It is also between the different labs, is there good correlation, how do I know if this company offering this test is doing it the right way? . . . But suppose you send your blood overseas to do a test, Singapore government cannot be responsible for that. Do we assume that if you send anywhere in the world you will be okay or not? What are the standards there? How do we know that that particular company in their own country has actually been regulated well?

Commercially available genetic tests fall into two different categories. The first category (i.e. direct to consumer genetic testing) may not only be the result of an uncontrollable or unregulated market but could induce unnecessary anxiety in patients due to the lack of an expert opinion on the implications of disease risk. Issues with the second category (i.e. genetics tests ordered through doctors) may sometimes overlap with the first. First, the lack of corresponding treatments puts the utility of having the genetic test in question, and, second, there is an absence of quality assurance due to the lack of stringent validation by local health authorities.

Privacy concerns and the potential for genetic discrimination at the level of the individual and the group

Patient confidentiality is a key pillar of ethics in medical practice. The professional ethics mean that health care providers are required to keep a patient's personal health information private unless the patient consents to releasing it to other parties. Information obtained from genetic testing is part of a patient's personal health information and its confidentiality should be protected. However, germline mutation is inheritable, and, hence, such information has implications for not just the patient being tested but individuals who are biologically related to him or her. If the test reveals that the patient carries a gene variant that predisposes him or her to a certain disease, should the information also be made known to the biological relatives so that they might consider undergoing genetic testing themselves? Dr. Koh explained this ethical dilemma as such:

> [W]hen that data becomes available, who should have access to it? . . . right now, only the individuals have access to it, because of privacy issues, only the individual has access to it, but, someone may make the case that family should have access to it, because the families could be involved, right? The families, as in biological families, who are related to that individual, cause they could have inherited the same mutation, if it's an inheritable mutation. So those things are all very . . . very tricky, in terms of who should have access to this kind of data.

In the case of communicable diseases, there are public interest grounds for limited disclosure of a patient's information without his or her consent to prevent the spread of the disease. Should the same principle apply with regard to genetic information? Dr. Liang was uncertain about this:

> [E]ven communicable diseases, in many places, even that information is also protected; in Singapore, the protection is a little bit less, and there's more skewed toward protecting the public, but nevertheless, it's along that line of spectrum, . . . I mean, predisposition doesn't necessarily have to do with sort of public health issues, but it can affect other individuals.

On the other hand, there is the "right not to know" argument. There are individuals who prefer not to know whether they are predisposed to certain diseases, so that they do not have to live with anxiety for the rest of their lives. If an individual chooses to undergo genetic testing for a germline mutation, and the test results have implications for his or her relatives, should the relatives be consulted and be provided with genetic counseling as well? Dr. Chong explained that ultimately the patient's autonomy should be respected:

> [At] the end of the day it's patients' autonomy. They may not want to know. Okay, my mum's got [the] BRCA mutation, I don't want to know, I don't want to mastectomise myself, I don't want to remove my breasts, I want to live my life happy. If I get breast cancer, so be it, I die. I don't want to live under this cloud, I don't want to live under this cloud of going around without what I deem to be an important part of my body. It is legitimate. So to me, at the end of the day, there is a completely private dimension to this, but unfortunately, the private clashes with [the] commercial, with the reimbursement, with payment. That's when all the conflict starts.

A further complication to the issue of "right not to know" is that of what is termed "incidental (unintended) findings." For example, an apparently healthy subject has his or her DNA tested as part of a GWAS, but the test reveals that he or she possesses a genotype that is associated with elevated risk of developing a completely different disease. Should the information be revealed to the subject? Dr. Wu explained the moral dilemma:

> [W]hen you do a larger, broader panel, you may find things that you didn't expect to find. . . . [W]e may find a genetic germline syndrome that's not expected – these are the incidental findings. The incidental findings like you see someone, who's old, and has got breast cancer, you wouldn't have suspected it, but then you've picked it up incidentally because it's part of your genetic testing panel that you do, either in a research setting or in a clinical practice setting. And how do you handle that. I think there needs to be certain frameworks and guidelines that are out there. . . . Cause there are many extremes [positions] that're taken, there're ethical views that [if] this is done in a research setting, you do not need to inform the patient, and also you're not sure whether your result is right, or wrong, and you may cause unnecessary anxiety. There is also the ethical counterpart which says that because you're doing it in a research setting, but you have a possibility that the patient has got a particular genetic syndrome, you are obliged to inform the patient of that possibility.

Dr. Chong's point above about "private clashes with [the] commercial" brings us to the issue of genetic discrimination, a situation in which an individual is treated less favorably than others because of an apparent or perceived genetic variation from the normal human genotype. Areas with high likelihood of genetic discrimination are employment and insurance.

Most importantly, potential discrimination can be exercised not only against the individual, but also against racialized groups. As Dr. Chong wisely pointed out:

INTERVIEWER: [I]n the clinical trials, sometimes the patients sign away their rights. . . . [D]o they know what they sign away?

DR. CHONG: When the trials are being crafted up, the Ethics Board will say you must have all these security measures to make sure the data is kept intact and everything, but you see, what happens is, like what you mentioned, we do the trial in Singapore, and suddenly we find that a lot of "Indians" happen to have this gene, that predisposes them to a certain cancer at a very young age, then what have we done? We say, no we've done good, we will now screen Indians at [an] earlier age for this cancer, and all that, but we may also open the Pandora's box! Employers may say that, if you're Indian, before we employ you, go for this genetic test. On the one hand we have raised the awareness, we look after their health, on the other hand, we have also made them a possible target for prejudice and stigmatization. So is it a benefit, is it a risk?

In the scenario that Dr. Chong sketched, employers may decide to make genetic screening mandatory for all potential "Indian" employees. Moreover, it is not unreasonable to hypothesize that the "Indians" who refuse to get tested, and those who get tested and happen to carry that gene, will automatically be denied the employment opportunity. Yet, this gene can be present in individuals from other ethnic groups, even if it is statistically less likely. Moreover, as articulated by PuruShotam (1998), "who is an Indian" is already a problem to begin with. Similarly, Leong (1997:86) puts it this way to explain the official labeling and simplification of ethnic categories:

> The CMIO categories were convenient labels for bureaucratic functions of form-filling and rational administration, but the British recognised much finer distinctions in census surveys. In the census of 1881, forty-seven ethnic groups were named; these increased to fifty-six in the 1921 census (PuruShotam, 2000). The reduction of ethnicity to four categories and the use of these narrow classifications in official policy began when Singapore was granted sovereign and independent status on 9 August 1965.

The "Indians" today were comprised of Bengalis, Dogras, Gujeratis, Mharattis, Marwaris, and so on during the colonial period. Even then, the elaborate list of ethnic categories was itself socially constructed (PuruShotam, 1998).

Dr. Chong painted a worrying possibility that might materialize with advancements in genetics research:

> I think we will come to a point in the future, I don't know when, especially if the GWAS data for healthy people becomes very robust, for certain cancers, common cancers, insurance, employers, may even ask you to go for a test, before you are hired or enrolled onto an insurance plan. Heaven forbid that, but there's still a point that I can't rule out.
>
> . . . [I]f you genotype cancer patient[s] and you find that it's something potentially transmissible, in terms of genetics, to the next generation, then

that would actually be causing a lot of problems for your kids, your siblings, because, again, insurance may wise up to the fact and ask, [have you had this test done]? Maybe they'll say all policy buyers have to go for [a] BRCA test first, or you'll be loaded.

[T]his is where people's personal agenda, and business clash. If this was just a matter about you knowing whether or not you have the gene, and therefore your risk of your siblings and your children having the gene, then it's just that. But it's now tying in with the economics of healthcare – who pays? Third party pays, [but] third party doesn't want to pay, third party wants to carefully select who they insure – they only want to insure the best that they can insure so it's free money to them. So this is why the collision happens, right?

It is a personal thing, the collision only happens when it ties in with reimbursement or remuneration, in the sense of if your mother has BRCA, and now, you are going to be hired by a multi-national corporation, are you supposed to declare that? Because if you develop breast cancer due to the BRCA from your mum, the multinational company is off the hook for your bill.

Some countries have put in place legislation to prevent genetic discrimination. The United States enacted the Genetic Information Nondiscrimination Act (GINA) in 2008. The GINA prohibits health insurers from requesting genetic information from an individual or from the individual's family members and from using this information to make decisions regarding coverage, rates, or preexisting conditions. The GINA also prohibits most employers from using genetic information for hiring, firing, promotion, or making employment decisions. However, GINA's nondiscrimination protections do not extend to life insurance, disability insurance, or long-term care insurance (U.S. Department of Health and Human Services, 2009). It should also be noted that this legislation does not completely eliminate concerns about discrimination – patients in the United States are still worried about sharing their genetic information with their employers and insurance companies despite the GINA (McGowan, 2014).

A cursory review of application forms for health or life insurance in Singapore suggests that the insured are required to declare details of genetics test results that suggest predispositions for disease. Since insurance companies are in the business of pricing risks, it is likely that someone who declared that she has a BRCA mutation will be charged a higher premium or have breast cancer excluded from coverage. Below are examples of clauses found in application forms:

Have any of your immediate family members (parents or siblings only) suffered from cancer of any form or any known *hereditary disease or disorder*? [emphasis added]

Any other ailment, impairment, Bodily Injury, Accident, condition(s), *medical investigations*, or Hospital treatments not mentioned above? [emphasis added]

I/We are aware and acknowledge that the *failure to provide all relevant details* in each of the Sections of this Application Form may prejudice any claim(s) that may be made by Me/Us in the future. [emphasis added]

It soon becomes clear that this awareness of disease predisposition may entail discriminatory practices in society, specifically in terms of purchasing insurance or getting a job. In view of this, should one be open about results when such personal data can potentially be used against oneself?

Should genome-based pharmaceuticals be the primary approach to treating cancer?

In 2014, Dr. Christopher Wild, Director of the International Agency of Research on Cancer (IARC), pointed out that "despite exciting advances . . . we cannot treat our way out of the cancer problem." According to Anand et al. (2008):

> Only 5–10 percent of all cancer cases can be attributed to genetic defects, whereas the remaining 90–95 percent have their roots in the environment and lifestyle. The lifestyle factors include cigarette smoking, diet (fried foods, red meat), alcohol, sun exposure, environmental pollutants, infections, stress, obesity, and physical inactivity. The evidence indicates that of all cancer-related deaths, almost 25–30 percent are due to tobacco, as many as 30–35 percent are linked to diet, about 15–20 percent are due to infections, and the remaining percentage are due to other factors like radiation, stress, physical activity, environmental pollutants etc.

However, despite the understanding that cancer is a product of both genetics and the environment, it seems that the idea of "personalized medicine" is almost synonymous with genome-based pharmaceutical products, with significantly much less emphasis on environmental causes and prevention, and some doctors are voicing their concerns, including Dr. Neo:

> So Polaris[3] is happening . . . again they are taking the approach for more common stuff . . . yes I agree with the overall approach that we need to raise the infrastructure so that when we find out what mutation it is, patients can have targeted therapy. But my question is these are all patients with developed cancers, stage three, stage four. . . . I am saying that it is equally important, Polaris attends to the group where there is genetic predisposition to cancer, whether the pediatric group, or the adult population.

Indeed, identifying environmental risk factors is important, as research has shown that more than 50 percent of cancers can actually be prevented. At the same time, such environmental interventions also bear more extensive benefits than cancer drugs, as they not only improve quality of life but also target a broad spectrum of cancers and chronic diseases rather than just a specific organ (Colditz, Wolin, and Gehlert, 2012; Sze, 2010). Yet, several push and pull factors have contributed to the current trend of focusing on genetics and treatment over environment and prevention. One significant factor is the potential financial gain that pharmaceutical products can bring. Dr. Soh argued:

> [Pharmaceutical companies] will naturally design drugs, to run the trials in a population where they are going to make money. That's all, they are a private company.

At the same time, the uphill task in isolating environmental sources may serve as a deterrent to research in this area. For instance, gathering DNA data is seen as relatively easy, while the environment is perceived as constantly in flux, and epidemiological studies require large databases of personal information, as Drs. Xie and Wee pointed out:

DR. XIE: The environment is actively changing . . . the PSI [Pollutants Standard Index], tomorrow, you know . . . again, different.

DR. WEE: Our genes are the same from the day one we are born . . . it's actually [an] easy task to measure the gene, the genetic information. But environment. Today I drink soya bean, tomorrow I drink coffee, so it's . . . ever changing. . . .

As Dr. Tang put it, although prevention is a well-established and cost-effective method of reducing cancer incidence, it is difficult to incorporate it into personalized medicine without first knowing the root cause:

> So if we don't know what the cause is, how do you prevent? There is no way to prevent. So that is the most challenging one to achieve. Finding a more effective treatment for established cancer is not easy, but it's not as difficult as trying to find ways to prevent the lung cancer.
>
> So, most of the efforts are now concentrated on treatment rather than prevention. For simple reasons because they know that finding the etiological agents is near to impossible that's the current thinking, but I don't think it is totally impossible.

These inherent complications of research on environmental causes and difficulties in obtaining results have resulted in a lack of financial support. Dr. Murphy shared how he is caught between a rock and a hard place:

> I think it's harder now to get funded to study the environment and lifestyle, and that's because it's very difficult to do. It's very expensive and it's very difficult; whereas genetic studies are actually much easier now.

To further complicate matters, the environment and biology are always interacting with one another, and such interactions make it even more difficult to differentiate and categorize observations as effects of purely biological or environmental causes. Dr. Yuan drew an analogy between understanding cancer and the English language to highlight the interplay between biology and the environment:

> I think that the first step is trying to understand the alphabet . . . so sequencing the human genome and then sequencing the genome of different cancers is just the beginning of the alphabet.
>
> Once you've got the alphabet, you need to try and string it into sentences that are meaningful. And then once you string things into a sentence, you then have to see whether it fits into the paragraph. Because all three can be taken out of context [i.e. the environment].

Moreover, Dr. Yuan pointed out, while the current state of personalized medicine tailors cancer treatment based on the expression of molecular signatures, looking exclusively at the molecular signature based on a single test/sample can also be misleading:

> [D]epending which part of the tumor one samples, there could be differences. . . . And then to cap it all off, one feature of cancer is that cancer spreads. . . . [B]etween the original tumor removed from the patient's breast, and later if it spreads to say, the lung or the liver, up to 20 percent of the metastasis can have a different signature.

In a similar thread, Dr. Hsu warned against overlooking the effect of the passage of time:

> [T]he primary and secondary tumor may be different. The chance of the discordance is 15 percent . . . therefore your so-called testing and all that is at one frame in time, but there is a longitudinal dimension that is not captured.

However, even if the personalized treatment matches the molecular signature, each individual's response can still be affected by the cumulative effect of his or her body's health status and lifestyle choices, as Dr. Yuan described:

> [Our] livers may be built differently, and our kidneys may be built differently. And we may have different underlying diseases.
>
> . . . [A]bout 10 percent of the oriental population, if we, if we don't have the vaccination program, are Hepatitis B carriers. . . . That means 1 in 10 people have potentially abnormal liver. And we put the drug, the way the drug is metabolized is different.
>
> . . . [I]f patients have underlying kidney dysfunction. . . . And if, so if the kidney is also affected because of some childhood illness that goes on to adulthood. Again the ability to clear. . . .
>
> Well, it's diet and the whole issue of supplements . . . anything that you take has an effect . . . anything that we take by mouth has to go to the liver

has to go to the kidneys. And there are *numerous* examples whereby what you take will interfere with the drug. So you give chemotherapy and you get a side effect, and you don't know what it's due to.

Even though we know that "we cannot treat our way out of the cancer problem," there is less emphasis on prevention for a variety of reasons. They include, but are not limited to, financial gains from pharmaceutical products noted in Chapter 3 and the strong belief in the relative ease in "controlling the genetic variable" as compared to environmental factors.

Conclusion

Socio-economic factors are, ultimately, related to ethical issues. And it's precisely this relationship that this chapter highlights. A relatively unique feature of personalized medicine is that it can be prohibitively expensive; but, at the same time, it is not curative. Contrary to popular expectations, generally, the new genome-based medicine serves only to prolong the patient's life for a few months or years. As such, doctors have raised a number of concerns. They have articulated that, in some instances, prescribing genomic medicine has become a new norm. In some cases, genetic tests are routinely being ordered regardless of whether patients can afford the medicine. Thus, these doctors wonder whether they should take into account the high cost of the medicine when deciding on treatment. In particular, when faced with patients from economically disadvantaged backgrounds, doctors have found themselves pondering questions of how or if they should tell a patient that all of this is available. It becomes a judgment call based on professional knowledge, but it also presents an ethical dilemma.

Physicians have different ways of resolving or handling these ethical dilemmas. Some may think, No, I would not tell the patient. I would look at the situation, and I would not tell them. This is because they do not want to put the burden on the patients to struggle with this issue. Given awareness of such expensive short-term treatment, the patient or the patient's loved ones may begin to ask: "Should I sell the house? Should I borrow from relatives to come up with 50,000 dollars or 200,000 dollars to prolong life for six months to one year when one eventually will die?" However, this consideration from the doctor may not be appreciated by patients and their loved ones. There may be loved ones who feel that $200,000 or $600,000 over one year is completely worthwhile, just to be with this person for one more year. Who is to decide what the most appropriate way is of handling such a dilemma?

These are common questions that doctors struggle with, and have to think over, because their decisions can potentially be challenged by patients and patients' families. Their compassionate decision to withhold such information "because it's costly" may become problematic if patients happen to be informed about the available medicine and demand: "There is all of this medicine. Why didn't you recommend it? Aren't you supposed to save my life? Why didn't you recommend this medication?" On the other hand, potential users may also find themselves caught in an ethical dilemma. For example, should the patient sell the house in order to acquire such medicine? Answers to these tough questions do not come easily for doctors or patients and their loved ones.

Beyond creating an awareness of genetic tests, oncologists have raised additional concerns such as who should be expected to interpret and conduct genetic tests (i.e. whether direct-to-consumer testing should be available) and how much emphasis should be given to genetic testing vis-à-vis environmental factors (i.e. since cancer can be a context-dependent manifestation).

The ethical dilemma exists not just for doctors, patients, and patients' families, but for governments and societies as a whole (in deciding what to pay for through government subsidies/taxes). As noted in this chapter, some ask why the government cannot subsidize these treatments or why few subsidies exist in their county compared to others. However, if the government does subsidize these expensive treatments and tests, where does it end? Should the public subsidize a very costly medicine that will prolong an 85-year-old grandmother's life for 3 months or a year? How about subsidies for genomic medicine pertaining to other diseases such as heart failure or diabetes? And, if all of these subsidies are approved, how would the government raise sufficient funds to deliver what is promised?

A downstream implication of genetic testing involves addressing issues of patient confidentiality and potential discrimination against an individual or a racialized group in areas of employment and insurance. For example, how should insurance companies use genetic information about a particular person or group? Should they require potential customers to go for a test? Should all people above a certain age, or belonging to a racial/ethnic group, go for specific kind of genetic testing when they acquire medical insurance or seek employment? If one has the genetic propensity for a particular disease, why should the insurance company raise the premium for everyone? Should results of genetic testing be available only to the individual or not? Who should have access to such personal genetic information?

Having confronted such a variety of dilemmas in relation to adoption and implementation of genomic medicine, some physicians have taken a step back and questioned the validity of focusing only on genes in addressing the complex problem of cancer. Focus should also be placed on the other side of the story – that is, on understanding environmental factors that contribute to cancer incidence in the first place (Sze, 2010). These physicians have suggested that research focusing on nongenetic factors should be funded as well in order to devise preventive strategies that will ultimately benefit everyone, regardless of wealth.

Notes

1 FoundationOne is a commercially available molecular diagnostics test for all solid tumor types, which analyzes routine clinical specimens for somatic alterations in relevant cancer-related genes. The test costs US$5,800. Nanos, Janelle. 2014. "Google To Offer FoundationOne Cancer Tests to Employees." *BetaBoston*, November 15. Retrieved December 15, 2015. (http://www.betaboston.com/news/2014/11/05/google-to-offer-foundationone-cancer-tests-to-employees/).

2 *The Straits Times*, February 14, 2014, "No Stock of Cancer Drug." For the reply from the National Cancer Centrem Singapore, see *The Straits Times*, February 14, 2014, "Stock Limited as Drug Is New."
3 The POLARIS (Personalized Omic Lattice for Advanced Research and Improving Stratification) is a program established in 2013 to pilot the application of clinical genomics in the treatment and diagnosis of medical diseases in Singapore and the region. Retrieved April 2, 2016. (https://www.a-star.edu.sg/polaris/).

References

Anand, Preetha, Ajaikumar B. Kunnumakara, Chitra Sundaram, Kuzhuvelil B. Harikumar, Sheeja T. Tharakan, Oiki S. Lai, Bokyung Sung and Bharat B. Aggarwal. 2008. "Cancer Is a Preventable Disease that Requires Major Lifestyle Changes." *Pharmaceutical Research* 25(9):2097–2116.

Aronson, Naomi. 2015. "Making Personalized Medicine More Affordable." *Annals of the New York Academy of Sciences* 1346:81–89. doi: 10.111/nyas.12614.

Chieng, Wei-Shieng and Soo-Chin Lee. 2006. "Establishing a Cancer Genetics Programme in Asia – the Singapore Experience." *Hereditary Cancer in Clinical Practice* 4(3):126–135

Colditz, Graham A., Kathleen Y. Wolin and Sarah Gehlert. 2012. "Applying What We Know to Accelerate Cancer Prevention." *Science Translational Medicine* 4(127):127. doi: 10.1126/scitranslmed.3003218.

Cornetta, Kenneth and Candy Gunther Brown. 2013. "Perspective: Balancing Personalized Medicine and Personalized Care." *Acad Med* 88(3):309–313. doi: 10.1097/ACM.0b013e3182806345.

Khalik, Salma. 2011. "Subsidised Drug List Reviewed Every Year." *The Straits Times*, February 15. Retrieved January 09, 2016 (https://www.healthxchange.com.sg/News/Pages/Subsidised-drug-list-reviewed-every-year.aspx).

Leong, Laurence Wai-Teng. 1997. "Commodifying Ethnicity: State and Ethnic Tourism in Singapore." Pp. 71–98 in *Tourism, Ethnicity and the State in Asian and Pacific Societies*, edited by M. Picard and R.E. Wood. Honolulu, HI: University of Hawaii Press.

Lim, Jeremy. 2013. "Who Should Be Subsidised?" *Today*, January 14. Retrieved January 09, 2016 (http://www.todayonline.com/commentary/who-should-be-subsidised?singlepage=true).

McGowan, Michelle L., Richard A. Settersten Jr, Eric T. Juengst and Jennifer R. Fishman. 2014. "Integrating Genomics into Clinical Oncology: Ethical and Social Challenges from Proponents of Personalized Medicine." *Urologic Oncology: Seminars and Original Investigations* 32(2):187–192.

Ministry of Health. 2011. Standard Drug List (SDL). Singapore: Ministry of Health. Retrieved December 15, 2015 (https://www.moh.gov.sg/content/moh_web/home/pressRoom/Parliamentary_QA/2011/Standard_Drug_List_SDL.html).

Ministry of Health. 2012. "Healthcare 2020: Improving Accessibility, Quality, and Affordability." Healthscope 1. Retrieved December 15, 2015 (https://www.moh.gov.sg/content/dam/moh_web/healthscope/archive/2012/MOH%20Healthscope_July-August%202012%20Issue.pdf).

Ministry of Health. 2015. Drug Subsidies. Singapore: Ministry of Health. Retrieved December 15, 2015 (https://www.moh.gov.sg/content/moh_web/home/costs_and_financing/schemes_subsidies/drug_subsidies.html).

Nanos, Janelle. 2014. "Google to Offer FoundationOne Cancer Tests to Employees." BetaBoston, November 15. Retrieved December 15, 2015 (http://www.beta boston.com/news/2014/11/05/google-to-offer-foundationone-cancer-tests-to-employees/).

Pfister, David G. 2013. "The Just Price of Cancer Drugs and the Growing Cost of Cancer Care: Oncologists Need to Be Part of the Solution." Journal of Clinical Oncology 31(28):3487–3489.

PuruShotam, Nirmala Srirekam. 1998. Negotiating Language, Constructing Race: Disciplining Difference in Singapore. Berlin: Walter de Gruyter.

PuruShotam, Nirmala Srirekam. 2000. Negotiating Language, Constructing Race. Berlin: De Gruyter Mouton.

Swiss Academy of Medical Sciences (SAMS). 2012. "The Potential and Limits of Personalized Medicine." Retrieved December 15, 2015 (https://www.google.ca/url?sa=t&rct=j&q=&esrc=s&source=web&cd=1&ved=0ahUKEwiJivT999_JAhW n6IMKHWPAALsQFggbMAA&url=http%3A%2F%2Fwww.samw.ch%2Fdms%2 Fen%2FPublications%2FStatements%2Fe_PersMedizin_PosPapier.pdf&usg=AFQj CNEyp3VtddW9YDqoeFD74xixPRuacA&cad=rja).

Sze, Julie. 2010. Noxious New York: The Racial Politics of Urban Health and Environmental Justice. Cambridge, Massachusetts: The MIT Press.

Toh, Han Chong. 2014. "Stock Limited as Drug Is New." *The Straits Times*, February 26. Retrieved January 09, 2016 (http://yourhealth.asiaone.com/content/stock-limited-drug-new).

U.S. Department of Health and Human Services. Office for Human Research Protections (OHRP). 2009. Guidance on the Genetic Information Nondiscrimination Act: Implications for Investigators and Institutional Review Boards. Washington, D.C: U.S. Department of Health and Human Services. Retrieved December 16, 2015 (http://www.hhs.gov/ohrp/policy/gina.html).

7 Conclusion

Personalized medicine and population-based genetic/ genomic studies

Following the sequencing of the human genome in 2003, the curtains of a new century of medical advancement opened to reveal the development of a personalized medicine or precision medicine (PM) paradigm. In the words of Willard (2013:5), genome-based personalized medicine refers to:

> [A] rapidly advancing field of healthcare that is informed by each person's unique clinical, genetic, genomic, and environmental information. The goals of personalized medicine are to take advantage of a molecular understanding of disease to optimize preventive healthcare strategies and drug therapies while people are still well or at the earliest stages of disease. Because these factors are different for every person, the nature of disease, its onset, its course, and how it might respond to drug or other interventions are as individual as the people who have them. In order for personalized medicine to be used by healthcare providers and their patients, these findings must be translated into precise diagnostic tests and targeted therapies. Since the overarching goal is to optimize medical care and outcomes for each individual, treatments, medication types, and dosages, and/or prevention strategies may differ from person to person – resulting in unprecedented customization of patient care.

According to Trent (2012:32), "the US President's Council of Advisors on Science and Technology reported in 2008 that interest in personalized medicine stems from its potential for: 1. Improved patient care; 2. Disease prevention; 3. Reduction in health costs, and 4. Stimulating new drug development." In this book, I note that effective treatments for a few types of cancer – lung, colorectal, and liver are prominent examples – has been improved by genome-based personalized medicine.

At the same time, this book suggests that the construction and identification of racially and ethnically labeled populations have become integral parts in the development of the aforementioned aspects of personalized medicine. For example, with respect to stimulating new drug development, I demonstrate in Chapter 3 that in order to identify patients likely to participate in clinical trials and to maximize the chances of a successful trial, pharmaceutical companies routinely seek information (such as prevalence rates of a specific genetic variant) among racialized and ethnicized populations. Moreover, while the economic impact of pharmacogenomic interventions and associated companion diagnostics at the macro-level remains unclear (Shabaruddin and Payne, 2014), I draw attention in Chapter 4 to cases such as those in Singapore, in which the construction and identification of the prevalence rates of a specific genetic variant among local ethnic populations is a key component in cost-effectiveness studies of pharamacogenomics.

Indeed, as noted in the introduction, "while contemporary genomic research promises personalized medicine (or measures of risk) targeted at the individual, it is primarily the comparison of groups and populations that drives human genome research" (Hinterberger, 2012:74). As such, I pay particular attention to claims-making and potential contradictions between the goals of "individualized medicine" and the continuing search for population-related genetic markers and regions.

The key argument this book advances is that while ethnic and racial categories emerge as a result of social processes of (self-)othering, in the process of creating, marketing, and regulating genomic medicine, such categories have come to be believed by some scientists to indicate the biological existence of racial and ethnic groups. Specifically, in the pursuit of personalized medicine, some scientists and medical researchers building the reference population datasets and/or conducting population-based genetic studies use race and ethnicity as proxies for human genetic diversity, or to calculate allele frequencies or to interpret the significance of any genotype information. This problematic usage occurs even when the scientists themselves articulate the social nature of such categories. Ironically, it undermines biologists' own understanding that there is only one race: the human race. Moreover, one of the key questions that this book addresses is, what are the consequences of the molecularization of race and ethnicity for personalized medicine in Asia and beyond? The interviews with physicians (mostly oncologists) suggest that there are serious issues and ethical dilemmas in translating such racialized and ethnicized knowledge about human genome variation at the level of clinical practices of PM. Thus, in sum, the evidence in this book suggests that race/ethnicity is a specious proxy for both human population genetic/genomic diversity and for individual genotype in clinical decision-making.

While this book focuses on personalized medicine for cancer, the lessons learned could potentially be useful for the development of personalized medicine for other diseases. As the World Health Organization announced:

> [C]ancer figure[s] among the leading causes of morbidity and mortality worldwide, with approximately 14 million new cases and 8.2 million cancer related deaths in 2012. Moreover, the number of new cases is expected to rise about 70 percent over the next two decades to 22 million new cases. More than 60 percent of [the] world's total new annual cases occur in Africa, Asia and Central and South America. These regions account for 70 percent of the world's cancer deaths
>
> (Stewart and Wild, 2014).

The estimated toll of cancer on human lives highlights the importance of looking into the benefits and potential ethical, legal, and social issues involved in the fight against cancer in this postgenomic era. In the sections that follow, I begin by summarizing that the definition of population in population-based genetic/genomic studies is not only context-dependent but fluid and arbitrary. The fact that definitions of race and/or ethnicity are in a perpetual state of indeterminacy should make us worry about the emergence of ethnically and/or racially based medicine, billed as "personalized medicine." Specifically, I emphasize again the regional racialization of genetics/genomics and the molecularization of ethnicities in Asia. Finally, I identify some ethical, social, and legal issues raised by the findings, and the challenges of treating and preventing complex diseases, such as cancer, in an era of postgenomic medicine.

The definition of population in population-based genetic studies is context-dependent

In the context of a *global* pharmaceutical industry, as described in Chapter 3, I found that the population categories that matter are racial (e.g. Asian and Caucasian) and ethnic (e.g. Chinese). How do these racial/ethnic categories matter? Pharmaceutical companies do not, generally, make ethnic-specific medicine because they prefer drug indications to be as broad as possible, so that medicine can be sold to as many people as possible. However, it is revealed that companies do actively seek knowledge regarding distributions of allele frequencies and other genotype information among ethnically or racially labeled population groups as a strategy to deal with potential failures of multi-billion-dollar investments in drug development. The story of IRESSA serves as a prime example: the only way forward in "salvaging" the drug was through racializing clinical trials – Asians vs. Non-Asians. Even though further analysis found that it was EGFR mutations that contributed to the responsiveness to the drug, the spotlight was already on IRESSA as an "Asian-focused" medicine for lung cancer patients. As Dr. Chong pointed out:

> I mean, you know, especially in [the cases of] all these very costly targeted drugs like IRESSA and everything, it's best to enrich your population for those [for] whom you will see a response, so whilst it's not Chinese and non-smokers per se, rather EGFR, but there is a very close association between the two, so by first purifying your population with these non-genetic tests, i.e. check[ing] gender, check[ing] race, you make it more likely that your trial will produce meaningful results.
>
> But of course, there are some of these trials nowadays where, to get registration in China, they are obliged to recruit x number of patients from China. There's one particular trial that we're involved in now, they opened it up to Singapore only because they needed to get non-Mainland Chinese into the trial. So there's all these overlapping things, politics and business, you know, you're trying to get registration with the drug.

I further show that two population groups – "Asians" and "Caucasians" – are of particular interest to pharmaceutical companies, as they seek to maximize profits by channeling resources to the increasing affluence of the "Asian" market and, later, to the perceived core (i.e. "Caucasian") market. Despite apparent problems in defining racial categories, the population categories of "Asian" and "Caucasian" were found evident in all four phases of clinical trials, including Phase IV, post-marketing surveillance (PMS). Drawing on extensive interview data, I suggest that concerns about winning regulatory approval and greater access to overseas markets propel drug companies to naturalize socially constructed concepts of race and ethnicity into biomedically relevant objects.

In the context of a globalized genome science, geneticists in Asia also play a key role in marshaling big datasets and defining population categories along racial and ethnic lines. In particular, I suggest that a closer examination of how the HUGO Pan-Asian SNP Consortium (in Chapter 2) constructed population categories illuminates the emerging regional racialization of genomics and molecularization of ethnicity in Asia. First, the Consortium was established primarily to address gaps found in international genomics projects, such as the use of only Chinese and Japanese DNA as "Asian" samples. In an effort to address this problem of a lack of representativeness of samples, and to counter the perceived hegemonic scientific authority of the West, the HUGO PASNP Consortium members gathered to take control of the definition of "Asian" genome variation. Second, host and guest nations collaborated and shifted the supposedly disease-oriented study into one concerned with population migration. Moreover, Consortium members used contemporary ethnic categories as population sampling frames and proxies for genetic diversity in studying migration histories. As Duster (2005:1050) notes, "particular groups of individuals chosen to represent each region of the world are often chosen because of their convenience and accessibility," and this is no less true in Asia. Finally, even though political, logistical, and financial (i.e. nonbiological) factors contributed to this shift from a study of disease susceptibility to a study of migration history, "scientific" or biological claims with serious epistemological and medical consequences for the development of therapeutics were being made based on ethnic and racial differences between and among Asians.

Cancer is the leading cause of death in Singapore, with about 30 percent of deaths attributed to it (Ministry of Health, 2015). In the context of national public health policy-making, I show that the categories that matter are current census ethnic categories of Chinese, Indian, Malay, and Others (CMIO). How and when do such categories matter? In Chapter 4, I demonstrate that they are key elements in cost-effectiveness studies aimed at promoting optimal management of scarce public health resources. There are certainly valid reasons for making use of genetic data calculated at the population level, such as controlling cases of adverse drug reactions and cost-benefit analysis of various genetic tests to decide which drugs to subsidize and screening programs to fund. However, the use of genetic data calculated based on prevailing CMIO census population categories remains questionable. As Loveman (2014) demonstrates, census racial categories are a function of the shifting agendas of the ethnoracial and economic elites who do the categorizing.

The case of Irinotecan, discussed in Chapter 4, is an example of how implementation of personalized medicine is associated with the CMIO categories. Past research on personalized medicine found that patients with two variants of UGT1A1*6 and UGT1A1*28 are at an increased risk of adverse reactions to Irinotecan. This information was taken one step further by population-based research to include the statistical prevalence of these two gene variants across different ethnic groups in Singapore – a move toward creating aggregate data for cost-effectiveness analysis. The key issue lies here: why was ethnicity adopted as a population category when aggregated data can be conceptualized and analyzed in various ways that have been associated with toxicity (such as utilizing categories based on weight range, types of diet, etc.)? Further prompting revealed that distribution of risk alleles based on ethnicity was adopted due to existing administrative routines and convenience of such categories for data collection and analysis. In other words, it was the availability of categorical data (i.e. CMIO categories) – as opposed to biomedical considerations – that prompted the use of ethnicity in assessing whether a patient is likely to suffer from toxic effects in taking Irinotecan. Moreover, the reliance on race and ethnicity as frames for calculating risk-allele frequency is consistently illustrated through a review of cost-effectiveness studies of drugs such as IRESSA, Irinotecan, and carbamazepine in selected countries in Asia.

In short, as is demonstrated in Chapters 2, 3, and 4, the kinds of population categories that matter in population-based genetic studies are context-dependent. Moreover, while Bliss (2012) illustrates "antiracist racialism" – that is, that racialization in genomic science in the United States is primarily a function of geneticists' good intentions to include racial and ethnic minorities in their research – the interviewees in this study did not explicitly voice social justice concerns. Rather, I draw on interview data to argue that the usage of racially and ethnically labeled population categories serves multiple purposes, including getting studies published in the highly competitive scholarly community, working with pharmaceutical companies' capital investments, and saving public health care costs. Furthermore, as is shown in Chapter 5, in the interviews with clinician-scientists in Singapore, many, in fact, explained that the usage of race and ethnicity in research settings stems from clinical observations, and that the use of these as proxies for genetics is not ideal and is merely a temporary tool, a means to the end of finding a molecular target. Once the molecular cause of disease susceptibility or drug response is identified, racial and ethnic identifications are mostly irrelevant in the clinical setting – indeed, the interview data suggest that using race/ethnicity as a proxy for administering drugs is a last resort only in cases in which other options are limited. One scenario might be when genetic testing is unavailable or unaffordable, or when the relationship between genotype and medical outcome is not clear. If genetic tests are unavailable, physicians sometimes take race/ethnicity into account based on prior clinical observations of inter-ethnic differences in terms of drug responses and/or toxicities.

However, such clinical observations and decisions are not based on science but on what Dr. Teo called "intuition." Furthermore, such "intuition" is generally used only initially, because in some cases, patients cannot afford the time to take genetic tests and wait for results when their conditions are severe and require more immediate treatment.

Despite the limited and problematic usefulness of racial and ethnic identifications in clinical practice, the CMIO census categories continue to be widely used as population categories in genetic/genomic research projects in Singapore, while "Asian" and "Caucasian" continue to be popular categories used in studies at the international level. Evidently, however, the persistence of the usage of race and ethnicity to construct and identify human populations in genomics is due to non-biological reasons, including, but not limited to, convenience sampling, scientists' intuition, bureaucratic inertia, and the multiple political-economic purposes highlighted earlier.

The definition of a population is not only context-dependent but also fluid and arbitrary

Definitions of population categories rely on more than just "others" observed through a "Western"-centric lens. With the advancement of medical science in Asia, there is a growing prominence of scientists and clinician-scientists from previously marginalized scientific communities taking steps toward the construction, reinforcement, and circulation of an "Asian" identity. This serves to counter the perceived Western ethno-centrism and, in turn, introduces a cycle of self-othering processes, which, ironically, reproduce cognitive categories generated in the West.

To begin with, scholars have produced a vast and growing literature that documents race as a social/historical/cultural construct: a system of ideas, identities, and material relations that emerged slowly in the context of Western European imperialism and colonial expansion beginning in the fifteenth century. The first laws designed to establish and patrol racial boundaries and hierarchy did not appear until the middle of the seventeenth century (Smedley, 2007). As indicated in the first chapter of this book, racial and ethnic categories emerge out of the othering/social-boundary-making process, as an "ongoing strategic effort to make a difference in space among the movements of people, money or products" (van Houtoum and van Naerssen, 2002:126). During the colonial era, race/ethnicity was a product of colonial administration: artificial boundaries were created to meet the exigencies of daily rule. For instance, as Spaan, von Naerssen, and Kohl (2002:163) write, "the colonial economy marked the origin of the Malaysian multi-ethnic society" – a person of each "race" had certain characteristics or mannerisms that made him "suitable" to be working in certain occupations in the eyes of the colonial administrators, and "real or imagined attributes such as language, customs, religion and indigenousness (were codified)" (Spaan, von Naerssen, and Kohl, 2002:163). Similarly, Loveman's (2014:44) study shows that in Latin America the census in the colonial era functioned to justify "orderly extraction of agricultural, mineral and labor resources" by indigenous and imported slave laborers for elites from and in Spain and Portugal.

The Swedish naturalist Carolus Linnaeus published the tenth edition of *Systema Naturae* in 1758 and classified human beings as part of the animal kingdom. Linnaeus designates four basic races of humans – American, European, Asian, and African, and his influence on racial thinking remains obvious today (Goodman, Moses, and Jones, 2012). Gissis (2011) argues that two modes of discourse and visualization played a significant role in the emergence of "race" as a new scientific category during the eighteenth century: one involving society, civility, and civilization (as found primarily in the travel literature), and the other involving nature (as found in natural history writings, particularly botanical classifications). That is, the European colonizing enterprise resulted in an extensive flow of new objects at every level. Visual representations of these new objects circulated in the European cultural world and were transferred and transformed within travelogues and natural history writings. Over the course of the century, the discourse on society, civility, and civilization collapsed into the discourse on nature. Humans became classified and visually represented along the same lines as flora, according to similar assumptions about visible features.

In addition, the advent of the nation-state necessitated the formation of the "native" and the "other." States trying to create "nations" require the creation of a myth of being, and who-we-are-as-a-nation is always relational (Göl, 2005). I provide an example in Chapter 2 of the historical and political construction of the "Japanese."

From historically othered to contemporary self-othering

At the same time, it must be added that the "othered" takes part in the othering process. For instance, as previous chapters show, social actors in contemporary times uncritically have adopted the notion of "Asian" and reinscribed it at the molecular level. In particular, there are at least three ways in which the notion of "Asian" – "regionally-Asian" (Chapter 2), "geographically-Asian" (Chapter 3), and "nationally-Asian" (Chapter 4) – is constructed by social actors participating in the creation and development of genomic medicine in Asia. Moreover, ethnic categories created during the colonial era have been taken for granted and reinscribed in the twenty-first century. For instance, Chapter 4 illustrates the formation process of the "Malay" category during the period of British colonial rule. Soon, this constructed identity – that stood out against other groups like Chinese and Indians – was internalized by the people. The definition of being Malay, however, is different from that in Malaysia just across the causeway in Singapore: being Malay in Singapore is not limited to those having a "Malay" ancestor, but acceptance by the Malay community. This case study points again to the fluid definition of race and ethnicity.

Thus, I suggest not only that definitions of populations are context-dependent, but that they are fluid and arbitrary. How does it play out in genomics in Asia? In the following paragraphs, I reiterate some of the main examples. For instance, the definition of Caucasians is contested, as is evident from the following quotes from researchers:

DR. ZHAO: Well, I think in this sort of study done in Asia . . . I think it's just basically anybody from European heritage or American heritage.

Dr. Tang further added that geography does not really contribute to the definition of who is Caucasian and who is not Caucasian. Interestingly, he briefly pointed out that physical appearances matter and can serve as differentiation markers:

INTERVIEWER: What about Europeans?

DR. TANG: Those that are in Europe. Australians are considered to be of European descent. . . . [U]sually, it's more of the racial thing rather than . . . geography.

INTERVIEWER: How [are] Western European[s] different?

DR. TANG: Caucasian appearance.

INTERVIEWER: Not location based?

DR. TANG: No. Like Chinese migrants who migrate to Europe or [the] US will not be considered . . . Western European. They will still be called East Asian in [terms of] their ethnicity.

There are clearly no objective criteria or processes to define and identify one's race or ethnicity. Dr. Rajaratnam stated that he would use identification cards to directly check on race and ethnicity, though he had other concerns as well:

Verbally asking them, and by their IC [i.e. national registration identification card]. Because that is their national identification. So that's the only proof we have.

One thing I am very careful of is with Indonesians. Indonesians, they may have Malay names, but they can be Chinese, they can be Indians. But all of them, their names are Malay. So I am very careful. If the Indonesian patient is clearly a Chinese, I mean, you can also see.

I am very careful, unless I can get at least two people to verify for sure that that person, that Indonesian is a Chinese or Malay, [and] Caucasians also. . . .

Names, however, may not match how researchers and/or doctors expect a patient to look. Dr. Wee brought up an example similar to Dr. Rajaratnam's attempts to be careful with racial/ethnic identification:

I always shared this joke that, during my reservist military service, one day I was running a clinic in an army camp. Then my medic would help me call Mr. Chong Ah Gow. The person [who] came in [was] an Indian. 'Cause his mum is an Indian. He looks exactly like [an] Indian, but he is Mr. Chong Ah Gow. [Interviewer: You would have thought he is Chinese]. So your father is Mr. Chong? Ya. Correct, my mum is an Indian. But he looks exactly like [an] Indian.

Such situations arise precisely because race and ethnicity are social and fluid constructs. There is no essence in "being" "Caucasians," "Asians," or "Malays." However, in using them in research and analysis, researchers sometimes act as if these categories are unproblematic and coherent. Dr. Poh, for instance, said that he identified who was "Caucasian" based on what his colleague told him:

> Because one of my colleagues is from Germany . . . and he gave us samples. Normal German, Caucasians. . . . They tell us.

Additionally, the category of "Caucasian" is often used in comparison with the category of "Asian." However, definitions of both categories remain vague and contested. This can be seen in this particular example: Dr. Huang suggested a geographical gauge for what could be included under "Asian," though eventually he gave up on coming up with a precise definition:

> . . . so anything that is 6 hours flight from here [Singapore]. . . . I mean I think that the easy ones are easy. Thailand is Asia. South Korea is Asia, then you get . . .
> . . . I would consider Japan Asia . . . maybe not South-East Asia. So . . . I would say anything that's not Western Europe or North America. . . .
> . . . Is Russia Asia or not? That becomes a bit of a blurry line. So it's a, it's a nice title to have [for a scientific paper presentation]? But obviously, where does Asia end? Is Australia part of Asia, I don't know [laughs].

In the case of Singapore, Dr. Zhang defines "Asian" based on existing racial categories: Chinese, Indian, and Malay.

DR. ZHANG: Okay, our "Asian" probably refers to Chinese, Indian, and Malay.
INTERVIEWER: So if a Caucasian lives in Singapore, which is part of Asia, he/she is not Asian?
DR. ZHANG: [He/she]'s not Asian.

Other researchers define "Asian" similarly in their studies, with respect to the specific races:

DR. ZHUANG: [T]he category of "Asian" is very heterogeneous. [S]o . . . although we generally put down "Asian" . . . in our patient selection criteria, we would have to define [it] . . . to the specific races. Whether we're talking about Chinese, we're talking about Malay, we're talking about Indian. We tend not to group them together. So, when we do an Asian study, that study may include Chinese, Malay or Indian, or sometimes just Chinese alone.

Undoubtedly, neither "Asia" nor "Asians" is objectively defined nor delineated. "Mapping Human Genetic Diversity in Asia" (HUGO Pan-Asian SNP Consortium, 2009) is a high-impact publication that has informed and lent support to "Asians" being conceptually "one people" after the mapping of genetic variations and migration patterns of 75 populations from 10 countries: Japan, Korea, China, Taiwan, Singapore, Thailand, Indonesia, Philippines, Malaysia, and India (excluding Australia). Definitions of ethnic groups in the study, however, were left to the scientists' discretion. This is problematic as it glosses over the fact that these ethnic categories are historically, politically, and socially constructed. An analysis of the emergent and fluid nature of the label "Japanese" in Chapter 2 serves to remind us of this point. Two additional categories used in the study are Han and Korean. Here are how these ethnic populations are subjectively defined by Consortium members:

Han Chinese:

DR. CHUA: We use . . . three generations. So this is for HUGO Pan-Asian. And also our definition of Han Chinese. In all my studies when we talk about Han Chinese, this is the definition. For us, [it is] difficult to get . . . 4 generations because nobody knows . . . 4 generations. Difficult to find. I mean . . . you know your parents are Chinese, your parents will know whether their parents are Chinese, but your grandparents may not be there to know the fourth [generation]. . . .

Korean:

DR. KANG: The way we define the Koreans [was] at that time, people who had three generations of knowledge that they have been in Korea, no external influence, and people who are from two cities, one called Ansung, the other one Ansan. . . . We took the original samples from a previous study in Korea, Korean Study, so they collected this. So essentially they just defined geographically, these two cities.

The problematic usage of these racial/ethnic categories in human genetic/genomic studies has been carefully examined due to their wide- and far-reaching implications, including, but not limited to, how such categories become molecularized in labs and then packaged to be sold to the uninformed public. Dr. Rajaratnam pointed out that use of statistics on the prevalence of certain alleles in relation to race and/or ethnicity is also part of public health decision-making rubrics:

The prevalence of double heterozygotes (*6/*28) in Singapore is 6.9 percent, 1.2 percent and 2.9 percent in Chinese, Malays and Indians, respectively. . . . [W]hat I meant was ethnic group matters . . . because this involves . . . regulatory bodies introducing the test. The FDA [in the USA] did not introduce *6 testing because it is totally absent in Caucasian[s]. Whereas [the] HSA introduced both *6 and *28 testing. That's where ethnicity matters.

Upon closer inspection, race and/or ethnicity is used for data analysis because existing data is already provided and defined by the government along those lines, as Dr. Ballheimer said:

> 70 percent of Singaporeans are Chinese. We need to do a model that's representative of the population. . . . We just use allele frequencies based on what the government gives us. And they give us frequencies based on Chinese, Singaporean, Chinese, Malay, and Indian. So we just use it. If they gave it to us in a different way, we would analyze it in a different way. . . .

Definitions of ethnicity in Singapore are not entirely consistent across all doctors and/or researchers interviewed. There is, however, a tendency to use self-identification and the identifications of three generations (the individual, his/her parents and grandparents) to categorize an individual. As Drs. Yuan and Wang explained:

DR. YUAN: When we do studies, if ethnicity is involved, we usually ask for three generations. So okay that's how we define. So . . . you know, how did your parents define themselves, how did your grandparents define themselves? So if the grandparents, parents and, and the patient, or the human subject, all declare themselves as Malay, then the person is classified as Malay.

DR. WANG: In these studies, the definition of Asian, definition of ethnic group is based on three generations. And what is written on the national registration identity card of these patients. So it's more or less a self-declared ethnic group. And of course we excluded those individuals that . . . we're a bit uncertain of. In other words, if the patient were to say that my mom and my dad are Chinese and my grandparents are Chinese, we are okay. You're Chinese. If my mom and dad are Chinese, my grandparents one of them is not a Chinese . . . okay, you are not a Chinese.

In short, the definition of any racial or ethnic group, whether "Caucasian," "Asian," or "Han," is not based on biology and is never static. Different social actors can define a racial or ethnic group differently and verify such identification in various manners.

The regional racialization of genetics/genomics and the molecularization of ethnicity in Asia

At a ceremony announcing the completion of the first draft of the human genome in 2000, President Bill Clinton declared: "I believe one of the great truths to emerge from this triumphant expedition inside the human genome is that in genetic terms, all human beings, regardless of race, are more than 99.9 percent the same" (The New York Times, 2000). I suggest, however, that in the process of creating, marketing, and regulating genomic medicine, such categories have come to be believed by some to indicate the biological existence of racial and ethnic groups. As Duster (2005:4) points out, "by accepting the prefabricated racial designations of stored samples and then reporting patterns of differences in SNPs between those categories, misplaced genetic concreteness is nearly inevitable." Such an insight can also be applied to situations in which molecular geneticists use ethnicity as a proxy – that is, now there is misplaced genetic concreteness of ethnic categories. For instance, HUGO PASNP member scientist Dr. Sato said, "one of the biggest findings from the Pan Asian Consortium is just [that] ethnic classification corresponds to the genetic classification very well," and HUGO PASNP member scientist Dr. Lee remarked, "What is the implication of demarcation? Well, *ethnic populations are genetically different. It's true*. Right, if you talk about even Koreans and Chinese, you can still see difference, the point is how different [when] you talk about on the world scale" [emphasis mine].

Scientists should not really be surprised to find interracial or inter-ethnic differences in genetics due to historical discriminatory practices against particular groups (TallBear, 2013) and the practice of endogamy. More importantly, as Feldman and Lewontin (2008:93) put it:

> [I]t must be borne in mind that the taxonomic problem cannot be inverted. That is, while clustering methods are capable of assigning an individual to a geographic population with a high degree of certainty, given that individual's genotype, it is not possible to predict accurately the genotype of an individual given his or her geographical origin. . . . There are gene alleles that appear only in one group . . . but there does not exist any gene for which one major geographical cluster includes 100 percent of one genotype while another major geographical cluster has 100 percent of another genotype.

Furthermore, as noted earlier:

> When researchers claim to be able to assign people to groups based on allele frequency at a certain number of loci, they have chosen loci that show differences between the groups they are trying to distinguish.
>
> (Duster, 2006a:434)

"Race is best understood as a relationship and, more specifically, a relationship between social groups in conflict over resources," writes Duster (2002:549), "Serbs and Croats become white when they get to New York, Capetown or Melbourne, but when they return to the Balkans the salience of their whiteness recedes, even dissipates." Having gathered the interview data with social actors in different settings, I suggest that clinician-scientists and molecular geneticists exhibit different levels of faith and considerations concerning the genetic basis of fundamentally historically and socially constructed racial and ethnic categories. At one end, some researchers believe that there is definitely a genetic basis to race, and, at the other, some believe that there is absolutely no such basis. Many researchers in Singapore repeatedly emphasized that race and ethnicity identifications will become irrelevant once the molecular target affecting the disease or drug toxicities or drug effectiveness is found, suggesting that they do not believe that there is a genetic basis to race/ethnicity. Indeed, one clinician-scientist who studies inter-ethnic differences and drug responses, Dr. Wang, actually lamented, "I think the BiDil story is a very sad one. Shouldn't have happened. It's kind of one drug company, Nitromed, trying to make some money."

That said, I have presented data to suggest that the molecularization of race and ethnicity is occurring when researchers use such categories as proxies or calculate allele frequencies or interpret the significance of any genotype information for various purposes, regardless of whether they actually believe that there is a genetic basis to race. In addition, as Tallbear and Bolnick (2004)'s article on "Native American DNA tests" suggests, "now that genetics carries such cultural power, we face several pressing questions: Will Native American identities and rights that have been reckoned through a combination of kinship ideas, law, and policy now be reckoned increasingly through DNA? Will DNA tests be required in law and policy? Will prevailing cultural notions of kin, race, and genetic ancestry undermine tribal notions of kin that emphasize a close cultural connection to the tribe? How will the focus on DNA affect ongoing U.S. negotiations with tribal nations? Tribes need to consider these possibilities carefully." One can raise such questions with respect to the molecularization of ethnic groups in Asia as well.

The specter of ethnic medicine

Through extensively describing the political and regulatory landscape at the time, Kahn (2013) explains how the social-political landscape was the driving force for the racializing of BiDil. He focuses particularly on patent laws and elucidates that "patent law is supposed to promote the invention of new and useful products. In the case of BiDil, patent law did not spur the invention of a new drug, but rather the recharacterization of an existing therapy for a particular segment of society – in short, the repackaging of the drug as ethnic" (Kahn, 2013:66). Kahn further points out that, "while clinical trials and drug development may sometimes look at an array of factors, including social and economic variables, they also frequently look *only* at biomedical variables. . . . When a drug's efficacy or safety is correlated to racial or ethnic categories, it opens the door to reifying those categories as genetic" (Kahn, 2013:68) [emphasis mine].

As noted above, race and ethnicity are used as surrogates for genetics, but there are differences in opinion regarding whether race/ethnicity serves as a "good" surrogate. For instance, Dr. Chong said: "this [i.e. race/ethnicity] is just a lousy surrogate for a genotype. So at the end of the day, you have to drill down to the genotype, you know. I don't think anyone is going to start prescribing medicine that says that ABC is the preferred choice for Chinese, high blood pressure patients."

While Dr. Chong and many of his colleagues suggested that it is not possible for drug prescriptions to be based on race/ethnicity, the existence of IRESSA in Asia and BiDil and the history of sickle-cell anemia screening made mandatory for African Americans should serve as stern reminders for what may develop in the future with the advent of racially/ethnically labeled population-based genetic studies (Wailoo, 2001; Duster, 2003; Kahn, 2013).

Cancer genomics in the clinic

Genetic testing and genome-based personalized medicine have been adopted across three dimensions of clinical decision-making: drug efficacy, drug toxicities, and preventive medicine. In line with the view of personalized medicine as a beneficial development, interviewees generally agreed that such targeted treatments not only maximize therapeutic benefits and minimize potential adverse drug reactions for patients, but also can reduce health care costs for society as a whole.

At the same time, interviewees continually emphasized that laboratory science and clinical practice are different worlds. The former seeks to investigate a clear relationship between an independent variable (presence of a genetic marker) and dependent variable (responsiveness to a drug treatment or susceptibility to a particular disease), while the latter requires an overall assessment of a patient beyond this proposed parsimonious relationship. This partially explains why the statistically significant relationship observed within a study population might not be applicable in a clinical setting.

It seems to us that "probability medicine" is a more accurate term than "precision medicine" or "personalized medicine." To begin with, clinicians have pointed out that genetic mutations tested are strongly correlated with – but not precisely determinative of – a drug's efficacy and toxicity. That is, even if a drug has been shown to be effective against a particular mutation, the targeted drug does not work effectively for everyone with the particular mutation. As noted in Chapter 5, Dr. Tang explained: "About 70 percent of the [local] patients will carry the EGFR mutation. Of those patients who [have the] EGFR mutation, you do expect that 80 percent of them will respond to the drug [IRESSA], so 20 percent that will not respond – meaning that they [the tumors] either remain the same or they may even grow with the treatment." As far as drug toxicities are concerned, the situation is similarly complex. For example, genetic testing for two genes, CYP2C9 and VKORC1, serves to help determine the appropriate dosage of Warfarin to be administered to a patient. However, an adverse reaction (i.e. bleeding) to Warfarin could also be caused by many nongenetic factors (i.e. drinking of herbal tea) that genetic testing may not account for.

Ogolla describes race-based medicine as synonymous with personalized medicine (Ogolla, 2010). He further suggests that categorizing groups "on the basis of race and ethnicity to benefit their health is desirable" (Ogolla, 2010:47). However, the interview data suggest that oncologists believe that clinical medicine *cannot* profitably use race/ethnicity as a proxy in the administering of medicines to diverse ethnic and racial populations. Hence, I argue that using race/ethnicity as a framework to make clinical decisions about genomic medicine is *not* desirable and may actually cause harm for several reasons. First, as the doctors' consensus seems to indicate, when information on particular genetic variants/mutations have been identified, patients' race/ethnicity becomes irrelevant. It might be useful at the research stage if variants are not known. However, a drug that effectively targets a mutation should work similarly across all patients, regardless of ethnicity. As Dr. Yeh put it: "It is the driving mutation. It does not respect ethnic boundaries."

Results from a clinical trial that uses race/ethnicity as a framework may reveal the probability, for example, that patients from a particular ethnic group face a higher chance of having a mutant/variant gene. However, such a probability statement is not very helpful in guiding treatment decisions because it is only when the patient actually goes through genetic testing that he/she knows whether he/she carries the mutant/variant gene. Likewise, even if trial results show that a particular ethnic group is less likely to carry a particular mutant/variant gene, this does mean that there is not a chance that a particular patient of that ethnicity does carry that mutant/variant gene. Thus, the frequency of a mutation within a particular ethnic group does not matter; all patients should go for genetic testing because there is always the chance that a patient might have the specific mutation. To proceed without genetic testing because of race-based probability statements could result in medical misdiagnosis or treatment (Witzig, 1996; Anderson et al., 2001; Garcia, 2004; Barr, 2005; Braun et al., 2007; Acquaviva and Mintz, 2010; Megyesi, Hunt and Brody, 2011). The interviews with oncologists suggest that, for example, even though the prevalence rate or the frequency of the EGFR mutation may be higher in the "Asian" or "Chinese" population, this does not mean that the doctors should not offer EGFR genetic testing to an "Indian" or "Caucasian" lung cancer patient. In fact, the physicians interviewed emphasized that EGFR mutation testing should be done for each lung cancer patient, irrespective of ethnic identity. Thus, the finding lends support to what Cooper, Kaufman, and Ward (2003:1167) point out, "if you really need to know whether a patient has a particular genotype, you will have to do the test to find out." To reiterate, we need to be wary of situations, where race and ethnicity is used, unfortunately, as the poor man's genomic test. As far as preventive measures are concerned, interview data suggest that race- or ethnicity-based estimates are less convincing than a patient's family history, and there is a need to discuss what is meant by clinically relevant risk percentages.

Bioethics in practicing personalized medicine

The reality of genome-based personalized medicine, particularly in oncology where it is most extensively applied, is that personalized drugs offer the potential to prolong patients' lifespans but not to cure their diseases. When personalized medicine becomes heavily promoted, patients may be led to mistakenly expect that it will cure them. Thus, it is important to manage expectations about personalized drugs. In the first place, as Roberts (2011:165) puts it, "when patients hear about a drug indicated specifically for their race, they may assume that it is 'just right for me.'" Next, one serious concern about these drugs involves high costs. Therefore, patients need to be clear about the fact that, should they opt for personalized drugs, they will be paying a very high cost not to be cured, but to prolong their lifespans.

The high costs of personalized medicine create a dilemma for doctors in terms of how they ought to work though treatment decisions with patients. While genetic testing is increasingly a norm in clinical practice, test results may not be useful, particularly in cases in which patients are unable to afford the specific drugs to be taken. First, although the cost of each genetic test seems low, for lower income patients, the cost is still financially significant. Moreover, as more and more different genetic tests become available, the total cost of genetic testing also grows. Some interviewees suggest that physicians should instead assess the financial backgrounds of their patients and recommend treatments that are affordable, rather than the most advanced (and, therefore, costliest), so that patients and their families will be spared the moral question of the value of the extra months of life. Even with state subsidies, personalized medicine remains very expensive for low income patients and those who are not covered by private health insurance. Thus, doctors feel pressure to prescribe genomic medicine, as it is the "new norm" in medical advancement, but they also face situations in which patients are unable to afford such advanced treatment. Should it be the physician's right to withhold treatment information out of good intentions in order to handle such an ethical dilemma? What if a patient's family was willing to find the means to pay the steep cost for a few more months with the patient, but was not informed about this possibility?

Making genetic testing and genomic medicine equally affordable for all patients entails a difficult discussion of how finite resources for public health care should be distributed and how various stakeholders are affected. As it is, it would seem that citizens would end up bearing the bulk of the cost through higher taxes and higher insurance premiums, and to convince the public to accept this would be a challenge. Even if they are agreeable, what about subsidies for diseases other than cancer? It appears to be a challenge for governments to fund all subsidies.

Another issue is that doctors sometimes lack the latest knowledge about genetics to properly interpret genetic testing results that will ultimately inform their clinical decisions. In situations in which patients ask about areas about which a doctor is unsure, should he or she hide ignorance or risk providing incomplete or inaccurate information? Moreover, given the rapid rate of development and launching of new drugs and diagnostics from pharmaceutical companies, doctors find it challenging to continuously process all of this information and decide which drugs should be applied in the clinical setting. It has been suggested that studying genomics could be incorporated into the curriculum of medical education, and perhaps a cohort of doctors could become medical geneticists who specialize in this area in order to be able to interpret more complex test results, such as those for direct-to-consumer (DTC) genetic testing products.

There are also serious concerns about privacy and potential genetic discrimination against individuals or particular groups that the literature on "citizen science" has alluded to. Technically, genetic testing results are personal information to be kept confidential. However, in cases of germline mutations, which are inheritable, such information has implications for both the patient and his or her biological relatives. Should these relatives be given such information so that they might consider undergoing genetic testing themselves? What if individuals prefer not to know if they are predisposed to certain diseases to avoid having to live with anxiety? Or, for healthy individuals who go through genetic testing, if it so happens that a test reveals a certain predisposition for developing a disease other than that which the test was intended to find, would the doctor need to reveal this information? Such awareness of disease predisposition might also entail discriminatory practices in society. For example, employers and insurance companies may ask individuals or individuals belonging to a particular ethnoracial group to go for genetic testing before employing them or enrolling them in insurance plans. Let's hypothesize that it is found that the Malays as a population group have a higher proportion of a manifesting tendency toward certain kinds of diseases – say 60 percent of the "Malay" as compared to 30 percent of the "Chinese" group. This information provided to an insurer, if what is said about Malays is uncritically accepted, could lead to consequences for individuals identified as "Malay": (1) not being able to enroll in a particular insurance plan, (2) enrollment in an insurance plan that excludes coverage for any expenses related to diseases they are supposedly predisposed to have, and (3) enrollment in an insurance plan that also insures against such diseases but charged a higher premium. In general, the revelation that one has a predisposition to a certain disease might result in denial of job opportunities or higher insurance premiums. So, should individuals be open with such information? Should employers or insurance companies be entitled to such information? Why or why not?

Lastly, cancer is a complex disease and has genetic, environmental, and lifestyle causes. According to Anand et al. (2008):

> [O]nly 5–10 percent of all cancer cases can be attributed to genetic defects, whereas the remaining 90–95 percent have their roots in the environment and lifestyle. The lifestyle factors include cigarette smoking, diet (fried foods, red meat), alcohol, sun exposure, environmental pollutants, infections, stress, obesity, and physical inactivity. The evidence indicates that all cancer-related deaths, almost 25–30 percent are due to tobacco, as many as 30–35 percent are linked to diet, about 15–20 percent are due to infections, and the remaining percentage are due to other factors like radiation, stress, physical activity, environmental pollutants etc.

Some cancers may also result from interactive effects of genes and the environment. Yet, in the postgenomic era, the focus seems to have been placed on "curing" cancer through genome-based pharmaceutical products, sometimes under the banner of "personalized/precision medicine," as opposed to preventing cancer through tackling environmental and lifestyle causes.

While genetics, not race/ethnicity, should be the basis on which precision medicine should be developed, I caution against genetic determinism. As one interviewee, Dr. Wee, put it, "genetics is not destiny," and the fact that even targeted medicine is not always effective further attests to this statement. Environmental problems, diet, and certain lifestyle practices can be detrimental to health, and, thus, the context of cancer as a multifactorial disease is significant.

I warn against the dangers of seeing race as a biological/genetic concept, as this legitimizes racial discrimination (which has health consequences) and, on a broader level, treads into the dangerous territory of genetic determinism (Nelkin and Lindee, 1995). Moreover, the focus on pharmacogenomics has overshadowed our collective ability to better understand the role of modifiable and preventable nongenetic/environmental factors, which have a strong potential to result in interventions that actually benefit all individuals regardless of socio-economic status.

To fully capitalize on the potential benefits of genomic medicine, in-depth interdisciplinary discussion is vital for the proposal and implementation of complementary and/or alternative solutions. In the following section, I raise the importance of interdisciplinary collaboration and discussions among different social actors, particularly at the initial stage when scientists are formulating the variables, including that of "population," in their human genetic or genomic studies (Kaplan, 2014).

Upstream engagement and regulatory guidance

To help elucidate the processes of naturalization of socially derived concepts of race and/or ethnicity, Duster (2006b:1) recommends that social scientists "turn greater attention to an analysis of data collection at the site of reductionist knowledge production." Through illustrating how molecular geneticists use racial and ethnic categories, one can penetrate the logic there and then help shed light on the internal debates and arguments among molecular geneticists during the process of such knowledge production. In the pages of this book, a few researchers' responses also reveal their dilemmas, as on the one hand, they recognize that race and ethnicity are constructed socio-culturally, but on the other hand, they believe in certain technologies, such as Ancestry Informative Markers (AIMs), to analyze race/ethnicity biologically. Several studies serve as models for how social scientists can work with molecular geneticists to provide a fuller picture of the process of scientific knowledge production and the "molecularization of race" in labs (Fullwiley, 2007, 2008; Fujimura and Rajagopalan, 2011; Shim et al., 2014). For instance, insofar as AIMs are concerned, Fullwiley (2008:706) concludes:

> It should be clear by now that the very continents and people chosen for this product [ancestry determination] were selected due to their perceived proximity to what we in North America imagined race to be. . . . In other words, the assumed bounded groups on which the AIMs draw (African, European, Native American and Asian) correspond to American cultural ideas of race, which, in the case of many scientists, also ends up shaping where across the globe they collect the DNA of "populations."

In the absence of clear professional statements from molecular geneticists and/or medical researchers that race/ethnicity is not a genetically or biologically determined category, an interdisciplinary research team is even more necessary in order to delineate systematically the discussions and possible impacts of both using and *not* using race/ethnicity as a proxy in genomic science.

With respect to clinical practices, according to Guttmacher et al. (2010:164):

> [I]dentifying information that may be of clinical significance to the individual patient will be impracticable without the use of automated systems and clear guidelines. There are not enough clinical geneticists to help patients interpret whole-genome sequencing results, and research shows that primary-care physicians lack the knowledge and expertise to help patients understand even single-gene genetic test results; they certainly are not prepared for whole-genome counseling.

Good sampling methodologies and management of data require foresight that can be aided by interdisciplinary dialogue. Moreover, critical assessment of the presentation of data is important, for example, in the framing of data to highlight the significance of a particular study, or in assigning factors as either the "cause" or the "effect" in a cause-and-effect relationship, as both can drastically impact the outcome and perception of importance/implications of studies. For instance, in the case of hypertension, as Duster (2007:703) notes,

> Michael Klag and his associates showed that, in general, within the African-American community, the darker the skin colour, the higher the rate of hypertension. Klag argued that the correlation between skin colour and hypertension was not biological or genetic in origin, but biological in effect due to stress-related outcomes of reduced access to valued social goods, such as employment, promotion, housing stock, etc.

In addition, states and relevant authorities (including research governance bodies) have important roles to play in terms of regulations because guidelines influence the actions of scientists and doctors. Jasanoff's (2003) comparisons of regulations concerning biotechnology in Britain, Germany, and the United States lead her to argue that "regulatory choices invariably affect the degree to which publics can unpack and deliberate on the underlying purposes of innovation." Lee (2003) criticizes the lack of bureaucratic/governmental guidance and support (e.g. FDA, HUGO Ethics committee), asserting that current regulation "further embeds race and race thinking into the research process":

> The [USA] federal government has sidestepped critical examination of these local meanings of race.
>
> [The draft guidance by the US FDA] cites its sister institution . . . and emphasizes the need for administrative continuity. Without consensus on the definitions of the census categories, much less their validity as scientific variables. . . .
>
> While [The HUGO Statement in Benefit-Sharing] reflects increasing concerns over the impact of genetics research on social justice, these guidelines lack legislative enforcement.

I further note in Chapter 3 that these US FDA regulations – the Demographic Rule (CFR 314.50 d(5)) in 1998 and a guidance document in 2005 on collection of race and ethnicity data in clinical trials – have problematic global consequences. That is, as pharmaceutical companies try to get their products registered with the US FDA, these administrative rules can inadvertently give rise to the development of race-specific or ethnic-specific medicine via non-Western routes. In order to avoid such pitfalls, regulations need to be informed by the concerns and controversies surrounding the usage of race and ethnicity in biomedical settings.

As Lee (2003:389) points out, although race is a "socially and historically contingent concept [that] should not be eliminated from medical research," there is a need for multidisciplinary dialogue and the creation of policies to address the role that race should play in scientific research in order to distribute benefits equitably. As Lee, Mountain, and Koenig (2001:47) add:

> The ever-changing taxonomy of race is a reminder that any research utilizing the concept of race and/or ethnicity must include an interrogation of the economic, political, and cultural factors that inform the struggle over how these categories are defined and used.

Should using race/ethnicity as a temporary proxy be unavoidable, for example, in the absence of better proxies and an understanding of probable molecular causes of disease susceptibility and drug response, or when necessary data were collected in the past using race/ethnicity as categories, the public needs to be informed that such categories were adopted due to methodological convenience and accessibility. If the adoption of an automated system is the future, then it seems that it would be instructive to further investigate whether, how, and why a patient's ethnicity/race is included in such an electronic health care system. This study has focused on the key actors in the biomedical industrial complex (e.g. geneticists, clinician-scientists, pharmaceutical companies, public health policy-makers, etc.), but it is also important for future researchers to understand how patients and their significant others (families, friends, etc.) receive, interpret, and act on the results of genetic testing.

What I have attempted to describe is a nuanced and complex situation concerning the development of so-called "personalized" or "precision" medicine in cancer prevention and treatment. In the (post)genomic era, will medicine be "personalized" according to an individual's unique genetic makeup, or will medicine be developed and administered in relation to an individual's racial and ethnic identities? While their primary intention is to develop drugs to treat various types of cancer and alleviate the physical suffering of cancer patients, but in the process of coming up with personalized genomic medicine, many molecular geneticists, cancer geneticists, and physicians do not realize the unintended consequences of their actions regarding the molecular reinscription of race and ethnicity.

Moreover, it seems that "precision medicine" or "personalized medicine" could be misleading terms, and actually it may be more accurate to call "precision medicine" "probability medicine," as a patient's genetic information only provides clinicians with an additional layer of information to make probability statements. Furthermore, the interview data in Chapter 5 show that it is largely not advisable for race/ethnicity to be used as a proxy for administering drugs. Such a framework is considered appropriate only as a last resort when options to treat patients are limited. Many of the doctors interviewed did recognize that races/ethnicities are categories with social origins. Additionally, the doctors understood that the labeling of someone as a member of a certain race suggests social and cultural elements, such as certain dietary preferences. Thus, they knew that ethnic/racial information is not equivalent to genetic information, and that the racial/ethnic proxy is very limited in its usefulness in clinical decision-making about genomic medicine. Finally, due to the high cost of genome-based personalized medicine, there is a double-risk for individuals living in middle- and low-income countries: they may be enrolled in clinical trials, but they cannot afford the medicine that eventually comes out of such trials. While individuals in resource-poor settings and marginalized groups do need adequate medical attention to ensure that their health status is optimized, I suggest that race- and ethnic-specific medicine is *not* the way to go. Instead, we should embrace the fact that cancer is a complex disease. Funding sources need to support research to advance our knowledge of both its genetic and non-genetic causes, rather than nudging researchers to yield to the molecular imperative even in the context of gene–environment interaction research (Darling *et al*, 2016). While we cannot escape categorization and classification, in the context of genomic science and medicine, we need to pay attention to the questions of why the categories of race and ethnicity are used as the population sampling frame, and who gets to define race and ethnicity and with what possible dire consequences.

As an era of genome-based personalized medicine dawns upon us, and as the processes of molecularization of race and ethnicity unfold, it is of utmost importance that the public, policy-makers, clinicians, and scientists understand this: that race and ethnicity serve as a dubious proxy for human genetic diversity in population-based genomics research and for individual genotype in clinical decision-making, and that there is no genetic basis to racial and ethnic identities.

References

Acquaviva, Kimberly D. and Matthew Mintz. 2010. "Perspective: Are We Teaching Racial Profiling? The Dangers of Subjective Determinations of Race and Ethnicity in Case Presentations." *Academic Medicine* 85(4):702–705. doi: 10.1097/ACM.0b013e3181d296c7.

Anand, Preetha, Ajaikumar B. Kunnumakara, Chitra Sundaram, Kuzhuvelil B. Harikumar, Sheeja T. Tharakan, Oiki S. Lai, Bokyung Sung and Bharat B. Aggarwal. 2008. "Cancer Is a Preventable Disease that Requires Major Lifestyle Changes." *Pharmaceutical Research* 25(9):2097–2116.

Anderson, M.R., S. Moscou, C. Fulchon and D.R. Neuspiel. 2001. "The Role of Race in the Clinical Presentation." *Family Medicine* 33(6):430–434.

Barr, D.A. 2005. "The Practitioner's Dilemma: Can We Use a Patient's Race to Predict Genetics, Ancestry, and the Expected Outcomes of Treatment?" *Annals of Internal Medicine* 143(11):809–815.

Bliss, Catherine. 2012. *Race Decoded: The Genomic Fight for Social Justice.* Redwood City, CA: Stanford University Press.

Braun, Lundy, Anne Fausto-Sterling, Duana Fullwiley, Evelynn M. Hammonds, Alondra Nelson, William Quivers, Susan M. Reverby and Alexandra E. Shield. 2007. "Racial Categories in Medical Practice: How Useful Are They?" *PLOS Medicine* 4(9):e271. doi: 10.1371/journal.pmed.0040271.

Cooper, Richard S., Jay S. Kaufman and Ryk Ward. 2003. "Race and Genomics." *New England Journal of Medicine* 348(12):1166–1169.

Darling, Katherine Weatherford, Sara L. Ackerman, Robert H. Hiatt, Sandra Soo-Jin Lee, Janet K. Shim. 2015. "Enacting the molecular imperative: How gene-environment interaction research links bodies and environments in the post-genomic age." *Social Science & Medicine* 155: 51-60. doi: 10.1016/j.socscimed.2016.03.007.

Duster, Troy. 2002. "Caught Between 'Race' and a Hard Place" *Ethnicities* 2(4):547–553.

Duster, Troy. 2003. *Backdoor to Eugenics.* 2nd ed. New York and London: Routledge.

Duster, Troy. 2005. "MEDICINE: Enhanced: Race and Reification in Science." *Science* 307(5712):1050–1051. doi: 10.1126/science.1110303.

Duster, Troy. 2006a. "The Molecular Reinscription of Race: Unanticipated Issues in Biotechnology and Forensic Science." *Patterns of Prejudice* 40(4–5):427–441. doi: 10.1080/00313220601020148.

Duster, Troy. 2006b. "Comparative Perspectives and Competing Explanations: Taking on the Newly Configued Reductionist Challenge to Sociology." American Sociological Review 71 (1): 1–15.

Duster, Troy. 2007. "Medicalisation of Race." *The Lancet* 369(9562):702–704.

Feldman, Marcus W. and Richard C. Lewontin. 2008. "Race, Ancestry, and Medicine." Pp. 89–101 in *Revisiting Race in a Genomic Age*, edited by B.A. Koenig, S.S. Lee and S.S. Richardson. New Brunswick, New Jersey and London: Rutgers University Press.

Fujimura, Joan H. and Ramya Rajagopalan. 2011. "Different Differences: The Use of 'Genetic Ancestry' Versus Race in Biomedical Human Genetic Research." *Social Studies of Science* 41(1):5–30.

Fullwiley, Duana. 2007. "The Molecularization of Race: Institutionalizing Human Difference in Pharmacogenetics Practice." *Science as Culture* 16(1):1–30.

Fullwiley, Duana. 2008. "The Biologistical Construction of Race: Admixture Technology and the New Genetic Medicine." *Social Studies of Science* 38(5):695–735.

Garcia, R.S. 2004. "The Misuse of Race in Medical Diagnosis." *Pediatrics* 113(5): 1394–1395.

Gissis, Snait B. 2011. "Visualizing 'Race' in the Eighteenth Century." *Historical Studies in the Natural Sciences* 41(1): 41–103. doi: 10.1525/hsns.2011.41.1.41.

Göl, Ayla. 2005. "Imagining the Turkish Nation through 'Othering' Armenians." Nations and Nationalism 11(1):121–139. doi: 10.1111/j.1354–5078.2005.00195.x.

Goodman, Alan H., Yolanda T. Moses, and Joseph L. Jones. 2012. *Race: Are We So Different?* Hoboken, NJ: Wiley-Blackwell.

Guttmacher, Alan E., Amy L. McGuire, Bruce Ponder and Kári Stefásson. 2010. "Personalized Genomic Information: Preparing for the Future of Genetic Medicine." Nature Reviews Genetics 11:161–165. doi: 10.1038/nrg2735.

Hinterberger, Amy. 2012. "Investing in Life, Investing in Difference: Nations, Populations and Genomes." *Theory, Culture and Society* 29(3):72–93.

Jasanoff, Sheila. 2003. "Technologies of Humility: Citizen Participation in Governing Science." *Minerva* 41(3): 223–244.

Kaplan, Judith B. 2014. "The Quality of Data on 'Race' and 'Ethnicity': Implications for Health Researchers, Policy Makers, and Practitioners." *Race and Social Problems* 6(3): 214–236. doi: 10.1007/s12552-014-9121-6.

Kahn, Jonathan. 2013. *Race in a Bottle: The Story of BiDil and Racilized Medicine in a Post-Genomic Age.* New York: Columbia University Press.

Lee, Sandra Soo-Jin. 2003. "Race, Distributive Justice and the Promise of Pharmacogenomics: Ethical Considerations." *American Journal of Pharmacogenomics* 3(6):385–392.

Lee, Sandra Soo-Jin, Joanna Mountain and Barbara A. Koenig. 2001. "The Meaning of 'Race' in the New Genomics: Implications for Health Disparities Research." *Yale Journal of Health Policy, Law, and Ethics* 1:33.

Loveman, Mara. 2014. *National Colors: Racial Classification and the State in Latin America.* Oxford, UK: Oxford University Press.

Megyesi, M.S., L.M. Hunt and H. Brody. 2011. "A Critical Review of Racial/Ethnic Variables in Osteoporosis and Bone Density Research." *Osteoporosis International* 22(6):1669–1679.

Ministry of Health. 2015. Principal Causes of Death. Singapore: Ministry of Health. Retrieved on January 25, 2016 (https://www.moh.gov.sg/content/moh_web/home/statistics/Health_Facts_Singapore/Principal_Causes_of_Death.html).

Nelkin, Dorothy M. and Susan Lindee. 1995. *The DNA Mystique: The Gene as a Cultural Icon.* New York: Freeman Press.

Ogolla, Christopher. 2010. "Racial Discrimination in Medicine Versus Race-based Medicine: What Are the Ethical, Legal and Policy Implications on Health Disparities?" *Georgetown Journal of Law and Modern Critical Race Perspectives* 3(1):59–107. Retrieved January 25, 2016 (file:///C:/Users/I/Downloads/fulltext_stamped.pdf).

Roberts, Dorothy E. 2011. *Fatal Invention: How Science, Politics, and Big Business Re-create Race in the Twenty-first Century.* New York and London: The New Press.

Shabaruddin, Fatiha H. and Katherine Payne. 2014. "Evaluating the Cost-Effectiveness of Pharmacogenomics in Clinical Practice." Pp. 779–811 in *Handbook of Personalized Medicine: Advances in Nanotechnology, Drug Delivery, and Therapy,* edited by V. Vizirianakis. London: CRC Press, Taylor & Francis Group Ltd.

Shim, Janet K., Sara L. Ackerman, Katherine Weatherford Darling, Robert A. Hiatt and Sandra Soo-Jin Lee. 2014. "Race and Ancestry in the Age of Inclusion Technique and Meaning in Post-genomic Science." *Journal of Health and Social Behavior* 55(4):504–518.

Smedley, Audrey. 2007. "The History of the Idea of Race. . . and Why It Matters." Paper presented at the conference "Race, Human Variation and Disease: Consensus and Frontiers," sponsored by the American Anthropological Association (AAA) and funded by the Ford Foundation, March 14–17, Warrenton, Virginia. Retrieved January 26, 2016 (http://www.understandingrace.org/resources/pdf/disease/smedley.pdf).

Spaan, Ernst, Ton Van Naerssen and Gerard Kohl. 2002. "Re-imagining Borders: Malay Identity and Indonesian Migrants in Malaysia." *Tijdschrift voor economische en sociale geografie* 93(2):160–172.

Stewart, B.W. and Christopher. P Wild, ed. 2014. *World Cancer Report 2014.* Lyon, France: International Agency for Research on Cancer, World Health Organization. Retrieved on January 26, 2015 (http://whocp3.codemantra.com/Marketing.aspx?ID=WCR2014&ISBN=9789283204299&sts=b).

Tallbear, Kim. 2013. *Native American DNA.* Minneapolis: University of Minnesota Press.

TallBear, Kim and Deborah A. Bolnick. 2004. " 'Native American DNA' " Tests: What Are the Risks to Tribes?" *The Native Voice* Dec. 3–17, pp. D2.

The New York Times. 2000. "Text of the White House Statements on the Human Genome Project." *The New York Times,* June 27. Retrieved on January 25, 2016 (https://partners.nytimes.com/library/national/science/062700sci-genome-text.html).

Trent, Ronald J. 2012. *Molecular Medicine: Genomics to Personalized Healthcare.* 4th ed. Willard. London, UK: Elsevier Inc.

van Houtum, Henk and Ton Van Naerssen. 2002. "Bordering, Ordering and Othering." Tijdschrift voor economische en sociale geografie 93(2):125–136.

Wailoo, Keith. 2001. *Dying in the City of the Blues: Sickle Cell Anemia and the Politics of Race and Health.* Chapel Hill, NC: University of North Carolina Press.

Willard, Huntington F. 2013. "The Human Genome: A Window on Human Genetics, Biology, and Medicine." Pp.4–27 in *Genomic and Personalized Medicine.* 2nd ed, Vol. 1, edited by G.S. Ginsburg and H.F. Willard. London, UK: Elsevier Inc.

Witzig, Ritchie. 1996. "The Medicalization of Race: Scientific Legitimization of a Flawed Social Construct." *Annals of Internal Medicine* 125(8):675–679. doi: 10.7326/0003–4819–125–8–199610150–00008.

Appendices

Appendix A

A brief socio-history of ten societies in Asia

	Governance prior to Colonial Times	Prior to the Nation	Year of Nation-State
People's Republic of China		Dynasty-ROC (1911–1949)-PRC (1949 onwards)	1949 (PRC)
India	Company Rule (East India Company) [1757–1858]	British Crown Rule (1858–1947)	1947
Indonesia	Company Rule (Dutch East Indies) [1619–1800]	Dutch Colony (1800–1942), [Japanese Occupation, 1942–1945] (1945–1950)	1945
Japan	Shogunate (Feudal Society) (1192–1867)	Imperial Rule [The Empire of Japan] (1868–1945)	1947
Korea	Japanese Protectorate (1905–1910)	Japanese Colony (1910–1945)	1948
Malaysia	Malay Sultanate	British Colony (1874–1957) [Japanese Occupation, 1941–1945]	1957
Philippines	Spanish Colony (1521–1898)	American Colony (1898–1946) [Japanese Occupation, 1941–1945]	1946
Singapore	Sultanate (Johor-Riau) [1699–1867] [Trading settlement established in Singapore by the British since 1819]	British Crown Colony (1867–1963) [Japanese Occupation, 1942–1945] Federation of Malaya (1963–1965)	1965
Taiwan (Republic of China)	Cheng Ch'eng-kung regime, 1661–1683 Chinese Dynasty (Ch'ing Empire, 1683)	Japanese Rule (1895–1945)	1911
Thailand	Siam Kingdom	Siam Kingdom	1932

Appendix B

Key characteristics of the scientists and clinician scientists interviewed

Pseudonyms		Institutional affiliation (public or private)	Work in the research lab and/or clinic?
First name	**Last name**		
Satoshi	Hiro	Public	Research lab
Eugene	Lee	Public	Research lab
Kenneth	Cheung	Public	Research lab and clinic
Jun Wei	Yeoh	Public	Research lab
Paul	Lin	Private	Research lab and clinic
Jun	Park	Public	Research lab
Daniel	Yeh	Public	Research lab and clinic
Jerome	Yuan	Public	Research lab and clinic
Wei Sheng	Zhuang	Public	Research lab and clinic
Wei De	Wang	Public	Research lab and clinic
Jun Yuan	Chua	Public	Research lab
Josiah	Huang	Public	Research lab
Frank	Ballheimer	Public	Research lab
Jun Jie	Liang	Public	Research lab and clinic
Zheng Wei	Teo	Public	Research lab and clinic
Aaron	Zhao	Public	Research lab
Yi Jun	Wee	Public	Research lab and clinic
Jun Hao	Hsu	Private	Research lab and clinic
Wei Jie	Zhang	Public	Research lab and clinic
En Quan	Tang	Public	Research lab and clinic
Zhi Hong	Poh	Public	Research lab and clinic
Vijay	Rajaratnam	Public	Research lab
Christina	Neo	Public	Research lab and clinic
Michael	Wu	Public	Research lab and clinic
Wei Yang	Koh	Private	Research lab and clinic
Claire	Xia	Private	Research lab and clinic
Desmond	Deng	Public	Research lab and clinic
Han Wei	Soh	Public	Research lab
Alex	Xie	Public	Research lab and clinic
Gabriel	Chong	Private	Research lab and clinic
Cong Ming	Sim	Public	Research lab

Appendix C
Eugenic policies and practices in selected countries in Asia

Japan

The idea of "eugenics" and eugenic movements first surfaced in Japan in the Meiji era (1868–1912) (Matsubara, 1998; Kato, 2009). According to Robertson (2002:195):

> [E]ugenics, coined by Francis Galton in 1883, was translated into Japanese as the [R]omanized *yuzenikkusu* and as the neologisms *yu'seigaku* (science of superior birth) and *jinshukaizengaku* (science of race betterment). These terms were used synonymously with two terms coined a little earlier: "race betterment" (*minzoku/jinshu kairyo*) and "race hygiene" (*minzoku/jinshu eisei*).

In addition, there was the belief in the concept of "pure blood" as a criterion of authentic "Japaneseness" in the 1880s (Robertson, 2002). The eugenicists were keen on preserving the "Yamato blood" that was deemed a superior substance due to its association with the imperial household and ability to dominate other racial groups (Robertson, 2002).

The Japanese practiced eugenic marriages, which meant that a "pure-blood Japanese" selected a partner who was healthy physically and psychologically for the sake of the nation (Robertson, 2002). Eugenic marriage counseling centers were set up in Japan, with the first opening in Tokyo in 1927. While center staff advocated mixed blooded marriages among the "white" and "yellow" races, they discouraged some. For instance, center staff tried to prevent marriages between Japanese women and Korean men who were working as laborers following Korea's colonization (Robertson, 2002). The words of one survey report filed in 1942 read, "the Korean [male] laborers brought to Japan, where they have established permanent residency, are of the lower classes and therefore of an inferior constitution. . . . By fathering children with Japanese women, these men could lower the caliber of the Yamato *minzoku*" (Robertson, 2002:205). Caprio (2014) elaborates on how some medical scientists, such as Kubo Takeshi, used "scientific inquiry to biologically define Koreans."

To make a long story short, the racial Eugenic Protection Bill was drafted (Morita, 2001; Kato, 2009). It should be emphasized that the proposal was specifically made under the influence of the German Sterilization Law of 1933, as the Japanese considered Germans to be dominant in the field (Morita, 2001; Kato, 2009). The initiation of the bill can also be attributed to the pro-German atmosphere following Japan's military pact with Germany in 1937 (Matsubara, 1998). However, little scientific justification for such policies was provided to the public.

This bill, which aimed to sterilize persons with "hereditary diseases," was introduced as the National Eugenic Bill and passed as the National Eugenic Law (NEL) in 1940 (Matsubara, 1998; Morita, 2001). The law articulated the legal procedure for eugenic sterilization surgery for people with mental and physical "hereditary diseases" to prevent them from reproducing (Kato, 2009). All "undesirable features," including behaviors such as "alcoholism, rape, narcotic use and robbery," which were considered to be bad for society, were associated with the concept of "heredity" and included as reasons for eugenic sterilization (Matsubara, 1998; Kato, 2009).

With the fall of Japan in World War II, the country was in economic and industrial ruin and facing a baby boom (Matsubara, 1998; Kato, 2009). This led Japanese leaders to believe that the "racial crisis" was much more urgent than before; some criticized the NEL as too mild and the sterilization procedures as too troublesome, rendering the law ineffective. They advocated for a powerful eugenic policy as the only option for Japan's reconstruction. They also asserted that the protection of mothers' health and keeping families small were important to enhance the health and well-being of offspring.

As such, the Eugenic Protection Law (EPL) was enacted in 1948. The objective of the law was similar to that of the NEL, with the addition of protecting life and health of the mother (Kato, 2009). However, "inferior descendants" were defined as not only descendants of patients with hereditary diseases, but also those with infectious diseases such as leprosy. In other words, nongenetic diseases and other mental diseases were included. In 1953, the Eugenic Protection Law was enforced by the Ministry of Health and Welfare; a eugenic operation could be performed against the patient's will if the council judged it necessary.

In 1996, the EPL was revised again to remove all eugenic aspects, and its name was changed to the Maternal Protection Law (Robertson, 2002).

Korea

According to Shin (2006), as noted previously in this chapter, the "Korean nation was 'racialized' through a belief in a common prehistoric origin," of being the purest descendants of the mythical figure Dangun. Even today, pure bloodism (*sunhyol*) – a pseudoscientific ideology – is justified as "defensive nationalism" (Pai and Tanherlini, 1998) and functions as a key resource in Korean politics and foreign relations. Recently, Shin's (2006) study on national identity revealed that 93 percent of survey respondents believed that "our nation has a single bloodline."

In 2007, the United Nations Committee on the Elimination of Racial Discrimination (UNCERD) asked South Korea not to use the myth of pure blood and to "prohibit and eliminate all forms of discrimination against foreigners, including migrant workers and children born from inter-ethnic unions" (FIDH, 2007). South Korea's aspirations to be globally competitive and adhere to global standards have had the effect of rendering the myth unacceptable in the country (Kim, 2011:9). However, xenophobia remains intense (Choe, 2009; UN News Centre, 2014). Unlike in Japan, there have been no policies explicitly termed "eugenic" in South Korea. However, according to Kim (2011:9), the South Korean state's "overarching goal is the reproduction of Korean nationals, based on the idea of 'purity of blood' and understood exclusively as the paternal line."

People's Republic of China

The People's Republic of China was established in 1949. In 1986, there were guidelines and provisions targeted at preventing people with histories of mental illness, retardation, or hereditary diseases from procreating (Rodgers, 1999). The Ministry of Health issued a "Guiding Criteria for Classification of Abnormal Cases," listing groups of people deemed "unfit" to reproduce (Rodgers, 1999). The National Eugenics Law in China, enacted in 1995, is also known as the Maternal and Infant Healthcare Law (Sleeboom-Faulkner, 2010:126). Here, I will pay particular attention to the history of a law prohibiting the reproduction of the intellectually impaired in the Gansu Province to illustrate the operation of "negative eugenics" and the larger point about the danger of treating a socially determined category ("the intellectually impaired") as if it were a biological category. Gansu, in northwestern China, is one of the least developed provinces (Chung, 2011). It was selected as the testing ground for the national eugenics law, and a closer look at its history helps us understand how the sterilization law came about.

According to Johnson (1997), the law in Gansu can be translated as "The Prohibition of Reproduction by Intellectually Impaired Persons." It was adopted on November 23, 1988, took effect on January 1, 1989, and was suspended on January 22, 2002, supposedly due to criticism of its eugenic motives. The main aim of the law is to "improve the quality of the population and reduce the burden on society and on the families of the intellectually impaired persons" (Johnson, 1997:221). Under the law, intellectually impaired persons were required to undergo sterilization and were defined as having all of the following characteristics (Johnson, 1997):

(1) They are affected congenitally by hereditary causes, marriage of close relatives, or their mothers and/or fathers have been influenced by external factors; and
(2) They have moderately or severely limited intellectual capacity with an IQ of 49 or below; and
(3) Their speech, memory, orientation, thinking, etc., are impaired.

In addition, the law stipulated that mentally handicapped individuals were not allowed to marry unless they sterilized. The law was greatly supported by the government, with then Prime Minister Li Peng strongly believing that the intellectually impaired were incapable of caring for themselves, were a burden to their families, and that they would produce more of themselves and, thus, affect the quality of the population (Kristof, 1991). The law was praised and further adopted in other provinces and, eventually, led to the drafting of the National Eugenics Law in 1995.

At the same time, it has been suggested that the majority of intellectual impairment cases in Gansu Province were due to "poor prenatal care and birth procedures, or of dietary deficiencies like lack of iodine" (Kristof, 1991). As such, ensuring adequate resources for care and nutrition could have helped greatly reduce such cases (Johnson, 1997). In other words, rather than sterilization, it would have been better to bring attention to improving the conditions of the destitute and disease-plagued Gansu Province to effectively prevent the births of intellectually impaired babies.

Chinese geneticists claimed to have found higher rates of mental and physical handicap among the peasantry than the urban population, as well as among ethnic minority groups as compared to the majority Han (Qiu and Dikötter, 1999). However, Qiu and Dikötter (1999) argue that this is a scientized version of Han prejudice against a minority, as the Han "race" is also a socially constructed identity (Dikötter, 1997).

India

Early eugenic ideas and policies in India grew in the context of national population policy during the interwar period in the 1920s, when a discourse linking census, population, and progress began among Indian intellectuals (Nair, 2006). These ideas grew in the context of famine and deprivation among a growing population. India's large population was no longer seen as a sign of a healthy nation; rather, whether the nation was healthy was defined in relation to the proportion of nonproductive people (Buckingham, 2006). Census was used primarily as a means to "identify, classify, rank and categorize" society based on "religion, caste, sub-caste and profession" (Nair, 2006). International relations played an important role, as Indian intellectuals were exposed firsthand to British social, economic, and political movements, including the eugenics movement (Nair, 2006). These Indian intellectuals maintained organizational ties with the British by holding international conferences. Dr. Gopalji Ahluwalia was a biology professor who presented at an international forum on birth in 1922 (Nair, 2006). It was here that he drew an explicit connection between abject poverty and irresponsible and extensive breeding, and asserted that wealth was equated with superior racial qualities and that "subaltern populations" (tribal, lower caste, and Muslims) should definitely use birth control (Buckingham, 2006). Nonetheless, it is important to note that there was little evidence of widespread eugenic policies in India in the 1920s.

In the late 1940s, leprosy sufferers became central to biopolitical debates with regard to managing the health and welfare of the newly independent Indian population. Leprosy is a contagious, chronic, and highly stigmatized disease that affects one's nerves and skin, causing physical deformities largely on the limbs and face (Buckingham, 2006). It is not, however, a hereditary disease but an infectious one, so that patients tend to be isolated from their family members and social circle. Given that leprosy sufferers were reluctant to embrace vasectomy, in 1953, Srimati Lilavati Munshi proposed a bill to the House of People for compulsory sterilization of adults classified as "unfit" to reproduce. This was also the period when the discourse on eugenics and the issue of leprosy were both rapidly gaining traction internationally. The bill was withdrawn due to strong opposition from the Health Minister, but resurfaced again in 1968 as a "sterilization of the unfit bill" (Buckingham, 2006). This bill was intended not only to limit the births of disease sufferers, but also to "eradicate the race of unfit and unhealthy people" (Buckingham, 2006). Eventually, the bill failed to pass due to its "unscientific . . . impracticable . . . unethical" basis.

References

Buckingham, Jane. 2006. "Patient Welfare vs. The Health of the Nation: Governmentality and Sterilisation of Leprosy Sufferers in Early Post-Colonial India." *Social History of Medicine* 19(3):483–499. doi: 10.1093/shm/hkl046.

Caprio, Mark. 2014. "Abuse of Modernity: Japanese Biological Determinism and Identity Management in Colonial Korea." *Cross-Currents: East Asian History and Culture Review* 3(1):97–125. Retrieved January 18, 2016 (http://muse.jhu.edu/login?auth=0&type=summary&url=/journals/cross_currents_east_asian_history_and_culture_review/v003/3.3.caprio.pdf).

Choe, Sang-Hun. 2009. "South Koreans Struggle With Race." *The New York Times*, November 1. Retrieved January 18, 2016 (http://www.nytimes.com/2009/11/02/world/asia/02race.html?_r=0).

Chung, Yuehtsen Juliette. 2011. "The Postwar Return of Eugenics and the Dialectics of Scientific Practice in China." *The Middle Ground Journal* 3:1–50.

Dikötter, Frank. 1997. *The Construction of Racial Identities in China and Japan*. Honolulu, HI: University of Hawaii Press.

FIDH. 2007. "UN CERD Urges the Republic of Korea to Take Effective Measures in Order to Eliminate Discrimination against Foreigners." Worldwide Movement for Human Rights.

Johnson, Linda. 1997. "Expanding Eugenics or Improving Health Care in China: Commentary on the Provisions of the Standing Committee of the Gansu People's Congress Concerning the Prohibition of Reproduction by Intellectually Impaired Persons." *Journal of Law and Society* 24(2):199–234. doi: 10.1111/1467–6478.00043.

Kato, M. (2009). *Women's Rights?: The Politics of Eugenic Abortion in Modern Japan*. Amsterdam: Amsterdam University Press.

Kim, C. (2011). *Voices of foreign brides: The Roots and Development of Multiculturalism in Korea*. Lanham, MD: Rowman & Littlefield.

Kristof, Nicholas D. 1991. "Some Chinese Provinces Forcing Sterilization of Retarded Couples." *The New York Times*, August 15. Retrieved January 19, 2016 (http://www.nytimes.com/1991/08/15/world/some-chinese-provinces-forcing-sterilization-of-retarded-couples.html).

Matsubara, Yoko. 1998. The Enactment of Japan's Sterilization Laws in 1940s: A Prelude to Postwar Eugenic Policy. *Historia Scientiarum* 8(2): 187–201.

Morita, K. (2001). The Eugenic Transition of 1996 in Japan: From Law to Personal Choice. *Disability & Society 16*(5): 765–771. doi: 10.1080/09687590120070114

Nair, Rahul S. 2006. "The Discourse on Population in India 1870–1960." PhD Dissertation, Department of Humanities and Social Sciences, University of Pennsylvania. Retrieved from ProQuest Dissertation and Theses Database.

Pai, Hyung Il. and Timothy R. Tangherlini, eds. 1998. *Nationalism And the Construction of Korean Identity.* Berkeley: Institute of East Asian Studies, University of California.

Qiu, Renzong and Frank Dikötter. 1999. Is China's Law Eugenic? *The Unesco Courier* 52(9): 30–31. Retrieved January 23, 2016 (http://www.frankdikotter.com/publications/unesco.pdf).

Robertson, J. (2002). Blood Talks: Eugenic Modernity and the Creation of New Japanese. *History and Anthropology 13*(3): 191–216. doi: 10.1080/0275720022000025547

Rodgers, Gail. 1999. Yin and Yang: The Eugenic Policies of the United States and China: Is the Analysis that Black and White? *Houston Journal of International Law* 22(1): 129–168.

Sang-hun, Choe. 2009. "South Koreans Struggle With Race." *The New York Times.*

Shin, Gi-Wook. 2006. *Ethnic Nationalism in Korea: Genealogy, Politics, and Legacy.* Stanford: Stanford University Press.

Sleeboom-Faulkner, Margaret. 2010. Eugenic Birth and Fetal Education: The Friction Between Lineage Enhancement and Premarital Testing among Rural Housholds in Mailand China. *The China Journal* (64): 121–141.

UN News Centre. 2014. "Republic of Korea: UN Rights Experts Urges Adoption of Anti-Discrimination Law." *UN News Centre*, October 9. Retrieved January 18, 2016 (http://www.un.org/apps/news/story.asp?NewsID=49038#.Vp18BVmlTDo).

Appendix D
Is IRESSA available and subsidized in the ten societies that participated in the HUGO PASNP?

Japan

In Japan, IRESSA has been approved for the treatment of epidermal growth factor receptor (*EGFR*) mutation related cancers since 2002 (AstraZeneca, 2002; The Japan Times, 2013), with the drug being used for second-line and third-line treatment (Frampton and Easthope, 2005). Under Japan's National Health Insurance (NHI), Japanese citizens receive subsidies (co-payments range from 0 to 30 percent) for medicines that have been placed under the NHI's list of drugs, which is reviewed regularly to add new drugs (Cook and Kim, 2015). The Japanese government regulates prices of drugs through the NHI with the aim of preventing patients from suffering from crippling drug costs (Wiley Handbook of Current and Emerging Drug Therapies., 2007). Narita et al. (2015) conducted a cost-effectiveness analysis of IRESSA in Japan, in which the NHI subsidy seemed to be factored into the study. In other words, while there is no explicit mention of it, the study seems to suggest that IRESSA is on NHI's drug list, implying that it currently qualifies for a subsidy.

Various expensive drugs, such as Zevalin, are currently being subsidized in Japan (Okamoto, 2014). However, Japan's social security system (which encompasses the NHI) is being critiqued and labeled as potentially unsustainable (Yoshikawa, 2012), implying that there may come a time when various pricey drugs are removed from the NHI list.

South Korea

Like in Japan, IRESSA received approval for the treatment of *EGFR* mutation cancers in 2002 (Pao and Girard, 2009). South Korea also operates under the NHI paradigm of universal health care (Kang et al., 2012). As of 2014, 98 percent of the population was covered under NHI (Kim, Kim, and Kim, 2014), a proportion that rose to 99 percent in 2015 (Cook and Kim, 2015). Cook and Kim (2015) also state that, under the NHI, patients needing oncological drugs are only liable for a co-payment of 5 percent of the drug costs. The NHI prioritizes drugs that are deemed cost effective to receive subsidies (Williams, 2013). This list of subsidized drugs currently includes IRESSA (Ahn, 2012). It should be noted, however, that the introduction of subsidies for treating long-term conditions appears fairly new, and it appears that many expensive drugs have only recently been introduced into the NHI (Song, 2009).

Taiwan

As of 2011, IRESSA has been included in the NHI's list of drugs that receive a subsidy (The China Post, 2011; Taipei Times, 2011). As such, IRESSA is both available and subsidized in Taiwan.

China

As per the China Food and Drug Administration (CFDA), IRESSA has been approved for use to treat *EGFR* mutation cancers since 2014 (China Food and Drug Administration, n.d.)[1]. It does not seem that a state subsidy is available. However, the China Charity Federation (CCF), a Chinese non-governmental organization (China Charity Federation, n.d.) appears to be actively involved in providing, at the very least, patients in need of financial assistance with free doses of IRESSA as long as they have purchased and completed a six-month dosage of the drug (Xinhua Net, 2008; Zhu et al., 2013; Zeng et al., 2014). As such, while IRESSA does not appear subsidized, there seems to be a nongovernmental effort to provide relatively easier access to the drug.

India

IRESSA has been approved to treat *EGFR* mutation cancers since 2004 (Central Drugs Standard Control Organization, n.d.). However, the likelihood of the drug being subsidized is low. First, India's health care system has been criticized for its inefficiency, poor infrastructure, and inability to provide basic, primary health care to hefty portions of the population (Devadasan et al., 2011; Jayaraman, 2014), with an estimated 60 percent of the rural population and 40 percent of the urban population paying hefty sums out-of-pocket (Joe, 2015). Furthermore, the lack of basic coverage has come under criticism, with the parliament indicating to the government that the medicines covered, regulated, and capped under the National Pharmaceutical Pricing Authority (NPPA) are paltry, with the figure standing at a mere 348 out of thousands of drugs available in the country (The Telegraph, 2015).

Indeed, the update to the Gazette of India issued in 2013 and published in the NPPA does not include IRESSA in the list of drugs to be given a nationwide price cap (Ministry of Chemicals and Fertilizers, 2013).

Singapore

In Singapore, IRESSA was approved to treat and inhibit *EGFR* mutation related cancers in 2003 (Health Sciences Authority, n.d.)[2]. Furthermore, in response to an enquiry in *The Straits Times*, the Ministry of Health (MOH) mentioned that while the drug is not subsidized per se, individuals needing financial assistance can apply for help through the Medication Assistant Fund (MAF) (Au-Yong, 2013), a fund that physicians can help patients apply for to offset the costs of any expensive drugs deemed clinically necessary (Ministry of Health, 2012). Karen Au-Yong, then Deputy Director of MOH communications, justifies the MOH's stand by stating that IRESSA could only be given a subsidy if the supplier of the drug participated in the centralized purchasing program that allowed the state to purchase the drug in bulk (Au-Yong, 2013).

MOH's "Drug Subsidies" page, which collates a list of all subsidized drugs (i.e. not requiring patients to go through the additional step of requesting assistance through MAF), does not include IRESSA, indicating that it has not yet received state sanctioning for a subsidy (Drug Subsidies, 2015). As such, while IRESSA is available in Singapore and is not yet being given a subsidy, patients can still request financial assistance with regards to purchasing the drug through the MAF.

Indonesia

In Indonesia, IRESSA has been approved for the treatment of *EGFR* mutation cancers (Frampton and Easthope, 2005). The Indonesian NHI system is fairly new and currently operates under the name Asuransi Kesehatan (ASKES) (Thabrany, 2008; Wardani, 2010; Holloway, 2011; Husada and Tjandrawinata, 2013). ASKES has established a list of medicines that are sold with an enforced price ceiling. This list is known as *Daftar Platfon Harga Obat* (DPHO), which translates to Lowest Level Price Lists for medicines (Husada and Tjandrawinata, 2013). The DPHO has included IRESSA in the lists of medicines that require a price cap (*Daftar Platfon Harga Obat*, 2012).[3]

The Philippines

In the Philippines, IRESSA has been approved for the treatment of *EGFR* mutation cancers (Frampton and Easthope, 2005). The approval was received in 2003 after the clinical trials were deemed sufficiently successful (Gridelli et al., 2011), with the drug now being used for first-line treatment (PhilStar, 2010). The state's Department of Health (DOH) runs the National Center for Pharmaceutical Access and Management (NCPAM), an organization that sets the prices of drugs with the aim of assuring financial access (Department of Health, n.d.). It achieves this through the maintenance of the Philippine National Drug Formulary (PNDF), which only appears to list essential medicines as qualifying for state subsidies (Paje-Villar, n.d.; Department of Health, 2013). A search on the PNDF[4] for IRESSA (and gefitinib) yielded no results, suggesting that IRESSA is currently not subsidized in the Philippines.

Malaysia

In Malaysia, IRESSA first received approval as a second- or third-line treatment for *EGFR* mutation cancers in the early 2000 and in 2010, for first-line treatment (The Star, 2010). The drug also appears on the Malaysian government's National Pharmaceutical Control Bureau as an officially registered drug (National Pharmaceutical Control Bureau, n.d.). It is also likely that IRESSA is currently subsidized in the public health care system. This has been deduced by reviewing five sources.

First, the Malaysian public health care system is regarded as heavily subsidized, with the state footing roughly 98 percent of a patient's bill (The Malay Mail, 2015), with co-payments amounting to no more than 3 percent in most cases (Jaafar et al., 2013). Furthermore, the drugs available in the public health care system are regulated by the drug formulary (Hussain, 2008). One of the factors that influences whether or not a drug is listed on the formulary is if the suppliers agree to provide public health institutions their drugs at low costs (Hassali et al., 2014), hence allowing patients to access them at a low cost. Finally, the updated drug formulary lists IRESSA (Pharmaceutical Services Division, 2015), implying that it is currently available and subsidized in the public health care system.

Thailand

In Thailand, IRESSA was first approved as a second-line treatment of *EGFR* mutation cancers and has more recently been approved as a first-line treatment (Thongprasert, Tinmanee, and Permsuwan, 2012). As it currently stands, whether or not IRESSA is subsidized depends on where the individual patient is employed. Individuals employed in the public sector, an estimated 8 percent of the population, fall under the Civil Servants Medical Benefits Scheme (CSMBS) and are entitled to a full reimbursement of drugs regardless of whether or not they are listed in the National List of Essential Drugs (NLED) (Holloway, 2012; Rousseau, 2014). Non-civil servants, however, are only able to receive reimbursements for drugs that are on the NLED (Yoongthong et al., 2012). The 2012 NLED document, which appears to be the most current available, does not include IRESSA (Ministry of Public Health, 2012). Finally, while IRESSA has "been put on a special list to help patients" (Sarnsamak, 2012), the article does not clearly specify whom these patients are or what this "special list" is. Indeed, the same article also mentions that this "special list" has not had the effect of increasing access to the drug (Sarnsamak, 2012). As such, IRESSA is currently available in Thailand, but the subsidies and reimbursements only appear readily accessible to civil servants.

Notes

1 The China Food and Drug Administration has an e-portal that allows individuals to search if specific drugs have been registered in Singapore. It is accessible here: (http://app1.sfda.gov.cn/datasearcheng/face3/base.jsp?tableId=85&table Name=TABLE85&title=Database%20of%20approved%20Active%20Pharma-ceutical%20Ingredients%20(APIs)%20and%20API%20manufacturers%20in%20 China&bcId=13648913122665913246094 2000667).

2 The Health Sciences Authority has an e-portal that allows individuals to search to see if specific drugs have been registered in Singapore. It is accessible here: (http://eservice.hsa.gov.sg/prism/common/enquirepublic/SearchDRBProdct. do?action=load).

3 While the list provided is in Bahasa Indonesia, the medicines listed are in English. Furthermore, I asked an individual fluent in Bahasa Melayu, a language similar to Bahasa Indonesia, to translate the page for me. I was told that the page is the DPHO and belongs to ASKES.

4 The PNDF is accessible at http://ncpam.doh.gov.ph/index.php/pnf1/approved-pnf-medicines-samp/category/.

References

Ahn, J. 2012. *Health Technology Assessments in Korea.* Taiwan: Center for Drug Evaluation. Retrieved March 31, 2016 (http://www2.cde.org.tw/action/upload file/2012/0724/4.HTA%20Korea%202012%20Jeonghoon%20Ahn.pdf).

AstraZeneca. 2002. *AstraZeneca Secures First Market Approval For IRESSA™ In Japan.* AstraZeneca. Retrieved March 31, 2016 (http://www.astrazeneca.com/Media/Press-releases/Article/20020705—ASTRAZENECA-SECURES-FIRST-MARKET-APPROVAL-FOR-IRESSA).

Au-Yong, K. 2013. *MOH Committed To Keeping Medicines Affordable.* Ministry of Health. Retrieved March 31, 2016 (https://www.moh.gov.sg/content/moh_web/home/pressRoom/Media_Forums/2013/moh-committed-to-keeping-medicines-affordable.html).

Central Drugs Standard Control Organization. n.d. *List Of Drugs During 2004.* Central Drugs Standard Control Organization. Retrieved March 29, 2016 (http://www.cdsco.nic.in/writereaddata//list_of_drugs_approved_during_2004.htm).

China Charity Federation. n.d. *About Us.* China Charity Federation. Retrieved March 31, 2016 (http://cszh.mca.gov.cn/article/english/aboutus/).

China Food and Drug Administration. n.d. *Database of Approved Active Pharmaceutical Ingredients (APIs) and API Manufacturers in China.* China Food and Drug Administration. Retrieved March 31, 2016 (http://app1.sfda.gov. cn/datasearcheng/face3/base.jsp?tableId=85&tableName=TABLE85&title= Database%20of%20approved%20Active%20Pharmaceutical%20Ingredients%20 (APIs)%20and%20API%20manufacturers%20in%20China&bcId=136489 13122665913246094200067).

The China Post. 2011. *Gov't to Subsidize Lung Cancer Targeted Therapy.* The China Post. Retrieved March 31, 2016 (http://www.chinapost.com.tw/taiwan/national/national-news/2011/06/10/305651/Govt-to.htm).

Cook, G. and H. Kim. 2015. "From Regulatory Approval to Subsidized Patient Access in the Asia-Pacific Region: A Comparison of Systems Across Australia, China, Japan, Korea, New Zealand, Taiwan, and Thailand." *Value in Health Regional Issues* 6C:40–45.

Daftar Platfon Harga Obat. 2012. *Daftar Platfon Harga Obat.* KalGen Lab. Retrieved March 31, 2016 (https://kalgenlab.files.wordpress.com/2013/01/buku-dpho-2013-askes-lampiran-ii-pdf.pdf).

Department of Health. 2013. *The Philippine Drug Price Reference Index 2013.* Department of Health. Retrieved March 31, 2016 (http://www.doh.gov.ph/sites/default/files/DPR2013.pdf).

Department of Health. n.d. *About NCPAM.* National Center for Pharmaceutical Access and Management. Retrieved (http://ncpam.doh.gov.ph/index.php/about-ncpam/our-vission-mission-and-goal).

Devadasan, N., Criel, B., Van Damme, W., Lefevre, P., Manoharan, S., and Van der Stuyft, P. 2011. "Community Health Insurance Schemes & Patient Satisfaction – Evidence from India." *Indian Journal of Medical Research,* 133(1), 40–49.

Drug Subsidies. 2015. Ministry of Health. Retrieved (https://www.moh.gov.sg/content/moh_web/home/costs_and_financing/schemes_subsidies/drug_subsidies.html).

Frampton, J.E. and S.E. Easthope. 2005. "Spotlight on Gefitinib in Non-Small-Cell Lung Cancer." *American Journal of Pharmacogenomics* 5(2):133–136.

Gridelli, C., De Marinis, F., Di Maio, M., Cortinovis, D., Cappuzzo, F.,and Mok, T. 2011. "Gefitinib as First-Line Treatment for Patients with Advanced Non-Small-Cell Lung Cancer with Activating Epidermal Growth Factor Receptor Mutation: Review of the Evidence." *Lung Cancer* 71:249–257.

Hassali, M.A., Tan, C.S., Wong, Z.Y., Saleem, F., and Alrasheedy.A. A.2014. "Pharmaceutical Pricing in Malaysia." Pp. 171–188 in *Pharmaceutical Prices in the 21st Century,* edited by Z.-U.-D. Babar. Springer.

Health Sciences Authority. n.d. *PZ4972 INFOSEARCH – MEDICINAL PRODUCTS.* Health Sciences Authority. Retrieved March 31, 2016 (http://eservice.hsa.gov.sg/prism/common/enquirepublic/SearchDRBProduct.do?action=getProductDetails).

Holloway, K.A. 2011. *Indonesia: Pharmaceuticals in Health Care Delivery.* New Delhi: World Health Organization.

Holloway, K.A. 2012. *Thailand: Drug Policy and Use of Pharmaceuticals in Health Care Delivery.* New Delhi: World Health Organization.

Husada, R. and R.R. Tjandrawinata. 2013. "The Healthcare System and Pharmaceutical Industry in Indonesia." Pp. 134–151 in *The New Political Economy of Pharmaceuticals: Production, Innovation and TRIPS in the Global South,* edited by H. Löfgren and O.D. Williams. Basingstoke: Palgrave Macmillan.

Hussain, S.H. 2008. "Drug Control and Formulary Management in Malaysia." *Value in Health* 11:S158–S159.

Jaafar, S., Noh, K., Muttalib, K., Othman, N.H. and Healy, J. 2013. "Malaysia Health System Review". *Health Systems in Transition* (3)1, edited by Healy J. World Health Organization: Asia Pacific Observatory on Health Systems and Policies. Retrieved March 30, 2016 (http://www.wpro.who.int/asia_pacific_observatory/hits/series/Malaysia_Health_Systems_Review2013.pdf).

The Japan Times. 2013. *Lessons from the Iressa Case.* The Japan Times. Retrieved March 31, 2016 (http://www.japantimes.co.jp/opinion/2013/05/08/editorials/lessons-from-the-iressa-case/#.VgjxYxOqqkp).

Jayaraman, V.R. 2014. *5 Things To Know About India's Healthcare System Read More: http://forbesindia.com/blog/health/5-things-to-know-about-the-indias-healthcare-system/#ixzz3n20CEqrq.* Forbes. Retrieved March 31, 2016 (http://forbesindia.com/blog/health/5-things-to-know-about-the-indias-healthcare-system/).

Joe, William. 2015. "Distressed Financing of Household Out-of-Pocket Health Care Payments in India: Incidence and Correlates." *Health Policy Plan* 30(6): 728–741.

Kang, M.S., Jang, H.S., Lee, M., and Park, E-C. 2012. "Sustainability of Korean National Health Insurance." *Journal of Korean Medical Science* 27(Suppl):S21–S24.

Kim, L., J.-A. Kim and S. Kim. 2014. "A Guide for the Utilization of Health Insurance Review and Assessment Service National Patient Samples." *Epidemiology and Health* 36: e2014008. doi:10.4178/epih/e2014008.

The Malay Mail. 2015. *Despite Subsidies, Most Malaysians Still Save Money for Healthcare, Survey Finds.* The Malay Mail. Retrieved March 31, 2016 (http://www.themalaymailonline.com/malaysia/article/despite-subsidies-most-malaysians-still-save-money-for-healthcare-survey-fi).

Ministry of Chemicals and Fertilizers. 2013. *Gazette of India.* New Delhi: National Pharmaceutical Pricing Authority. Retrieved March 30, 2016 (http://www.nppaindia.nic.in/DPCO2013.pdf).

Ministry of Health. 2012. "Healthcare 2020: Improving Accessibility, Quality & Affordability". HealthScope, Issue 1, July – August 2012. Singapore: Ministry of Health. Retrieved March 30, 2016 (https://www.moh.gov.sg/content/dam/moh_web/healthscope/archive/2012/MOH%20Healthscope_July-August%202012%20Issue.pdf)

Ministry of Public Health. 2012. *National List of Essential Medicines.* Malaysia: World Health Organization. Retrieved (http://apps.who.int/medicinedocs/documents/s21586en/s21586en.pdf).

Narita, Y., Matsushima, Y., Shiroiwa, T., Chiba, K., Nakanishi, Y., Kurokawa, T., and Urushihara, H. 2015. "Cost-Effectiveness Analysis of EGFR Mutation Testing and Gefitinib as First-Line Therapy for Non-Small Cell Lung Cancer." *Lung Cancer* 90(1):71–77.

National Pharmaceutical Control Bureau. n.d. *Product Detail Information for MAL20033931AR.* National Pharmaceutical Control Bureau. Retrieved March 31, 2016 (http://portal.bpfk.gov.my/quest/search_result.php?type=t1&filter=C&searchtxt=iressa).

Okamoto, E. 2014. *Farewell to Free Access: Japan's Universal Health Coverage.* East Asia Forum. Retrieved March 31, 2016 (http://www.eastasiaforum.org/2014/02/22/farewell-to-free-access-japans-universal-health-coverage/).

Paje-Villar, E.B. n.d. *The Philippine National Drug Formulary.* Department of Health. Retrieved March 31, 2016 (http://uhmis2.doh.gov.ph/doh_ncpam/images/publication/pndf.pdf).

Pao, W. and N. Girard. 2009. "Clinical Applications of Kinase Inhibitors in Solid Tumors." Pp. 615–632 in *Handbook of Cell Signaling* 2nd ed., Vol. 1, edited by R.A. Bradshaw and E.A. Dennis. Amsterdam: Academic Press.

Pharmaceutical Services Division. 2015. *Senarai FUKKM.* Pharmaceutical Services Division. Retrieved March 31, 2016 (http://www.pharmacy.gov.my/v2/en/apps/fukkm).

PhilStar. 2010. *AstraZeneca's Gefitinib Gets FDA Approval.* PhilStar. Retrieved March 31, 2016 (http://www.philstar.com/science-and-technology/626492/astrazenecas-gefitinib-gets-fda-approval).

Rousseau, T. 2014. *Thailand: Social Health Protection.* COOPAMI.

Sarnsamak, P. 2012. *Govt Urged to Have Pharmaceutical Giants Reduce Price of Cancer Drugs.* The Nation. Retrieved March 31, 2016 (http://www.nationmulti media.com/national/Govt-urged-to-have-pharmaceutical-giants-reduce-pr-3018 4403.html).

Song, Y. 2009. "The South Korean Health Care System." *Japan Medical Association Journal* 52(3):206–209.

The Star. 2010. *Cancer Drug for Lungs: Gefitinib Approved as First Line Treatment for Lung Cancer Patients.* The Star. Retrieved March 31, 2016 (http://www.thestar. com.my/story/?file=%2F2010%2F5%2F2%2Fhealth%2F6159716).

The Star. 2010. *Targetting Lungs: With Advancements in Treatment, Patients Diagnosed with Advanced Lung Cancer Can Look Forward to Prolonged Survival with a Better Quality of Life.* Malaysian Oncological Society. Retrieved March 31, 2016 (http://www.malaysiaoncology.org/article.php?aid=775).

Taipei Times. 2011. *Taiwan News Quick Take.* Taipei Times. Retrieved March 31, 2016 (http://www.taipeitimes.com/News/taiwan/archives/2011/06/10/ 2003505438).

The Telegraph. 2015. *Cap All Drugs' Prices: Panel.* The Telegraph. Retrieved March 31, 2016 (http://www.telegraphindia.com/1150421/jsp/nation/story_15799. jsp#.VgkeZxOqqkp).

Thabrany, H. 2008. "Politics of National Health Insurance of Indonesia: A New Era of Universal Coverage." Paper presented at the 7th European Conference on Health Economics, July 23–26, Rome. Retrieved March 30, 2016 (http://www. un.org/en/ecosoc/newfunct/pdf/thabrany-nhip-program%20and%20politic- indonesia.pdf).

Thongprasert, S., S. Tinmanee. and U. Permsuwan. 2012. "Cost-Utility and Budget Impact Analyses of Gefitinib in Second-Line Treatment for Advanced Non-Small Cell Lung Cancer from Thai Payer Perspective." *Asia-Pacific Journal of Clinical Oncology* 8:53–61.

Wardani, S.M. 2010. "The Real Sector Effects of the Economic Crisis and Global Health in Southeast Asia: Study Case: Insurance Management in Indonesia." *AFBE 2010 Conference Papers*, pp 220–235. Retrieved March 30, 2016 (http://www. afbe.biz/main/wp-content/uploads/afbeconfpapers2010.pdf).

Wiley Handbook of Current and Emerging Drug Therapies. 2007. Pharmaceutical Pricing and Reimbursement in Japan. Hoboken, NJ: Wiley-Interscience, doi: 10.1002/9780470041000.cedt100

Williams, D.R. 2013. *The Funding of Biopharmaceutical Research and Development.* Philadelphia: Woodhead Publishing.

Xinhua Net. 2008. *CCF Distributes Free Drugs to Needy Lung Cancer Sufferers.* Xinhua Net. Retrieved April 1, 2016 (http://news.xinhuanet.com/english/2008–01/ 23/content_7481797.htm).

Yoongthong, W., Hu, S., Whitty, J.A., Wibulpolprasert, S., Sukantho, K., Thienthawee, W., Han, H. and Scuffham, P.A. 2012. "National Drug Policies to Local Formulary Decisions in Thailand, China, and Australia: Drug Listing Changes and Opportunities." *Value in Health* 15:S126–S131. doi:10.1016/j.jval.2011.11.003.

Yoshikawa, H. 2012. *Japan's Ageing Population and Public Deficits.* East Asia Forum. Retrieved April 1, 2016 (http://www.eastasiaforum.org/2012/06/21/ japans-aging-population-and-public-deficits/).

Zeng, X., Li, J., Peng, L., Wang, Y., Tan, C., Chen, G., Wan, X., Lu, Q., and Yi, L. 2014. "Economic Outcomes of Maintenance Gefitinib for Locally Advanced/ Metastatic Non-Small-Cell Lung Cancer with Unknown EGFR Mutations: A Semi-Markov Model Analysis." *PLoS ONE* 9(2): 1–9. doi:10.1371/journal. pone.0088881.

Zhu, J., Li, T., Wang, X., Ye, M., Cai, J., Xu, Y. and Wu, B. 2013. "Gene-Guided Gefitinib Switch Maintenance Therapy for Patients with Advanced EGFR Mutation- Positive Non-Small Cell Lung Cancer: An Economic Analysis." *BioMed Central* 13(39): 1–11. doi:10.1186/1471-2407-13-39.

Appendix E

Review of the Singapore Ministry of Health Standard Drug List (SDL): http://www.moh.gov.sg/content/moh_web/home/costs_and_financing/schemes_subsidies/drug_subsidies.html

Of the seven drugs reviewed, the minimum cost per month for usage is $3,300 and up. Some personalized cancer drugs are indeed subsidized by the Singapore Ministry of Health.

Drug	Function	Price*	Quantity	Subsidized by MOH?** (Ministry of Health 2014)
IRESSA/gefitinib	Lung cancer	$3,300–$6,000	Per month	No
Glivec/imatinib	Leukemia	$4,000–$6,000	Per month	No
Avastin/ bevacizumab	Colorectal cancer	$5,000–$7,000	Per dose	Yes
Rituximab	Lymphoma	$4,000–$5,000	Per dose	Yes
Herceptin/ trastuzumab	Breast cancer	$5,000–$6,000	Per dose	Yes
Nimotuzumab	Brain cancer	$15,000–$20,000	Per treatment cycle	No
Sutent/sunitinib	Kidney, stomach cancer	$8,000–$10,000	Per month	No

  * Please note that all prices are in Singapore dollars.
** As of April 1, 2014. It is not mentioned whether these prices stated are before or after MOH subsidy.

IRESSA/gefitinib

Leong (2006) reported that IRESSA pills cost $110.35 each, which costs about $6,000 a month for a patient who has to take two pills daily.

Khalik (2005b) reported that each IRESSA pill costs $115 and has to be taken daily, which adds up to a monthly bill of about $3,300 a month. This daily prescription may have to be taken for life.

Glivec/imatinib

Koh (2002) reported that Glivec costs patients about $5,000 to $6,000 a month.

Perry (2002b) reported that Glivec costs $4,000 a month or more.

Perry (2002a) also reported that Glivec costs at least $4,500 for a month's supply.

Avastin/bevacizumab

Teo (2014) reported that patients pay between $2,800 and $6,600 for each dose of Avastin. This figure is after a subsidy by the Singapore Cancer Society and before Medisave and Medishield deductions.

Chew (2012) reported that each dose of Avastin costs between $5,000 and $6,000, in addition to each cycle of chemotherapy, which costs between $2,000 and $4,000.

Khalik (2005a) reported that Avastin dosage depends on an individual's height and weight and costs about $6,000 to $7,000 a month.

Rituximab

Teo (2013) reported that each dose of rituximab costs about $4,000 to $5,000, and a full cycle of treatment usually consists of six to eight doses depending on body size.

Herceptin/trastuzumab

Teo (2014) reported that patients pay between $3,600 and $7,000 for each dose of Herceptin. This figure is after a subsidy by the Singapore Cancer Society and before Medisave and Medishield deductions.

Cheong (2009) reported that each injection of Herceptin costs between $5,000 and $6,000.

Nimotuzumab

Liaw (2008) reported that one treatment cycle of nimotuzumab, which lasts eight weeks, costs between $15,000 and $20,000.

Sutent/sunitinib

Tay (2007) reported that 30 Sutent pills, or a month's supply, costs between $8,000 and $10,000.

References

Cheong, June. 2009. "Cancer Patients, VIP Clients." *The Straits Times*, January 15.

Chew, Joan. 2012. "Ovarian Cancer Drug starves Tumour to Give Patients More Quality Time." *The Straits Times*, June 28.

Drug Subsidies. 2014. *Ministry of Health*. Retrieved October 6. (http://www.moh. gov.sg/content/moh_web/home/costs_and_financing/schemes_subsidies/ drug_subsidies.html).

Khalik, Salma. 2005a. "New Drug for Advanced Colorectal Cancer." *The Straits Times*, March 26.

Khalik, Salma. 2005b. "New Lung Cancer Drug More Effective on Asians." *The Straits Times*, April 23.

Koh, Boon Pin. 2002. "New Hope for Children with Rare Leukaemia." *The Straits Times*, June 16.

Leong, Sandra. 2006. "Always a Fighter." *The Straits Times*, April 23.

Liaw, Wy-Cin. 2008. "New Brain Cancer Drug Undergoing Clinical Trial." *The Straits Times*, September 13.

Perry, Margaret. 2002a. "New drug for leukemia patients here." *The Strait Times*, January 15.

Perry, Margaret. 2002b. "New Drug Offers Hope to Dying Cancer Patient." *The Straits Times*, March 15.

Tay, Sheralyn. 2007. "New Drug for Rare Stomach Cancer." *The Straits Times*, July 19.

Teo, Joyce. 2013. "Better Treatment on the Way." *The Straits Times*, May 23.

Teo, Joyce. 2014. "Drug Subsidy Boosts Cancer Treatment Fund." *The Straits Times*, August 25.

Index